WHISKY

Uisge Beatha • Water of Life

WHISKY

Uisge Beatha • Water of Life

Helen Arthur

FIREFLY BOOKS

To Dick with love.

A FIREFLY BOOK

Published by Firefly Books Ltd. 2000

First Printing

Library of Congress Cataloguing in Publication Data
is available.

Canadian Cataloguing in Publication Data

Arthur, Helen

      Whisky: the water of life=uisge beatha

Includes index.

ISBN 1-55209-425-1

1. Whiskey – History.   2. Whiskey.   I. Title.

TP605.A77 2000   641.2′52   C99-932188-9

Published in Canada in 2000 by
Firefly Books Ltd.
3680 Victoria Park Avenue
Willowdale, Ontario, M2H 3K1

Published in the United States in 2000 by
Firefly Books (U.S.) Inc.
P.O. Box 1338, Ellicott Station
Buffalo, New York, 14205

This book was designed and produced by
Quintet Publishing Limited
6 Blundell Street
London N7 9BH

Creative Director: Richard Dewing

Art Director: Simon Daley

Design: Isobel Gillan

Photography: Jonathan Russell Reed, Paul Forrester,

Laura Wickenden, Colin Bowden

Project Editors: Keith Ryan, Toria Leitch

Editor: Diane Pengelly

Typeset in Great Britain by
Central Southern Typesetters, Eastbourne

Manufactured in Hong Kong by
Regent Publishing Services Ltd
Printed in China by
Leefung-Asco Printers Ltd

Contents

Foreword
BY CHARLES MACLEAN

Nearly twice as many books about whisky have been published in English since 1990 than were published between 1645 and 1970; seventy-two titles in this decade, so far as I can ascertain, as opposed to thirty-eight in the previous two and a quarter centuries. Is there room for yet another whisky book?

Before I answer this, let us explore the literature. The earliest books in English appeared during the mid 1600s and were practical manuals for home and small-scale distilling. The most successful of such titles were *The London Distiller* (1652) and Ambrose Cupar's *Complete Distiller* (1750s). Both were reprinted many times, with slight variations and additions until the beginning of the 19th century. They provided instructions for distilling fermented mashes made from various grains and fruits, recipes for cordials, and directions for compounding or rectifying spirit with herbal infusions, sugar and the like, in order to make what we would now call liqueurs.

Interestingly, Cupar's recipe for *usquebaugh* (whisky) is a compounded liquor, not a single malt. A later edition of his book directs that half the spirit be re-distilled with mace, cloves, nuts, cinnamon, coriander seeds, ginger, and cubebs (berries from the pepper family), and run through a cloth bag containing English saffron. The other half is infused with a mixture of golden raisins, dates, and licorice. Mixed together, the batch is sweetened with one pound per gallon of sugar and put into a cask for "8 or 12 days." In his *Dictionary* (1755), Dr Johnson follows Cupar, defining *usquebaugh* as "a compounded distilled spirit, being drawn on aromaticks: and the Irish sort is particularly distinguished for its pleasant flavour. The Highland sort is somewhat hotter, and by corruption in Scotch they call it *Whisky*."

It was perfectly legal to distill at home – for your own consumption and from grains grown on your own land – until 1784, and after this was banned, private distilling, now illicit, increased. "The Smuggling Era," as this period is referred to by historians, was as brutal as it was romantic, but by the time it had finished, in the mid 1820s, it had given rise to the second thread in whisky literature – the "history," often somewhat fanciful accounts of the origins of distilling and its practise in Scotland. One such book was Samuel Morewood's *Inebriating Liquors* (1838). "By far the most interesting and complete [treatise on the origins of distilling], and all writers on the subject since that date rely largely upon him for their facts and data," wrote Alfred Barnard in his introduction to *The Whisky Distilleries of the United Kingdom* (1887). Morewood was an officer of the excise in Dublin, like his contemporary, Aeneas Coffey, the inventor of the patent still. Barnard visited every whisky distillery in Scotland and Ireland (and four in England for good measure), and supplies a history, a physical description (accompanied by numerous engravings), and an account of the operation of each. A monumental endeavor, matched only by his later *The Noted Breweries of Great Britain and Ireland* (1889-91) in four volumes. A more technical approach was adoped by the Elgin chemist J.A. Nettleton in *The Manufacture of Spirit as Conducted at the Various Distilleries of the United Kingdom* (1898), a book which applied late 19th century scientific principles to the alchemy of distilling, and which is even today considered a reliable guide by contemporary chemists. By 1900 no more than a score of books had appeared on the subject of whisky – I know of fourteen – all of them of a technical or semi-technical nature and many of them devoted to spirits in general.

During the 1930s a couple of books appeared which marked a new departure in their approach to the subject: *Whisky* by Aeneas MacDonald (1930) and *Whisky and Scotland* by Neil Gunn (1935). The former furiously bemoaned the total eclipse of malt whisky by blended whisky, and the latter, by one of Scotland's leading novelists, adopts a literary approach; apart from these two, I know of only four other books about whisky published during the first half of the century, and that includes Professor Sainsbury's *Notes on a Cellar Book* (1920), which devoted only a chapter to whisky.

Eight titles appeared during the 1950s, including Sir Robert Bruce Lockhart's *Scotch* (1951), and six in the 1960s, notably Professor R.J.S. McDowall's *The Whiskies of Scotland* and Professor David Daiches' *Scotch Whisky*. All three books are still in print. The writers now tie whisky closer to Scotland – the land and the people – and for the first time begin to discuss flavor and regional difference in malt whiskies. The books are good fireside reads, glass in hand.

The 1970s was an era of unprecedented confidence in Scotch whisky. Maturing stocks had never been higher, new distilleries were built, and old ones refurbished; the market seemed insatiable. Malt whisky began to be vigorously promoted for the first time. Although the traditional markets – the United States and the United Kingdom – were drinking less (owing to fashion in the U.S. and higher taxes in the U.K.) other markets, in Europe

and the Far East particularly, were booming. The demand for information about whisky – especially malt whisky – was reflected by the number of books published on the subject (around thirty titles during the decade and a further thirty during the 1980s).

So we reach the 1990s, during which some seventy books have already appeared on the subject of Scotch whisky: introductions and consumer guides; histories; personal recollections; anthologies; and essays. Is there room for another? What contribution does this new book by Helen Arthur make? First, curiosity about whisky – beginning with Scotch, and now Irish, bourbon and the rest (all of which are embraced by this book) – has never been greater. Second, readers approach the subject with varying amounts of knowledge, looking for answers to questions of differing complexity. Helen Arthur satisfies a broad audience and has written a text which is a thorough introduction to its subject, a personal view, and a detailed account of some aspects. So there is something here for all enthusiasts, from novice to whisky expert. The author has also

provided public relations and advertising consultancy to the whisky industry for over twenty years, and her chapter on the "culture" of whisky, as defined by the way the spirit has been represented in advertising, is of special interest. It is an aspect which is rarely addressed, and one which makes a fascinating social comment on how attitudes and fashions change in relation to a spirit which is perennial and perennially fascinating. This you will discover as you turn the pages which follow.

Helen Arthur has written an entertaining and informative book, styishly designed and attractively illustrated. I hope it will introduce many more people to the limitless pleasure and diversions available from the finest spirit known to man.

CHARLES MACLEAN
Edinburgh, Scotland,
September 1999

Introduction

In my early years working as a public relations consultant in the whisky industry, my job was to raise the media and consumer profiles of particular brands and not necessarily to know the inner workings of the industry. The best thing about landing a whisky account, my business partner, the late Patrick Gallagher, would say was that "before anything else happened they sent you a crate of the stuff to try and whisked you off to a distillery to see how it was made." These visits to places as far apart as Highland Park on Orkney, Laphroaig on Islay or The Glendronach in the eastern Highlands of Scotland will linger forever in my memory.

Anyone who has visited a distillery knows the distinctive smell of malting barley and the reek of peat smoke.

Crossing the threshold, I always feel a sense of wonder that something as wonderful as a single malt can be created by mixing water, barley and yeast.

Whisky has always been a sort of personal passport in this way, opening doors I would never otherwise have found. It sparks immediate discussion when I tell people that, among other things, I write books on whisky. The response is inevitably the same: "Which is your favorite?" I'm sure all whisky writers suffer this situation and the answer is never simple because of the range and variety of whiskies available. Will I be drinking whisky before a meal and, if so, what will I be eating? Or will I be drinking whisky at a cocktail party and will there be a selection of blended and single malt whiskies to choose from? The questions can go on and on.

Bottom: Bird watchers and whisky enthusiasts enjoy the idyllic setting of Dalmore distillery.

Left, far left and below: Peat fires and copper stills help create the pure spirit flowing through the spirit safe.

The second question often asked is, "Which whiskies would you recommend to start a whisky collection?" This is perhaps an easier question to answer. A selection of several single malts from Scottish islands, Laphroaig or Lagavulin from Islay for a really peaty malt, maybe Talisker from Skye for a little less peat and Highland Park, which is a good after-dinner drink. I would then choose a Speyside single malt such as The Glenlivet and a Highland, possibly Old Pulteney. For a sweeter taste you could include The Macallan or Glenmorangie finished in port pipes. Finish the collection off with Jack Daniels and Wild Turkey from the United States, Bushmills from Northern Ireland and a couple of blends and then enjoy your armchair travels around the world of whisky.

It was with these and many other questions in my mind that I started to write this book. In my early work with the whisky industry, I was often unaware of the legislative and economic pressures forcing changes worldwide – some of them not for the better. I tried to fill the gaps in my knowledge while researching my first book on whisky, *The Single Malt Whisky Companion*. With this book I have taken my research still further and have made some interesting discoveries.

From left to right: An engineer's dream: a pot-bellied still at Old Pulteney, polished copper nameplates, an old beam engine and gleaming copper stills (Blair Athol).

I have tried to gather as much material as possible from source, but with historical data there is bound to be some distortion over the years. I apologize for any errors or omissions which might appear, but I believe these are inevitable in a book with such an all-encompassing brief. Many of the comments are my own personal views and I hope readers won't find these irritating – there is absolutely nothing worse than reading a book and wishing you could wring the author's neck! Of course, a little controversy makes for interesting reading...

While working on this book, I have had the pleasure of tasting new whiskies, sampling some really old malts and meeting many people who share my enthusiasm, and dedicate their knowledge and skills to distilling, blending, marketing and selling whisky worldwide. One thing became clear very early on: whether cruising through the gorges of the Yangtze river, crossing the wilds of Siberia or lazing by a poolside bar in Barbados – no matter where you are in the world – where there's a bar, there's whisky, one of the greatest passports available.

So open a bottle of your favorite whisky, pour yourself a small dram and settle down with this book for a very unique journey.

Below: From single grains of barley a single malt is born.

Right: Spoilt for choice at The Canny Man in Edinburgh, Scotland.

Far right: A quaich and a hip flask, traditional whisky drinking vessels.

Author's Note:

While writing this book, a question of spelling was raised: "whisky" or "whiskey?"

The difference in spelling was said to indicate that rye grain was used in the distillation. Unfortunately, this idea doesn't work entirely – Canadians, who also use rye, call it by the traditional name of "whisky."

In most parts of the world – Australia, Brazil, Canada, India, Japan, Scotland, Spain, Turkey – it is "whisky." In the United States and Ireland it is usually "whiskey" although for a very long time the Irish didn't include the *e* either. Nor do all American distilleries include the *e* in their spelling. Maker's Mark, Old Forester and Early Times bottles, for example, bear "whisky" on their labels.

There are some 200 distilleries in the world of which only 21 are in the U.S. and Ireland. The confusion stems from the number of *brands* distilled by any one distillery (this is particularly true in the United States where old brand names are kept alive by small batch distillations). There are many more whiskies produced in the U.S. and for that matter other countries such as Canada, India and Ireland, than there are individual distilleries. Nonetheless, "whisky" remains the well-known and generally accepted spelling of the spirit.

The History of Whisky

Since the history of whisky is inextricably linked with Scotland and Ireland, this chapter explains the development of the art of distillation and the introduction of whisky distilling principally in these two countries. The growth of the industry, from its homestead base to today's familiar large corporations, is a fascinating story beset with political, legislative, social and economic problems. While immigration and expansion led to the economic development of new markets, whisky distillation spread to countries such as the United States and Canada, whose histories in turn influenced the growth of distillation in both Scotland and Ireland.

The art of distillation in the ancient world

Popular images of people drinking in the ancient past often involve Romans lying on sumptuous couches drinking wine. There seems to be no equivalent image of anyone drinking spirits. In ancient history, references to wine are far more common than those to alcohol. Noah was encouraged to plant a vineyard after the flood, and in the Bible there are some 450 references to the beneficial effects of wine, but very few concerning strong drink. In Proverbs 31:6 both wine and strong drink are mentioned as having advantageous properties – "Give strong drink to him who is perishing, and wine to those in bitter distress." But there are some disparaging comments too, as in Proverbs 20:1 "Wine is a mocker, strong drink is raging."

The art of distillation is indeed an ancient one. As early as 800 BC, the Chinese were using rice and millet to produce *sautchoo* and in Sri Lanka and India they used rice and molasses or palm sap to make *arrack*. Not only did these ancient civilizations distill alcoholic drinks, but they used a basic form of distillation to extract essences from herbs for medicines and flowers for perfumes.

Aristotle (384–322 BC) talks about distillation being used to create pure water by evaporation of seawater. Pliny the Elder (AD 23–79) describes the creation of turpentine from rosin (the natural gum from pine trees) by heating the rosin and collecting the steam on wool fixed to the underside of a basic still. The Romans and Greeks probably learned the art of distilling perfumes and medicine from the East. They developed their own medicines, yet one of the only recorded recipes specifies wine as its base. In the time of the Emperor Marcus Aurelius (AD 188–217) a cure for indigestion was a glass of wine sprinkled with pepper.

By the third century AD, Egyptians were distilling wine and herbs and with their influence this skill spread throughout Western Asia and Europe, specifically to the countries of Spain and France. As interest in wine and spirits grew, beautiful containers were created. One of the treasures of the National Museum of Scotland is a Roman flask made of glass dating from the fourth century AD. This lovely object with its decorated base and neck is sadly not normally on show. From AD 450 the Roman Empire went into decline and much of Europe was plunged into what historians call the Dark Ages.

Above and right: Old scales and a representation of an illicit still at the Glenkinchie Museum of Whisky Production, Scotland.

The first whiskies

At this time the only people keeping records of any description were the monastic communities, so written records on the subject of whisky are scarce. History was passed down by word of mouth, so it is difficult to substantiate exactly when distilling started in Ireland or Scotland.

From AD 500–800 Ireland became known for its saints and teaching. According to the Irish, the secret of distilling arrived around AD 500 with missionary monks who traveled from other monastic orders in France.

St Columba and his followers landed on the tiny island of Iona on the west coast of Scotland from Ireland in AD 521,

an important date in Scotland's religious history. Since there is no written evidence to support the claim, however, it is by no means certain that they brought the secret of distillation with them.

Apothecaries working at the famous medical school in Salerno, Italy, in 1100 developed the art of distillation from the medicine of ancient Greece and Rome. By using distillation, the apothecaries were able to extract the very essence or spirit of wine, cereals or herbs. Initially, liquid was heated in an earthenware vessel (glass vessels were developed later) and the vapor rising from the surface was condensed on the underside of an alembic or still placed over the receptacle. The condensed

vapor then ran into a tube and into a storage container. At the Salerno medical school the healing powers of wine were also investigated and it is said that above the door of the hospital was a sign engraved with the words "Drink a little wine."

For the next 100 years or so apothecaries, many of whom worked inside monasteries, used distillation to produce medicines. By adding sugar and spices to the essential oils they created medicines which were quite palatable. Many of these old herbal recipes today form the basis of liqueurs such as Benedictine and Green Chartreuse, and are still produced by monastic orders.

Top: Carrying a hogshead through town.

Right: An early still showing the coiled condensor for cooling the vapour to produce raw spirit.

Top right: Pluscarden Priory where monks brewed ale in the 1400s.

Far right: The heraldic coat of arms of the Surgeon Barbers of Edinburgh 1505.

The Benedictine monks from Pluscarden Priory were renowned for their brewing and distilling: in the 15th century the water was blessed by the abbot close to the site of Miltonduff distillery. This is referred to by Alfred Barnard, who recorded a tour of the distilleries of Scotland in his book *The Whisky Distilleries of the United Kingdom*: "Attended by his priors, palmers and priests, an aged abbot proceeded to the banks of the stream where kneeling on a stone with his hands outstretched to heaven, he invoked a blessing on its waters, and ever after the life-giving beverage distilled therefrom was christened 'aqua vitae'."

The Guild of Surgeon Barbers of Edinburgh was created by James IV in 1505 and among other things was given the monopoly on whisky distilling – "to mak and sell aqua vitae within the burgh." This was because distilling spirit was at that time principally for medicinal purposes. This monopoly did not last long because the practice of distilling spirit for drinking soon became widespread.

By the time the English invasion of Ireland by Henry II took place in 1170, there were many working distilleries. Henry's soldiers returned with a taste for drink, but had great difficulty in calling it by its proper name of uisge beatha. At Bushmills distillery in Country Antrim in Northern Ireland it is believed that as early as 1276 there were stories of spirit being produced in the area.

By this time alcoholic drinks were being made in what were then known as "The Low Countries" – Holland in particular – from wine lees. These *brandewijns* were the forerunners of today's *aqua vitaes*. The Black Death, which spread throughout Europe during 1348–50 seems to have stimulated increased alcoholic production, whether in the form of medicines or as a drink perceived to ward off the plague. Many doctors probably prescribed alcohol merely because it did induce a sense of well-being. By the 14th century distillers were taking over the role of producing spirits from apothecaries and in Germany rye spirit started to be produced. The Germans also became concerned about excessive brandy-drinking and introduced the first recorded tax on alcohol in 1360.

Little by little alcoholic drinks spread across Europe and across the North Sea to England where, apart from their use as medicines, they were used by cooks working for the nobility to produce flaming food to astonish their guests.

The first reference to making what we know as Scotch whisky dates from 1494 when one Friar John Cor of Lindores Abbey, near Newburgh in Fife, is cited as purchasing eight bolts of malt, which would have produced 35 cases of whisky. Home distillation, which was permitted under the law, was a logical part of a Scottish farmer's economy. During the summer, cattle were raised and barley grown to feed them in the winter months. Any surplus barley could then be used to produce a warming alcoholic beverage.

In England one of the triggers for alcoholic production was the dissolution of the monasteries by Henry VIII in the 1530s. This obliged many monk apothecaries to seek new occupations as distillers of medicines and alcoholic drinks. In 1527 the first English translation of a book on the art of distillation appeared – Hieronymus Braunschweig's *The Vertuose Boke of Distyllacion*. However, since alcohol was so expensive it continued for some time to be the prerogative of the rich, and Andrew Boorde reported in 1548 that "Ale was the natural drink of the Englishman." This was to change with the Elizabethan wars with the Dutch from 1558 onward when many soldiers are reported to have returned from fighting with a taste for strong liquor. Could this be the origin of the phrase "Dutch courage?"

In Ireland too whisky distillation was well under way. Sir Walter Raleigh recorded in his diary on his way to Guyana in 1584 that he had taken delivery of a "supreme present of a 32 gallon cask of the Earl of Cork's

home distilled Uisge Beathat ...." By the 1600s there were many mills with distilleries along the riverside close to the site of the Bushmills distillery today.

The Company of Distillers was incorporated in London in 1638 with virtually the same remit as the Surgeon Barbers of Edinburgh some 133 years before. The company retained control of the trade in distilled spirits until 1703 when Queen Anne came to the throne. In 1639 the Distillers Company published their first handbook on the art of distilling.

Several references to drinking whisky for medicinal purposes exist from around this time. Highland Bitters, a mixture of herbs and spices mixed with whisky, is one of the oldest cures for an upset stomach. "On the sideboard there always stood before breakfast a bottle of whisky, smuggled of course, with plenty of camomile flowers, bitter orange-peel, and juniper berries in it and of this he [Sir Hector Mackenzie] had a wee glass always before we sat down to breakfast, as a fine stomachic." Osgood Mackenzie: *A Hundred Years in the Highlands*.

Above left: Glenrothes Distillery close to the Lady's Well.

Above: Good food, ale, wines and whisky were the privileges of the rich.

Right: At Glenmorangie Distillery single malts are produced to traditional methods.

Dr Johnson compiled his famous *Dictionary* in 1755 and mentions whisky under the name of usquebaugh – "a compound distilled spirit, being drawn on aromaticks; and the Irish sort is particularly distinguished for its pleasant and mild flavour. The Highland sort is somewhat hotter; and by corruption in Scottish they call it whisky." He also refers to the medicinal qualities of whisky: "a dram much used in the Highlands as a stomachic, made from an infusion of aromatic herbs and whisky."

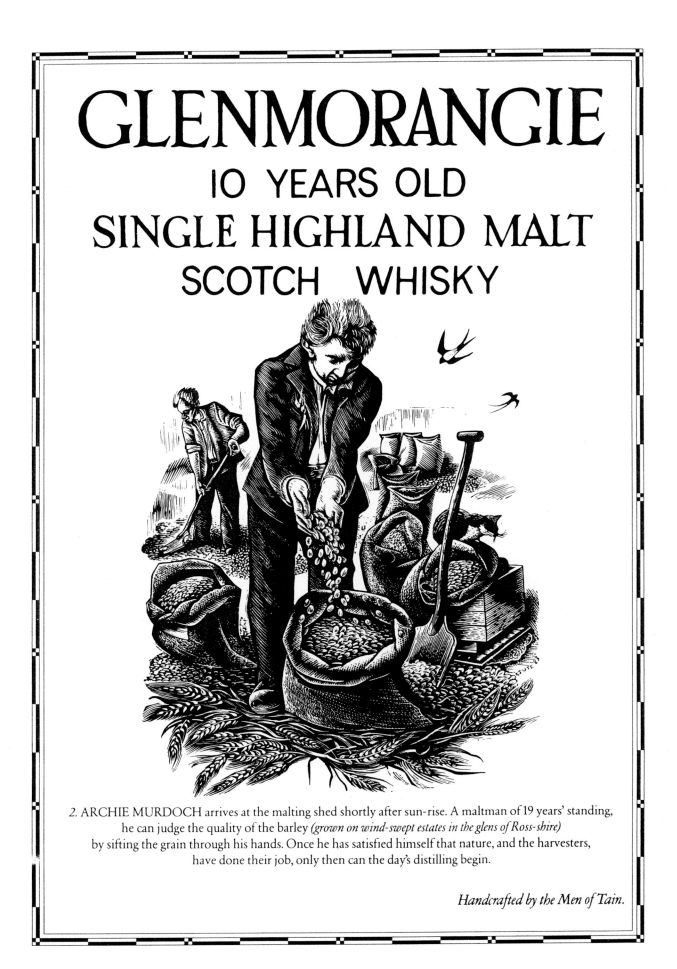

GLENMORANGIE
10 YEARS OLD
SINGLE HIGHLAND MALT
SCOTCH WHISKY

2. ARCHIE MURDOCH arrives at the malting shed shortly after sun-rise. A maltman of 19 years' standing,
he can judge the quality of the barley *(grown on wind-swept estates in the glens of Ross-shire)*
by sifting the grain through his hands. Once he has satisfied himself that nature, and the harvesters,
have done their job, only then can the day's distilling begin.

Handcrafted by the Men of Tain.

Taxes, wars and more taxes

The growth of whisky distilling in Scotland didn't meet with everyone's approval and in 1597 the Scottish Church tried to control its manufacture. In 1603 the Scottish King James VI became James I of England and the two countries started to form the basis of the present government system. (It wasn't until 1707 and the Act of Union that England gained control over Scotland.) In 1609 the Scottish parliament took steps to seize whisky in the Western Isles because of rioting between drunken gangs.

Following the Civil War in England in 1643, the puritanical government raised duty (taxes) on both the importation of spirits from The Netherlands and alcoholic beverages that were produced at home. Scotland was not controlled by the English government at that time, and so was unaffected by these taxes. However, on January 31, 1644 the Scottish government imposed a tax on spirits of 2s 8d (two Scots shillings and eight pence) per Scots pint (2 liters or 4¼ pints) in order to raise taxes to support the English parliament's fight against King Charles I. "...On everie pynt of aquavytie or strong watteris sold within the countrey," to raise money for "an armie to be sent into England." In 1693 the Scottish parliament again imposed duty on each pint of spirit produced.

In 1661 King Charles II imposed a duty of 4d (four pence) per gallon of whisky produced in Ireland – though the Irish took no notice at all.

At this time, whisky was not the preferred drink of the gentry in the cities of Scotland or indeed England: cognac and fine wines from France were more likely to be served at their tables. One reason for this was that the quality of whisky available was very variable, since stills often functioned for a very short time before they were moved on to evade the exciseman. There was one notable exception to this rule – Duncan Forbes' distillery at Ferintosh on the Black Isle, which began distilling in 1670. In 1689 his distillery was destroyed by supporters of James II, because Forbes had been a follower of William of Orange. With money given to him by William in compensation he set about refitting his distillery and was given the right to distill whisky "from grain grown on his own estate – upon payment of an annual sum of 400 merks." This special permission continued for some 95 years and during that time the Forbes family established other distilleries. In 1784 the arrangement came to an end with the payment to Forbes of a sum equivalent to 16 years' revenue, some £20,000 – a considerable sum at that time.

Collecting the taxes was difficult in Scotland, since there were few tax collectors and many of the distilleries for obvious reasons were situated in remote and inaccessible places. Whisky distillers saw the tax as a great imposition. Because it was levied on each pint produced, the amounts due would in some cases have been prohibitive, so for the most part they refused to pay. For the next 100 years or so smuggling became the accepted route for whisky sales and there are many colorful stories of moonlight exploits.

In 1707, when the Act of Union brought Scotland under English legislation, further attempts were made to control whisky distillation. Many laws were passed including the extension of the English Malt Tax in 1713. The imposition of British Rule caused widespread discontent within Scotland and this tax was seen as just another outrageous demand. The Scots tried to remove the British king and replace him with their choice, the "Old Pretender," the Catholic James Stuart. This led to the first Jacobite Rising in 1715, which ended at the Battle of Sheriffmuir in the same year. The situation became confused and inconsistent with distilleries being taxed at different rates. In 1725 the English Prime Minister Walpole raised taxes even higher and introduced a duty of three pence a bushel on malt. This would have netted a considerable sum for the government and further strengthened the Scottish view that the English were using taxes to impose their authority over Scotland.

Bonnie Prince Charlie's efforts to regain Scottish independence had serious repercussions on the whisky industry. After his defeat at Culloden in April 1746, the English government placed restrictions on the wearing of the kilt and other Highland clothing and outlawed anything associated with the Scottish clans. It also stepped up its efforts to collect taxes. A further setback was the introduction of a ban on distilling following bad harvests throughout England and Scotland in 1757. The ban wasn't lifted until 1760. Those distilleries that had been paying taxes and were thus seen as "legal" stopped producing altogether. Needless to say many of the illicit stills continued to produce whisky, and their sales increased.

In 1760 the English government tried again to enforce duty on Irish distillers and introduced a law to ensure that only those with a license could distill whisky. But all this achieved was to create a large illicit distilling industry with few legal contenders. Some names that are still familiar today were founded around this time, including Jameson and Power.

Whisky-making was an important part of the Scots' way of life, and efforts to curb its production were seen as persecution by the English oppressor. A Ross-shire minister wrote in the Statistical Account of 1796, "distilling is almost the only method of converting our victual into cash for the payment of rent and servants and whisky may in fact be called our staple commodity." For each of those who paid their taxes, hundreds did not. In Edinburgh in 1777, for example, there were eight legal distilleries and an estimated 400 more operating outside the law.

By the end of the 18th century the tax per gallon of still capacity had risen to £162. This was an excessive amount, which very few could afford to pay. Those distilleries situated in the Lowland region of Scotland could not evade paying taxes, because they were more accessible to the excisemen. Many of them went out of business. Most of the whisky available was still being distilled illicitly. In Ireland, despite the introduction of new legislation to license distilleries, there were some 2,000 operating illegally. Little by little the re-introduction of excise duty in Ireland had the effect of reducing the number of distilleries until only the largest remained.

The situation in 1822 when King George IV visited Scotland was not a happy one, although by that time whisky was perhaps the country's largest single

Left: Turn of the century mashing machine at the Glenkinchie Museum of Whisky Production.

industry. Taxes had forced some of the largest distillers out of business and the best whisky was in fact manufactured by illegal distillers. The King's first request when his yacht landed in Leith Harbour was for a bottle of "Highland whisky" and he and his host Sir Walter Scott drank together. On his arrival in Edinburgh the King again asked for a drink and this time he mentioned The Glenlivet whisky by name. This was a most ironical request, for he was asking for whisky from a distillery which operated illicitly by paying no taxes, at a time when his government was seeking to put such operations out of business. This illustrates how ineffective the activities of the excisemen and soldiers must have been in controlling the distribution of Highland whiskies; for it is clear that by then The Glenlivet had become well known in London. He also upset Elizabeth Grant of Rothiemurchus who was in charge of the cellars, for she

wrote that the request for The Glenlivet made her "...very cross. Lord Conyngham, the Chamberlain, was looking everywhere for pure Glenlivet whisky – the king drank nothing else – it was not be to had out of the Highlands. My father sent word to me – I was the cellarer – to empty my pet bin, where was whisky long in wood, long in uncorked bottles, mild as milk, and the true contraband gout [taste] in it. Much as I grudged this treasure, it made our fortunes afterwards, showing on what trifles great events sometimes depend ... ensured to my father the Indian Judgeship." The King was dressed in full Highland dress, which hardly flattered his portly figure and must have been quite an extraordinary sight.

In 1823 an act of parliament was passed that made distilling legal provided a license fee was paid and the distillery produced more than 40 gallons a year. This had the desired effect and

many distilleries were built on the same sites and using the same water supply as illicit distillers had been using for many years. Unfortunately, the government could not resist the temptation to raise more from whisky sales and in 1840 duty was imposed on each bottle sold by the distillery. Duty is still collected by the government from the distilleries on each bottle sold in the United Kingdom.

The first distillery to take out a license was incidentally The Glenlivet in 1824. The founder George Smith rented land from the Duke of Gordon who had pushed the legislation through. He was closely followed by Cardhu, The Glendronach, Old Fettercairn and The Macallan among others. Because of the lack of written records we can date the earliest commercial distilleries only from those few accounts that do survive. Those which appear to date back to the late eighteenth century include Bowmore (1779), Strathisla (1786), Highland Park (1795), Lagavulin (1784), Littlemill (1772), and Tobermory (1795).

In 1889 the Technical Institution Act was passed, which was designed to divert money gained from an extra duty of 6d (six pence) per gallon levied on spirits to assist technical and secondary education. The amount raised was used by county and borough councils and was known as "whisky money," which seems strange since the original levy had been put in place to compensate licensees of inns that had been closed.

Smuggling and blethermen, gaugers and redcoats

The introduction of taxes, particularly after the Act of Union in 1707 in Britain, led to many distillers going underground. Taxes were raised on the volume of spirits produced by a distillery and to assess this amount the exciseman used a gauging rod to measure capacity. The first recorded use of the word "gauger" to denote an excise officer or tax collector was in 1483, and it was soon widespread throughout England and Scotland. The task of collecting taxes was dangerous and many gaugers were injured or lost their lives in the course of their duty. The tax collector would be accompanied by English soldiers who offered some form of protection. The soldiers were called "redcoats," named for the color of their uniforms. Outwitting the redcoats became a national sport in Scotland and tales of heroism and cunning against them are woven into the history of individual distilleries.

Distilleries were usually small, and an illegal still could be broken down quite easily and removed, so detection was difficult. An illegal still comprised a metal pot in which the barley, yeast and water were boiled over a fire, a small length of coiled pipe known as a "worm" in which the steam was collected, and a barrel for the raw spirit. A persistent exciseman knew that all he had to do was wait in a secluded spot where he suspected illegal distilling was taking place and watch for a spiral of smoke rising. It is said that the fact that there are very few juniper trees in Scotland today is directly related to the history of illicit distilling; burning juniper wood makes very little smoke.

In 1736 people in Edinburgh held a demonstration at the execution of a smuggler. The town guard was led by a Captain Porteus who panicked because of the crowd and ordered his men to fire, killing several people. Porteus was tried and condemned to death. Before his sentence was carried out, however, it was rumored that he would be set free. So the townspeople captured him and arranged his hanging themselves.

Top: An illicit still reconstructed at Royal Lochnagar Distillery.

Right: Dipping the can into the washback enabled the distiller (and the exciseman) to test the alcoholic content.

Exciseman and poet

The most famous writer on the subject must be Robert Burns (1759–96), an exciseman and a poet. Robert Burns wrote "Scotch Drink" in 1785, a poem about the glories of whisky and the end of Ferintosh distillery's special tax-free immunity:

Let other poets raise a fracas
'Bout vines, an' wines, an' drucken
Bacchus,
An' crabbet names an' stories wrack us,
An' grate our lug:
I sing the juice Scotch bere can mak' us,
In glass or jug.

Burns was a great patriot and believed that the taxes were contravening the farmers' right to earn badly needed extra income from distilling. He wrote his poem "The Author's Earnest Cry and Prayer" in 1786 before he became an exciseman and it was sent as a plea to the House of Commons, the seat of Parliament in London. "E'er sin they laid that curst restriction, On aqua vitae... Freedom and whisky gang together..."

In "John Barleycorn – A Ballad" Burns gives the story of the making of whisky and clearly felt that drinking whisky would overcome all problems. John Barleycorn is a reference to barley.

In spiring bold John Barleycorn!
What dangers thous canst make us scorn!
Wi tipenny, we fear nae evil!
Wi usquebae, we'll face the devil!

His best-known poem is "Auld Lang Syne," in which singers are invited to "tak a cup o'kindness yet," surely this must be a whisky? And no Burns' Night Supper should be without his poem "To A Haggis!"

Although distilleries could be hidden, it was less easy to hide stocks of whisky. There are many tales of how precious stocks were saved from destruction or confiscation. In 1798, Magnus Eunson was distilling whisky at Highland Park in Orkney. A notorious smuggler and local preacher, he used to hide barrels of whisky in his church. On hearing that excisemen were in the area, the barrels of whisky were taken from the church and hidden under a white cloth in his house. While the excisemen searched the church, Eunson and his staff placed a coffin lid under the cloth and started a funeral service. One of Eunson's employees whispered that smallpox had been the cause of death and this was enough to make the excisemen flee in terror.

Another tale is told, taking place some years later, of a well-known Stirling hotelier who used a funeral cortege as cover to collect his whisky from the Highlands of Perthshire. His stock traveled the 20 miles from the Braes of Glenlivet to Dufftown at a slow pace while everyone who saw it pass by, including the exciseman, took off their hats.

Many smugglers chose to meet outside a town and wait for the arrival of agents who would sell their whisky for them. These agents were known as "blethermen" named for the Scots word blether meaning to chatter or speak continuous nonsense. John Grant, who worked for The Glenlivet distillery and had been a smuggler in his youth, talked of how "... the blethermen generally bought all we had but if we did not agree about the price we went on to another place and did the same thing... These blethermen acted as middle men or agents and were entitled to close the transactions with us, so that we did not generally see our real purchasers, the publicans."

While smugglers were generally circumspect about selling their whisky,

Above: The rooks at The Glendronach distillery were seen as a good luck charm as they made a noise when the exciseman came down the road.

Bottom left: Stoking the peat fire; an engraving from Laphroaig.

some were quite brazen on their return, as a Reverend Thomas Guthrie reported. "They rode on Highland ponies, carrying on each side of their small, shaggy but brave and hardy steeds, a small cask or keg as it was called of illicit whisky, manufactured amid the wilds of Aberdeenshire or the glens of the Grampians. They took up a position on some commanding eminence during the day, where they could, as from a watchtower, descry the distant approach of the enemy, the exciseman or gauger: then, when night fell, every man to horse, descending the mountains only six miles from Brechin, they scoured the plains, rattled into the villages and towns, disposing of their whisky to agents they had everywhere ... I have seen a troop of thirty of them riding in Indian file, and in broad day, through the streets of Brechin, after they had succeeded in disposing of their whisky."

The local courts were overloaded with prosecution cases against illicit distillers. Many magistrates' sympathies were with the distillers for not only did they

appreciate the whisky they produced but understood that earning additional income from its sales was vital. For most Scottish farmers life was one of grinding poverty, since barley was difficult to sell and their landlords demanded exorbitant rents. One well-known magistrate was William Grant, known as "the Cripple Captain" after an accident, who presided in Keith. "... Smugglers always liked to see the Earl of Fife and the Cripple Captain on the bench. When those gentlemen dispensed justice they were generally fined to the extent of half-a-crown [two shillings and sixpence] and sometimes as low as sixpence, which the Earl of Fife usually paid himself." Another magistrate known for his leniency was William Murray of Tain, a well-respected landowner who supplied distillers with barley from his estates. The offering of rewards for handing in illegal stills backfired because distillers saw this as a way of replacing their worn-out copper tubing. By taking the coiled "worm" to the exciseman they could claim five pounds for having seized an illicit still – then they would use the money to buy a replacement.

One of the most famous excisemen was the poet Robert Burns who worked in Dumfries from 1789 to 1796. As a poet he celebrated the distillation of

whisky and the role it played in the life of the Scots.

Spurred by the activities of the Duke of Gordon, a leading Scottish landowner, legislation was put in place in 1823 which would revolutionize distilling. The idea was that by making whisky distilling legal and charging only a modest license fee instead of a tax on every pint produced, distillers would set up more permanent sites and ultimately produce better-quality whisky. The Duke was also concerned that far too many troops were drafted to assist the excisemen. In 1820 over 14,000 raids on illicit distillers were made by gaugers and their accompanying soldiers, but for the most part these raids proved ineffectual and taxes were not collected.

With the introduction of legal distilling the role of the exciseman changed and he started to become part of the distillery establishment, so that he could verify the amount of whisky distilled. The life of a distillery exciseman became a far more comfortable one: he had his own cottage and a position in the local community. In April 1983 this was to change as distillery managers took over the responsibility themselves.

ECONOMIC REPERCUSSIONS AND NEW DYNASTIES

Whisky blends

W hisky distillation is not just a story of single malt distilleries producing whisky from single malt; other grains, essentially unmalted, were also used to produce spirit. The first continuous still was invented and patented by Robert Stein in 1826 and this meant that grain whiskies could be produced far more quickly than by the traditional pot still method. John Haig distilled grain whisky at Cameronbridge in 1828 and for quite some time the distillery sold its own single grain whisky. An excise officer who had an important impact on the Scotch whisky industry was Aeneas Coffey who worked as an exciseman in Ireland until 1824.

The invention of the Coffey patent still was the trigger for the development of grain whiskies and ultimately the growth of blended whiskies, since production could be quickly increased to meet demand. Several whisky dynasties were founded between the 1830s and 1850s and their names are still synonymous with blends today. Among these are brands such as Teacher's, Chivas and Cutty Sark. The stories of these blends and the families who promoted them are told in Chapter 4.

In 1827 George Ballantine had completed his apprenticeship with Andrew Hunter, an Edinburgh grocer, and set up on his own. His first shop was in the Cowgate, not the most fashionable part of Edinburgh, but a busy

thoroughfare nonetheless. From these humble premises he moved in 1831 to Candlemakers' Row and then again in 1836 to South Bridge off Princes Street, the most prestigious in Edinburgh. In those days grocers provided everything from dried goods through fish, to wine

and whisky. While his business expanded, George started to invest in supplies of malt whiskies such as The Glenlivet and Talisker. In 1853 Andrew Usher, a friend of George Ballantine, produced his first blend of malts of different ages. Bill Bergius, a director of

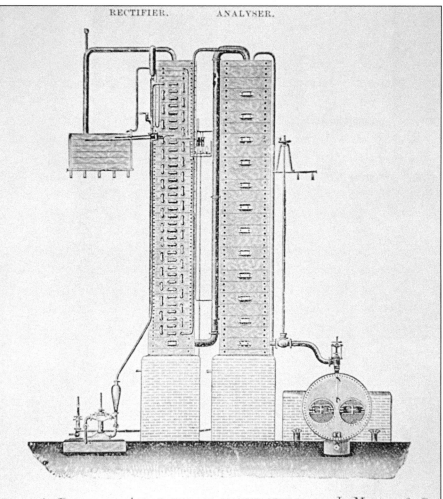

COFFEY'S DISTILLING APPARATUS, AS MANUFACTURED BY J. MILLER & CO.

trade relations at Ballantine's and himself a direct descendant of William Teacher (another famous blend), said "On the one hand people had been trying to produce a cheaper version of malt by adulterating it. At the time, there was no law about what Scotch whisky should be. Some unscrupulous traders were even diluting whisky with Spanish neutral spirit to increase their profit. In parallel with this unsavory side, there were reputable merchants such as Ballantine's who saw blending as an art form. They worked to create something lighter and more sophisticated, a high-quality product." Ballantine started experimenting with his own blends, using not only malts but the new grain whiskies being produced by Aeneas Coffey's patent still. He realized that the secret to a good blend was not just to mix different whiskies together but to discover something that was in itself special. Bill Bergius continues, "at first, they would perhaps stumble on a particularly fine combination. Customers who enjoyed the blend would ask them to repeat it, or sometimes bring a bottle of Scotch for their spirit merchant to reproduce. In this way, recipes and named blends evolved."

In 1869 George Ballantine handed over the running of his Edinburgh business to his eldest son, Archibald. George and his wife Isabella and the rest of the family moved to Glasgow to concentrate on building up a wholesale business from new premises at 100 Union Street. This was to herald a period of considerable growth for the company, boosted by expanding sales both overseas and throughout Britain.

Far left: The design of a Coffey still is virtually unchanged since this early example.

Above: Ordering a dram in a grocer's shop in Glasgow in the late 1800s.

Below: Single malts waiting for the blender's nose.

In Boswell's *Tour to the Hebrides* on October 23, 1773, he quotes Samuel Johnson (1709–84) as saying when calling for a gill of whisky, "Come let me know what it is that makes a Scotchman happy."

Charles Dickens (1812–70), the English novelist, wrote to a friend in 1852: "A man in Edinburgh supposed to be unparalleled in his whisky education has just sent me what they call in the City of London 'a small parcel' of what he recommends as rare old Glenlivet. Try the accompanying speciment..." In *Kidnapped* (1886) by the Scottish author Robert Louis Stevenson (1850–94), guests are welcomed by Duncan Dhu who "... made haste to bring out the pair of pipes that was his principal possession, and to set before his guests the mutton-ham and a bottle of that drink which they call Athole Brose and which is made of old whisky, strained honey and sweet cream, slowly beaten together in the right order and proportion."

One delightful quotation comes from Daisy Ashford's book, *The Young Visitors* (1919). This book was written when the author was aged nine and published when she was a grown woman. "Here Mr Salteena thourght he had better go to bed as he had had a long journey. Bernard always had a few prayers in the hall and some whiskey afterwards as he was rather pious but Mr Salteena was not very addicted to prayers so he marched up to bed."

John Buchan, a Scot, prominent barrister, Member of Parliament and 35th Governor-General of Canada was also a celebrated author. One of his books published in 1925 revolves around the story of John Macnab, a fictional character created by three "bored" pillars of the establishment, who sends letters to landowners saying that on a given date a deer or salmon will be poached on their land. Needless to say when the three conspirators, together with one of their servants, are drawing up their plans a dram of whisky is offered to help things along. The Macnab story was revived by *The Field*, a magazine published in the U.K. in June 1998 when it laid down a challenge to its readers to obtain a salmon, a brace of grouse and a stag within 24 hours keeping within the law. A great deal of fun ensued and several people achieved successful "Macnabs."

Above: A kingfisher perches by the side of the Dullan River near Dufftown Distillery.

As blended whiskies became more sophisticated and appealed to a wider audience (many had found single malts too harsh), an outbreak of phylloxera in 1863 in France started to decimate the vineyards. By 1879 most European vineyards had been forced to destroy their vines. The production of wine and, more importantly, cognac came to a halt. Customers had to look elsewhere for their liquor and attention turned to the homegrown product – whisky. During this time many new distilleries were built, such as Benriach in 1898, The Balvenie in 1892 and Dufftown in 1896. Irish whiskey also continued to gain a large share of the market in England, as people turned to lighter whiskies.

During his tour of whisky producers in the 1880s, Alfred Barnard also visited several grain distilleries. In fact his journey started at the Port Dundas grain distillery in Glasgow. In Bristol he wrote that he had visited the oldest distillery in England, which had been producing spirit since 1761. Other distilleries were sited in Stratford, in London and in Liverpool at the Vaux distillery built in 1781.

The Vat 69 blend was born in 1882. This was the result of a series of trials set up by William Sanderson. He produced 100 different blends to be tasted "blind" (from unlabeled bottles, each identified only by a number) by himself and a group of his friends. This was surely a phenomenal task: it must have taken some considerable time to make a choice. Ultimately the blend they liked the best was number 69. In the *War Office Times* and *Naval Review* of October 1905 the writer records, "Vat 69 is not a cheap whisky in the ordinary acceptance of the term, but at the same time, we consider the price low in view of the quality. Directly we sampled this whisky we said to ourselves: 'This is the ideal whisky so many of our Service readers have been looking for, and hitherto in vain.' … We have confidence in recommending it to our readers."

The growth in whisky sales was seriously affected in 1898 when Pattisons, a well-known blending company, went bankrupt. The Pattison brothers were given prison sentences and the collapse of their company had serious repercussions throughout the industry. Distilleries had been laying down single malts for Pattisons, who were then unable to pay for them, and the distilleries had to start looking for new customers. Unfortunately, this collapse coincided with a slump in the British economy and the combination of this general economic decline, under-capitalization and over-spending led to the closure of many distilleries. Malt whisky distillers were concerned by the continued growth in blended sales and sought to control this by seeking legislation stating that whisky could be produced only by them. The London Borough of Islington prosecuted two liquor retailers for selling whisky "not of the nature, substance and quality demanded" because their blends consisted of only 10 percent malts and the balance grain whisky. After the case a Royal Commission was set up to consider the whole question of what could legally be called whisky and in July 1909 the result was published. This stated that "Scotch whisky embraced malt, grain and blended whisky, no matter how little malt was incorporated in the blend."

One other legislative change that should be noted in this history is the Immature Spirit Act of 1915, which was introduced in England during World War I (1914–18). This stated that raw spirit had to be matured for two years before it could be sold and was part of the Chancellor of the Exchequer, Lloyd George's efforts to curb drinking during the war. Lloyd George would have prohibited the sale of alcohol completely if he could. He said in an address he made in Bangor, north Wales during February 1915 "We are fighting Germany, Austria – and Drink. And as far as I can see the greatest of these deadly foes is Drink!" Restricting sales of raw spirit changed the face of whiskey production in Ireland, affecting particularly those manufacturing grain whiskies in continuous Coffey stills. Many of these companies were forced to close their plants. Ironically when Lloyd George became Minister for Munitions he took over the Coffey stills for the production of spirit for the manufacture of explosives.

To ensure that the consumer was getting a properly matured spirit, some companies took unusual steps. William Teacher & Sons sent their whisky to Australia and back. The total journey took at least a year: six months to arrive and another six months to get back, so with an additional period in bond in Australia the whisky was guaranteed to be properly matured.

Below: Teacher's whisky traveled around the globe to reassure customers it was properly matured.

In 1913 William Teacher & Sons took the unprecedented step of introducing "The Self-Opening Bottle." The idea was invented by William Bergius and the company adopted the slogan "Bury the Corkscrew" to promote the new stopper. As recorded in the *Licensed Victuallers' Gazette* of June 1913, "This is the advice which Messrs William Teacher and Sons, the well-known whisky distillers are tendering to the trade, and they are showing the licensed victualler how he can economize time and save no end of trouble and worry by using the new self-opening device, which they have adopted for their several brands; and which, it is not surprising to hear, although it was only placed on the market on May 1st, has met with unqualified approval from the trade and the public. There is no need at this time of day to draw attention to the difficulty and often danger of drawing a cork by means of a corkscrew. Sometimes the neck of the bottle has come off, resulting in a cut hand, or the cork is rotten and away go the pieces in the liquor. The little device of Messrs Teacher is simplicity itself. It is in reality a cork stopper with a broad top which is made to fix securely on the mouth of the bottle, and all that one has to do is to give it a twist and hey presto! the cork is out. Nothing could be easier, at the same time there is perfect security of the contents of the bottle. The motto of the firm has long been, 'put the value in the bottle and let the contents speak for itself,' and there can be no question that the public appreciation of Highland Cream is due to its never-varying quality. What you have now is to 'get the value out of the bottle' with the minimum of trouble and delay; in short to make a point of using the 'self-opening' bottle … and save your expletives." In spite of

Main picture: A rare Teacher's bottle from 1860.

Left: Horses at the Mains of Balvenie Farm, Glenfiddich.

Below: The distillery team at Glenturret in the 1860s.

this roaring acclamation it took some 15 years for all the competition to adopt the new stopper.

The growth in popularity of Scotch blended whisky had a detrimental effect on Irish whiskey sales in England. The introduction of the Immature Spirit Act, also meant that sales of new grain whisky from Ireland were curtailed and many distilleries never recovered from the blow. After the Irish War of Independence in 1916 the country was divided by the English in 1919 and there followed a period of unrest until 1921. Duty was introduced by both Ireland and England by way of retaliation. This meant that Irish whiskey, which had recently started to lose its American

market with the introduction of Prohibition, also lost almost overnight its English and associated markets, such as the Caribbean, Australia, New Zealand and India. These two events were to have a devastating effect on the Irish whiskey industry and when Prohibition ceased in 1934 distillers were unable to respond because most distilleries were inoperative.

In Scotland from 1917 to 1919, during World War I, distilleries were forced to close because barley was needed for food. When the war was over many Scotch whisky companies, such as Watson's, who owned Ord Distillery in Ross-shire, went out of business rather than attempt to continue distilling.

The American story

When the first English Puritan settlers sailed to America one thing they did not take with them was whisky, for they forswore strong drink. So the first settlements in Massachusetts and New York were "dry" when the next wave of immigrants arrived in the early 1700s from Scotland and Ireland. They traveled westward into Pennsylvania, Maryland and Virginia and settled down to farming. Once they had produced sufficient grain for their food needs they turned to the natural by-product of excess grain: the distillation of whisky. The first reference is to the distillation of rum from molasses and subsequently brandy from fruits. The Scots and Irish discovered ample supplies of rye in Pennsylvania and started distilling whisky from this as well as barley. But when the settlers moved further westward they discovered that barley wouldn't grow so well and started growing Indian corn as their staple crop. By the end of the eighteenth century there were literally thousands of small home distilleries producing whisky from local grains.

The British government's predilection for imposing taxes on whisky distillation was not confined to the British Isles. The first tax was introduced in America very early in 1684, but as in Ireland it seems to have largely been ignored by the local population. The sheer size of the area to be covered meant that collecting taxes was a difficult and often dangerous task. On March 3, 1791 the local government tried again and introduced a law requiring that all stills in Pennsylvania be registered. This imposition was met with anger by the local farmers and led to the whisky rebellion of 1794. Fighting broke out in Pittsburgh and distillers attacked customs men. Private property was destroyed and some of the excise officers were tarred and feathered. The militia was called in and the rebellion was quashed by a contingent of 13,000 soldiers commanded by a distiller from Virginia – George Washington.

There are three principal whisky styles in the United States – rye, Tennessee sour mash and bourbon. The whisky-producing areas all follow a limestone belt which stretches through Maryland, Pennsylvania, Tennessee and Virginia. While Virginia grew in size the western part of the state developed into the ninth state, Kentucky, in 1792. Kentucky became a whisky state after Thomas Jefferson, who was then Governor of Virginia, granted settlers land for growing corn. Bourbon County is part of Kentucky. It was named after the French royal family in recognition of the support given to the rebels during the War of Independence. Ironically, today Bourbon is a "dry" county with no distilleries, but its name lives on in whiskies produced in towns such as Frankfort and Louisville in Kentucky.

Various distilleries can trace their origins back to this time. Jacob Beam started distilling in 1795 and Abraham Overholt founded a rye distillery in Westmoreland County which continued in production until the 1930s. The company was then purchased by the National Distillers Company which still produces Old Overholt rye whiskey at its plant in Frankfort, Kentucky.

Prohibition was to stop production in most distilleries in the United States, with devastating consequences. For by the time it was all over the American taste had changed from the big bold ryes and heavy bourbons to the lighter blended whiskies which had been smuggled in from Canada, Scotland and Ireland. Distilling stopped in Maryland and Pennsylvania, and in Kentucky many distilleries were never to re-open. As if one blow weren't enough, the Prohibition era was followed by the depression in America and the Wall Street Crash of 1929.

Above: Jim Beam founded the James B. Beam Distilling Company in 1935.

Prohibition, bootleggers and "the real McCoy"

Prohibition is defined by the *Encyclopedia Britannica* as "the legal prevention of the manufacture, sale or transportation of alcoholic beverages with the aim of achieving partial or total abstinence through legal means." Prohibition was by no means a new idea in 1919 when it was introduced in the United States. The Aztecs, ancient Chinese and feudal Japanese had introduced Prohibition as a means of regulating consumption of alcoholic drink. In more recent times Polynesia, Iceland, Finland, Norway, Sweden, Russia, Canada and India have experimented with Prohibition.

Canada introduced partial Prohibition in a few provinces during World War I, but efforts to extend it nationwide in 1918 failed. The experiment, which lasted for only eight months, proved highly unpopular and had a damaging effect on the whisky industry.

Prohibition in the United States grew out of the religious fervor of certain groups that became active in the 1830s. They sought to improve the lot of their fellow man by encouraging temperance and also by seeking the abolition of slavery. In 1838 Massachusetts introduced a law which prohibited the sale of spirits in less than 15-gallon quantities. Maine was the first state to introduce Prohibition in 1846 and many states introduced similar laws before the advent of the Civil War. In 1893

religious groups picked up the cudgel again and founded the Anti-Saloon League, which based its campaign upon fears for the growth of saloons and perceived corruption within them and also employees' safety at work. The production of American whisky declined in the United States when a temporary Wartime Prohibition Act was introduced, which effectively ensured that all grain went into food production. The Canadian failure to impose total Prohibition seems to have been largely ignored and the movement to introduce it in the United States continued to gain ground. However, it was not until October 28, 1919, that the National Prohibition Act was passed, also known as the Volstead Act named for congressman Andrew J. Volstead who was its chief proponent.

In the United States, the population in rural areas was sympathetic to Prohibition, but city-dwellers were less supportive. Criminal activities grew around the demand for liquor. One of the most celebrated gangsters was Al Capone, whose annual earnings were in excess of $60,000 – an enormous sum at that time. Gang warfare escalated, culminating in the St Valentine's Day Massacre in Chicago in 1929 when Capone's men shot dead seven members of "Bugs" Moran's gang. Supporters of Prohibition were by this time becoming increasingly alarmed at

the restriction of civil liberties imposed on the population by law enforcers trying to quash these criminal gangs.

Paradoxically, during Prohibition Scotch whisky sales increased rather than diminished. Visitors to the United States could obtain a special license to bring their own whisky with them, and alcohol could still be distilled for medicinal purposes. Sales of Laphroaig apparently continued throughout Prohibition, because its particularly peaty taste and aroma gave rise to the belief that it was in fact a medicine and not a whisky at all! Thomas Dewar of Dewar's blended whisky may well have encountered Laphroaig when visiting a province in Canada where Prohibition was in place at the time. He wrote that when he asked in a store "Do you sell whisky?" the reply was "Are you sick, mister, or got a medical certificate?"; "No" was Dewar's answer, which elicited "Then I can't do it; but I reckon our cholera mixture'll about fix you. Try a bottle of that." Dewar went on to report that the "cholera mixture" bore the label of a Scotch whisky distiller on the one side and instructions as to when the medicine should be taken on the other.

Veterinarians were allowed to buy whisky to use as a medicine for treating horses. Doc Wellbanks was a well-known vet who appears to have had a large number of sick horses on his

in the American market and increased their sales dramatically. Whisky entered the States through agents who set up businesses in places such as Nassau in the Bahamas. One agent was Captain William McCoy who worked with Berry Bros & Rudd, owners of the Cutty Sark brand. Although to all intents and purposes a smuggler or "bootlegger," Captain McCoy gained a reputation for providing quality whisky, hence the expression meaning "the genuine article," "the real McCoy."

Companies such as Hiram Walker, whose huge Walkerville headquarters in Canada are just across the river from Detroit continued to distill whisky and sell it to their American neighbors, albeit illegally. The river between Lake St Clair and Lake Erie effectively became an alcohol corridor with thousands of gallons being shipped under the noses of the American law enforcement agencies.

In the 1920s Sam Bromfman of Seagram's built the La Salle distillery in Montreal. This together with others, such as the company's original distillery built in 1857 at Waterloo and Amhertsburg in Ontario and Beaupré in Québec, were to make Seagram's the world leader it is today. Surely it was no coincidence that only a small percentage of the whisky produced was actually sold in Canada!

By 1932, the American Democratic Party had set out its election manifesto stating that one of its aims would be to abolish the Prohibition Act and when they won the presidential election that year repeal was inevitable. By December 5, 1933, Utah became the 36th state to ratify its repeal and national Prohibition was dead. Incidentally, the Prohibition Party, founded in 1869, is the oldest minor U.S. political party, and it is partly through its activities that there is still local Prohibition in some counties.

Above: In 1934 Berry Bros & Rudd started shipping whisky to America again: "Remove the cork and get the message" was the slogan for Cutty Sark, a whisky which grew during Prohibition.

rounds, judging by the amount of whisky he purchased. Veterinarians could also obtain supplies of alcohol to use in the making of animal medicines. Doc Wellbanks purchased raw alcohol for $2.60 a gallon and he added two gallons of water to each gallon to reduce it to the usual "whisky" strength. He then resold it as Doctor Wellbanks'

White Liniment for $5 a quart bottle – making an extremely handsome profit. The drink obviously bore no resemblance to whisky, but it was at least relatively safe to drink and certainly drove away the blues. By 1925 Doc Wellbanks had three boats and was working with Wes Kaiser who ran a fleet of fishing vessels, which seemed to catch very few fish and deliver a great deal of whisky.

Several whisky blends, such as Chivas Regal and Cutty Sark, gained footholds

Big fish and little minnows

During World War II, Scottish malt whisky distillers were again forced to close so that barley could be diverted into the production of food. At the end of the war many distilleries found themselves facing huge reconstruction bills. This was a period of great change with some distilleries closing and others changing hands. In spite of all these setbacks, the Scotch whisky industry was in better shape than that of Ireland or the United States. Scotch whisky blends in particular – Cutty Sark, Chivas Regal and Johnnie Walker – had increased in popularity especially in the U.S.

The 1950s and 1960s were good years for the Scotch whisky industry. This was the era of the well-respected upper-class salesman who traveled the world promoting whisky. Many were ex-Army officers who had served with the "right" regiments and wore old school ties from the best English schools. They didn't earn a great deal but their expense accounts were legendary. Whisky was very much perceived as a man's domain. This is perhaps ironic considering that many distilleries and merchants survived only because the owners' widows had taken over the helm. (On a personal note I remember visiting one whisky-distilling company that was quite perturbed when it became clear that it would be difficult to avoid entertaining me in the boardroom – until then, it had been an exclusively male preserve!)

Around this time demand far exceeded supply, and complacency started to creep into manufacturing. At the same time the key American distillers had started to revitalize their own industry and the Japanese had started again to distill whisky. The seeds were sown for a change in the world's whisky sales.

Today the ownership of whisky distilleries and worldwide blends rests with a mixture of multinational conglomerates, smaller companies and independent businesses; many are still family owned. There are some who would say that too many brands are in the hands of too few, but there is also the argument that this ensures that traditional single malts and blends continue to be produced and also allows room for old brands to be resurrected and new ones to be introduced to the marketplace.

Trying to unravel who exactly owns whom is not easy today. Takeovers and name changes of the companies themselves, not to mention distilleries which have also changed their names, amalgamations and disposals all make the task of exploring the histories of the larger organizations equally difficult.

For example Diageo, which was formed as a result of the merger of Grand Met and Guinness, has appeared in many guises. Companies that are now members of the group include names synonymous with famous blends and single malts such as Arthur Bell & Sons Ltd who owned Blair Athol. In 1925 Distillers Company Limited joined John Walker & Sons Ltd and Buchanan Dewar, owners of Black & White. Today the company has an annual turnover of £12 billion and employs around 80,000 people. Within its portfolio are some 31 single malt distilleries including famous names such as Glenkinchie, Cardhu, Lagavulin, Knockando, Dalwhinnie and

Above left: One of the oldest distilleries, Seagram's Strathisla founded in 1786.

Above: In 1848 Queen Victoria visited Lochnagar to taste the whisky.

SCOTLAND'S MALT WHISKY REGIONS

PEAT CUTTING

WESTRAY

THE NORTH SOUND

NORTH RONALDSAY

NORTH RONALDSAY FIRTH

Mull Head

SANDAY

WESTRAY FIRTH

EDAY

ROUSAY

SANDAY SOUND

HIGHLAND PARK
SINGLE MALT SCOTCH WHISKY
ORKNEY ✦ ISLANDS

STRONSAY

STRONSAY FIRTH

AUSKERRY SOUND

M A I N L A N D

FIRTH

Highland Park Distillery

Kirkwall

N

HOY SOUND

Old Man of Hoy
Rora Head

HOY

SCAPA FLOW

SOUTH RONALDSAY

PENTLAND FIRTH

STANDING STONE

THE ORKNEY ISLES

HIGHLAND PARK CIRCA 1890

© Crown Copyright

ORKNEY

Both pages: Highland Park and The Glenturret are both owned by Highland Distillers. Glenkinchie is part of Diageo's single malt portfolio.

Royal Lochnagar and a wide range of whisky blends such as the world-renowned Johnnie Walker, J. & B. and Bell's. The company also owns two grain distilleries and distilleries in the United States and other parts of the world.

There are other leading players. Allied Domecq has interests worldwide and 11 single malt distilleries, among them Laphroaig on the island of Islay in Scotland as well as the international blended whiskies Ballantines and Teacher's and two grain distilleries. Suntory of Japan, founded in 1889, achieved sales in 1997 of U.S. $9,446,979,000, employs nearly 5,000 people and owns Bowmore, Auchentoshan and Glen Garioch distilleries in Scotland. Seagram's has nine single malt distilleries, including The Glenlivet in Scotland, others in Canada and New Zealand, and brands such as Chivas Regal and Seagram's VO in its marketing mix. Jim Beam has

seven single malt distilleries in Scotland and other worldwide interests, not least of which is Jim Beam Kentucky Straight Bourbon Whiskey. The Brown-Forman Corporation produces Jack Daniel's Tennessee Whiskey, Canadian Mist and the ubiquitous Southern Comfort among others.

Other international companies with interests in whisky are Groupe Pernod Ricard, owners of Irish Distillers, Bushmills and Aberlour distilleries, and Bacardi, who purchased the Dewars blend from Guinness following the merger with Grand Met, and own distilleries such as Royal Brackla and Glen Deveron.

There are also a few companies in the United Kingdom that have an international face, but are still relatively small when compared to the multi-national conglomerates. One of these is Highland Distillers with single malt distilleries including Highland Park and Glenturret plus The Famous Grouse and

Black Bottle blends. Highland Distillers also operates and markets The Macallan distillery as part of a joint venture.

Then there are the smaller independent companies, examples of which can be found around the world. In this category names spring to mind such as J. & G. Grant of Glenfarclas distillery in Scotland, William Grant of The Glenfiddich also in Scotland, Lauchie Maclean of Glenora in Nova Scotia and Fritz Maytag of Old Potrero in California. Some of these smaller enterprises have long and distinguished pedigrees; others are new, reflecting the continued interest in whisky and enthusiasm of individual personalities. The Speyside distillery at Glen Tromie produces Drumguish single malt in Scotland and is the brainchild of George Christie. He and his family have built the distillery themselves – the project started in 1962 and was not completed until 1987.

In 1989 independent Irish whiskey production started again at a former alcohol plant at Cooley and began distilling both pot still malt and grain whiskies. The Cooley Distillery plc markets a range of brands including Tyrconnel Single Malt and Lockes Irish Whiskey. The barrels are stored at Lockes distillery in Kilbeggan where distilling no longer takes place, but where whisky had been produced since 1757.

What of the future? The changes in economic climates mean that last year's big consumers may no longer have the purchasing power and whisky manufacturers may have to look elsewhere, but on the whole the outlook is bright. Interest in single malt whiskies continues to grow worldwide and the demand for high-quality blends seems undiminished. So it is to be hoped that whisky distillation will continue to develop for many years to come.

The Anatomy of Whisky

ASK A DISTILLERY MANAGER WHAT MAKES HIS OR HER MALT DIFFERENT THAN THAT OF A NEIGHBOR AND HE OR SHE WILL CITE ANY NUMBER OF THINGS — THE WATER, THE TYPE OF BARLEY, HOW LONG THE BARLEY IS STEEPED IN WATER, HOW LONG IT IS DRIED, WHETHER OR NOT PEAT IS USED IN THE DRYING PROCESS, THE TYPE OF PEAT USED, THE FERMENTATION TIME, THE SHAPE AND SIZE OF THE STILLS, THE SPEED AT WHICH THE RAW SPIRIT IS COLLECTED, THE SIZE OF THE CASK USED, THE TYPE OF CASK USED — AND THE ENVIRONMENT IN THE WAREHOUSE. OTHER, MORE FANCIFUL REASONS FOR SCOTLAND'S PRODUCING SUCH FINE WHISKIES ARE OFTEN GIVEN, SUCH AS THE NORMALLY DAMP ATMOSPHERE OR THE WAY THE WIND BLOWS. PERHAPS IT IS SIMPLY THE MAGIC OF STILL AND CASK. IT IS PROBABLY FAIR TO SAY THAT ALL OF THESE CAN CONTRIBUTE, BUT NO ONE REALLY KNOWS THE ANSWER.

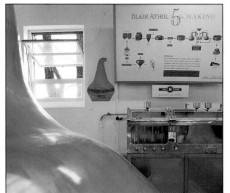

Distilling Malt Whisky

I t is not just serendipity that led to Scotland being such a large whisky producer. The country has an ideal environment for the industry, with everything required to make fine single malts. An early edition of the *New Scientist* magazine recorded that distilling whisky was "an art nobody had been able to reproduce outside Scotland." This assertion however is clearly not true, some exceptional whiskies are made in other parts of the world, but many of them are not well known outside their countries of origin.

Much has been written on the making of single malt whisky, but the fact that something so wonderful can be produced from the "ménage à trois" of water, malted barley and yeast makes it a story well worth the telling. Many distilleries do things just that little bit differently, which helps to explain why there is such a wide range of malts available. These refinements are not necessarily included in the general description that follows; indeed many of them are secrets still jealously guarded by individual distillers.

Sadly, some of the much-loved buildings of Scotland's oldest distilleries could change forever if supermarket chains succeed in imposing their own requirements that favor painted walls and clinical cleanliness over dusty

Right: Peat from Scotland's heather-clad hills has long been associated with fine malt whisky.

nooks and crannies, old equipment and silently-maturing barrels.

Single malts do not comprise the whole story: grain distilleries also make an important contribution to overall whisky production. When visiting a grain distillery it is hard to believe that this symphony of pipes can contribute so much to famous blended whiskies such as Chivas Regal, Teacher's and Johnnie Walker.

In Ireland, the U.S. and Canada, whiskies are also produced using different grains such as rye and corn. Using these other grains gives the resulting whiskies different tastes, as do the different climates which allow some whiskies to mature more quickly than others. American whisky distillers have

made good use of local ingredients and have developed different techniques to produce their fine whiskies – these techniques will be discussed later in this chapter.

All of this has a powerful influence on the all-important question: is it "whisky" or "whiskey?" As discussed in the introduction, generally speaking "whisky" is made in Scotland and throughout most of the world, and "whiskey" is made in Ireland and the United States, but there are exceptions. Where possible I have used the spelling attributed to the particular brand, so for example a Scotch single malt is always whisky, but when talking about American whiskies, Jim Beam is whiskey, but Maker's Mark is whisky.

For a whisky to qualify for the name "Scotch" it must have been produced in a distillery in Scotland and matured in Scotland. Whisky must be produced from water and cereals, distilled at an alcoholic strength by volume of less than 94·8 percent, and matured in casks of not greater than 185 U.S. gallons capacity for a minimum of three years from the date of distillation in a bonded warehouse.

A single malt whisky is distilled at an individual distillery and produced only from malted barley.

Grain whisky is produced using a continuous distillation process. Malted and unmalted cereals, which are cooked under steam pressure, are used and the resulting spirit is of a higher strength and matures more quickly than a malt whisky, since it has fewer constituent ingredients. Grain whiskies are usually used in blended whiskies.

Blended whiskies account for 95 percent of Scotch whisky sales. A blended whisky is created from both single malts and grain whisky. In the United States, Ireland and other countries most of the whiskies produced are also blends of pot still (the whiskies produced in pot stills could be made from a mixture of malted and unmalted barley as well as other grains) and grain whiskies.

Single grain whiskies are the product of a one-grain distillery. These whiskies are sold by several companies including Jim Beam (Invergordon) and United Distillers (Cameron Brig) in Scotland. Other whiskies that could qualify for this designation are those made from rye in the United States and Canada, although very few are made from 100 percent rye.

Left: New spirit flows into barrels to start its long maturation at Deanston Distillery, Scotland.

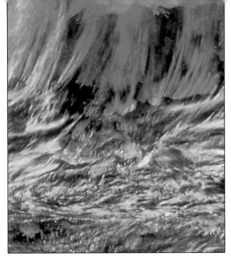

The ingredients

T here are in fact six ingredients (not just the three mentioned in the introduction) needed to produce a fine single malt whisky: water, barley, peat (although a few distilleries do not now use this), yeast, oak casks and the consummate skill and care of the distillery staff.

Below: Lochs of still, clear water provide distillers with the perfect source.

Water

The first requirement when choosing a site to build a malt whisky distillery is a pure, clear, water source. The water doesn't have to be free from minerals, but it certainly has to be clear of agricultural fertilizers, chemical wastes and other pollutants, which all too frequently find their way into the world's water supply. For this reason many distilleries are located in places of superb natural beauty in small villages on mountainsides, on the shores of islands or in the middle of large sweeping plains of open countryside.

The water must not only be pure, but a steady and continuous flow is essential throughout the year. Rivers that freeze in winter and run dry in summer are useless to the distiller wishing to produce whisky all year round, therefore most distilleries are

located by fast-flowing, sizeable streams or have access to a large lake. The water source, whether it is alkaline or acid, hard or soft, plays an important part in the taste and smell of the final single malt. When the water tumbles down from the Scottish hills or across peat bogs to the distillery, it carries with it a little of its birthplace and travels – peat, heather, granite and sandstone.

It is difficult to determine which elements are included in the water, and they can differ from one distillery to another. There are several cases of distilleries operating side by side and taking water from the same source yet producing completely different single malts, such as Clynelish and Brora, and Caperdonich and Glen Grant.

In Speyside, Scotland, the water travels over granite but the rock dates from different periods and has different constituent materials. Granite and basalt are volcanic rocks, laid down some 800 million years ago when volcanic activity twisted the rock strata and pushed up the mountains we know today. Much of the forests that covered this part of Scotland have been destroyed and the granite rocks are now close to the surface. Granite is tough and resilient and not much can grow on the bare rock, so water passes across the landscape unimpeded by vegetation, collecting small particles of minerals as it flows. Water flowing through granite will be acidic, but much of the acidity will be in the form of suspended solubles, which will disappear during distillation.

Chalk and limestone soils are alkaline and even if the water has flowed across peat bogs, which tend to be acidic, the alkalinity will reduce this acidity. Calcium and magnesium are essentially contained in water as bicarbonates, chlorides and sulfates. Some minerals remain after distillation; others disappear. Where the hardness of water

From left to right: Part of the secret of single malt – barley grown for the whisky industry, pure water, black peat dug from Islay and peat fires.

is caused by calcium bicarbonate, this will produce a calcium carbonate residue when distilled and will not remain in the whisky. In the northeast of Scotland, for example, near the Glenmorangie distillery, the basic rock is old red sandstone. Water running through sandstone tends to be hard with a high calcium and carbonate content. The water can also contain iron, which colors it red.

Traveling across to the Isle of Skye, the water crosses younger volcanic rocks thrust up when the British Isles separated from North America. This black rock contains magnesium, which will react with the copper in the still during distillation and may be one of the reasons why Talisker and other island single malt whiskies have such a unique taste. Water used for distillation on the Isle of Islay tends to be soft. On

the west coast of Islay the water flows over old sea beds and amphibalites, which are at least 1,600 million years old. Water on Islay is usually brown in color because it flows through peat, which also flavors the water.

Barley

Whisky companies the world over work closely with their grain producers to ensure that the grain meets their requirements. Some distilleries insist on a particular type of barley for their whisky, which they say imparts something special to their finished product. Different types of barley produce varying levels of sugar; this affects the alcohol level and can affect the final taste.

In Scotland malt whisky is produced from two types of barley – that sown in spring or that sown in winter.

Highland distilleries tend to prefer barley that was grown in summer. There are a number of different varieties specifically grown for the distiller, for example, Chariot, Prisma and Derkado are favored spring varieties and Puffin, Halcyon and Pipkin are preferred winter varieties. These specialist varieties meet the malt whisky distillers' requirements by having a high starch content; more starch means more sugar and thus more alcohol. The maltster looks for barley with a low nitrogen content, which is crucial for good fermentation, and a moisture content of not more than 16 percent, so the barley will be ripe and dry when it leaves the fields. In the silo, barley will dry to a moisture content of 12 percent and will enter a period of dormancy which will last approximately eight to 10 weeks before the barley can be malted.

Peat

Peat is decomposed vegetable matter, partly carbonized by chemical change. Peat forms very slowly at a rate of just over half an inch (about one and a half centimeters) per hundred years. So cutting peat is like cutting into history.

There are different types of peat. Bog peats have a water table, which defies all attempts to drain them – including the planting of trees on upturned turfs. Bog peats fed by rain tend to have quite a high acidic content. Fen or moss peats, which occur in the U.K. in Somerset and parts of Scotland and can also be found in other parts of the world such as Japan and Tasmania, are fed by rivers and streams, not rain; they remain underwater and are neutral. Both bog and fen peats, where the water table is high, continue to build up because no air can get into them. Peat can build up

to a good few feet (a meter or so) in depth in these wet areas. Shallow peat by contrast, which develops on mineral soil, may be alkaline or neutral. If the base is of sedges and grasses and the water does dry out, trees can grow on top of these shallow peat deposits. More often, however, as the peat builds up the plants that grow on it have more and more difficulty in sending roots down into the soil base below, and gradually acidity develops.

The basic composition of the peat will help to determine the final taste and aroma of the malt whisky. Peats from decomposed heather produce a lighter honeyed whisky than peats from decomposed mosses and sedges, which are slightly salty. The island distilleries are the ones most famed for their peaty flavors; Ardbeg, Lagavulin, Laphroaig, Bowmore and Highland Park, for example. Traditionally the only local fuel available to these distilleries was peat – there were no coal mines on the islands. Islay peat is composed of ferns, gorse, sphagnum moss and moorland grasses, all of which are compacted and have been sprayed by the sea. This unique combination of sea and moorland produces a singular style of whisky. Even on such a small island as Islay the quality of the peat can vary from the sandier, less efficient beds along the seashore to the black inland supplies, which are deeper and more effective as a fuel.

Peat had long been the traditional source of fuel for farming communities throughout Scotland and a peat cutter could cut about 1,000 peat blocks a day. Peat is not an efficient source of heat and to achieve any sense of warmth a typical family could use about 16,000 peats a year. Peat is no longer used domestically since there are more efficient fuels available and it is essential that the peat bogs are harvested carefully in order to preserve the fragile ecostructure of these ancient reserves.

Ideally, peat is cut during late spring, dried by the warm winds in early summer and brought to the distillery in high summer. Sometimes the weather simply doesn't allow this pattern to be followed. If it is too wet the peat cannot be lifted, and it will crumble if it is too dry. The distiller digs sufficient peat only for each year's production. Peat cutters always replace the turf carefully afterwards to ensure that supplies are protected. First a drainage channel is made and then the peat is cut out in neat rectangular shapes using a sharp triangular bladed spade. Cutting peat is a skilled art and, as with all traditional skills, opinions vary on the optimum size of each block and how it should be stacked to dry. The stacks are usually small to allow the air to flow through freely and the peat to firm up, so that it is easier to handle. On Islay the peats are soft, can be stacked straight away and can be left on site to dry, but on Skye and Harris they are wheeled to their drying position from the bank in a wheelbarrow.

Peat is no longer used to fire the stills: it would be uneconomical. When the railways opened up the Highlands and Lowlands of Scotland, coal could easily be transported from the fields of Wales and central England and it replaced peat as fuel in many distilleries. The resulting whiskies were less peaty and had a lighter taste and smell. Most Speyside distilleries only use lightly peated malt to produce their characteristicly sweeter whiskies. Very few distilleries still malt and dry their own barley over peat fires; those that do tend to be the island distilleries with easy access to peat, who take very seriously the need to protect the bogs and dig only what they need. The large

maltings that provide malted barley for most distilleries use peat smoke to dry a percentage of the barley as prescribed by the individual distillery's recipes. There are only a handful of malt whisky distilleries in Scotland that do not use any peat at all – Glengoyne is one.

Yeast

Yeast turns the sugar produced by the malting of the barley into alcohol. The distiller typically uses a mixture of brewers' and distillers' yeasts; one designed to increase the whisky's flavor; the other its alcoholic content.

Left: Peat drying next to the kiln.

Below: Feeding the peat fire so that smoke rises to the barley drying above.

Right: Peat on a barrow in the Museum of Malt Whisky Production at Glenkinchie Distillery.

Casks (barrels, pipes, hogsheads)

T he type of cask used by a single malt distiller certainly influences the final spirit produced. Oak is the only wood used for whisky casks, because it is permeable and the spirit can penetrate the wood and thus draw some flavors and aromas from it; the outside air will also seep into the whisky. If the air is salty, seaweedy, heather-scented, or pine-laden it will add flavor to the characteristics of the malt.

Making casks is a skilled art, since the 26 staves required to make a cask are fixed together simply by binding them tightly with iron hoops: iron nails, which would color the whisky, or glue, which would taint the flavor are not used. The staves are held over an open fire or steam so they bend to form the desired shape. The cask heads fit closely into grooves at the ends of the staves. A caskmaker, or cooper, would serve an apprenticeship of some six years and the day an apprentice finished would often be marked with much rowdy celebration. Danny Wood, who is Ballantine's Cask Supervisor and was an apprentice himself says "You are put in a barrel and everyone pours water over you. Then they cover you in wood shavings, eggs, flour – anything to hand and roll you up and down the cooper's

Top: The cooper's art is a very skilled one.

Right: Staves waiting to be made into barrels.

shop floor. You emerge looking terrible with your apprenticeship behind you and a career ahead, and celebrate by offering your workmates a whisky." Very few distilleries have their own cooperages now and casks are repaired at specialist workshops.

There is a wide choice of oak casks available to the whisky distiller, not only regarding size (which determines the barrel's name – butt: 132 gallons (500 liters); puncheon: 119 gallons (450 liters); hogshead: 66 gallons (250 liters); barrel: 55 gallons (200 liters); American barrels: 46 gallons (173 liters), but also their previous contents – malt whisky, bourbon, sherry, port or madeira. The names of the different sizes also reflect their origins. The word "barrel" comes from the French *barrique* and "firkin" and "pin" are Dutch in origin.

Some distilleries use sherry casks and this practice was first used to improve the quality of maturing whisky by William Sanderson of the VAT 69 blend. At present, The Macallan is the only single malt which uses all sherry casks to mature its world-renowned single malt. Bourbon, by law, can be matured only in new oak barrels by law. Some distilleries have taken advantage of this ready supply of American casks – the Laphroaig distillery in Islay, for example. Other distilleries use a mixture of new fill, bourbon and sherry casks. A few distilleries have recently been experimenting with different final maturation in port pipes, brandy and Madeira barrels – all of which impart their own special flavors to the single malt. Auchentoshan distillery has recently launched a single malt which is matured in old bourbon barrels for 10 years then spends a further year in Oloroso sherry casks and finally six months in Pedro Ximénez casks producing a whisky very different from the typical 10 year old Auchentoshan.

Above: Traditional cooper's tools on display at Glenkinchie Distillery.

The consummate skill of the distillery staff

Whisky-making still needs the careful attention and tender loving care of dedicated individuals. Many distillery staff have been working with the same company for years, indeed in some cases several generations of the same family have worked for the same company and their skills and traditions have been passed down from parent to child. Some distillery companies are owned by the families that founded them over a century ago.

The distillation process
for malt whisky

S electing the right ingredients is only the first part of the story. From there on the skill and expertise of the distillery manager and his team ensure that fine whisky is produced.

Malting barley

The production process starts with barley. On arrival at the distillery, the barley has a moisture content of approximately 10 percent and is stored in the loft until it is required. The barley is then transferred to a steep where it is left to soak or steep in water for a couple of days, by which time the moisture content will have increased to some 45 percent. The barley is then allowed to germinate. In a traditional distillery the wet barley was spread out by hand on a concrete malting floor, then left for about seven days. There are now fewer than a dozen malt whisky distilleries in Scotland malting a proportion of their own barley. These include Laphroaig and Bowmore on Islay, Highland Park on Orkney and Balvenie, Springbank and Glendronach on the mainland. During this period the barley is turned regularly to ensure the temperature is maintained at the required level and to control the rate of germination. At some distilleries the traditional wooden shovel or "shiel" is still used to turn the barley. At Glenkinchie distillery in the eastern Lowlands of Scotland there is a

museum where exhibits include a pair of canvas boots made by French prisoners of war during the Napoleonic Wars. Such boots were traditionally worn by workers who walked across the barley to turn it on the malting floor.

Most distilleries purchase their malted barley direct from maltings where the grain is turned mechanically in large rectangular boxes or cylindrical drums. The amount of barley that can be malted at any one time varies according to the size of the maltings. For example at Port Ellen Maltings on the Isle of Islay, 27½ U.S. tonnes of barley can be steeped at any one time. This compares with Laphroaig distillery where the capacity of the steep is only eight tonnes. At the commercial maltings the barley is placed in the germination receptacles and air is pumped through it to maintain the right temperature. The drums or boxes rotate every eight hours or so to ensure that the new shoots and rootlets do not become intertwined. A few distilleries have built their own mechanical maltings, known as Saladin boxes. One such distillery is Tamdhu.

When the barley starts to germinate, little rootlets and a shoot start to form, and each grain is soft and slightly sticky to the touch. Once the required level of germination has been achieved, the

Above: Malting barley can become very hot, so workers wore canvas boots to protect their feet.

Left: Barley is still turned by hand at Highland Park Distillery.

Below: Traditional wooden shiel for turning barley.

James Hogg

The Ettrick shepherd, James Hogg, is immortalized by John Wilson and he is recorded as saying in 1827: "Gie me the real Glenlivet, and I weel believe I could mak' drinking toddy oot o' sea water. The human mind never tires o'Glenlivet, any mair than o' caller air. If a body could just find oot the exac' proportion and quantity that ought to be drunk every day and keep to that, I verily trow that he might leeve for ever, without dying at a', and that doctors and kirkyards would go oot o' fashion." James Hogg, along with other writers such as Walter Scott, is seen as a chronicler of Scottish life. In *Sir Bingo Entertains the Captain and the Doctor* by Sir Walter Scott, the Captain says, "By Cot, it is the only liquor fit for a gentleman to drink in the morning, if he can have the good fortune to come by it, you see..." "Or after dinner either, Captain" added the Doctor, "It is worth all the wines of France for flavour and more cordial to the system besides."

All pictures: The pagoda shaped kiln chimneys and orkney peat fuelling the fire at Highland Park Distillery.

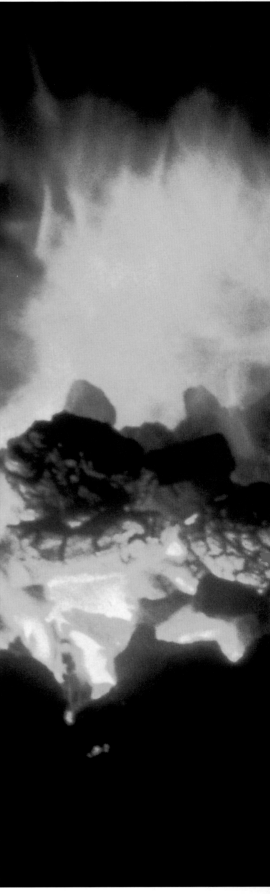

barley's natural enzymes are released. These produce soluble starch which converts into sugar during the mashing process. Germination is arrested by drying the barley either over a peat fire or with warm air. The barley is laid out in the kiln over a fine mesh floor above the fire and the smoke rises through the barley and out through the distinctive maltings chimney.

With its triangular-shaped roof and curved edges, this pagoda chimney is faintly reminiscent of Chinese temples and is now synonymous with whisky distilleries throughout the world. Yet when whisky distilleries were first built, the kilns had thatched roofs and were made from stone. Later designs show that some chimneys resembled more closely the conical shape of a hop kiln such as those seen in Kent or Herefordshire in England. The architect Charles Chree Doig from Elgin in Scotland was responsible for redesigning the chimney kiln and he and his family continued to refine their first designs, not just for pagoda chimneys but also for complete distilleries, from 1870 until as late as 1964. By constructing a chimney with a finely tapered tiled roof, the smoke could move around more freely and impart the traditional peat reek to the grain. Charles Doig's designs can now be found in the Elgin Library (Scotland) and were donated by Wilhe Brander, a retired architect whose own practice had taken over the Doig studio. In the 1890s when everyone was building distilleries, Doig was much in demand. His legacy can be seen in Scotland at Dailuaine, Abrfeldy, Craigellachie and Imperial among other places.

At the Bowmore distillery, the first 15–18 hours of the drying period take place over a peat fire. Barley dried over a peat fire absorbs phenols in the peat, which give Bowmore its characteristic peaty aroma and flavor. The barley is dried for a further 48–55 hours with warm air.

Above: Boiling water is added to the grist in the mash tun.

Near Right: The draff is taken away from the distillery for use as cattle feed.

Right: The wort is drawn off the mash tun and piped into the large wooden washbacks for fermentation.

Mashing

The dried malt is stored in malt bins and after a rest period is ground to a fine grist. The malt is dry and brittle and produces a large quantity of dust. Sometimes grit and other objects get into the malt and it is essential that before it is ground in the mill these impurities and as much of the dust as possible are removed. The dust is highly inflammable, and it is for this reason

that notices are displayed at all distilleries forbidding the use of flash photography. An article in *Distillers Magazine and Trade News* of September 1887 reports "I have known the miller get himself seriously burned by the bursting open of the malt elevators, and there is always the danger of fire to be apprehended. In a meal mill in Glasgow some years ago an explosion of this kind was attended with fatal results."

The malted barley is conveyed to the mill through grain elevators. At Glenkinchie the amount of malted barley placed in the mill is still counted in coups or bucket loads and the total entered in a handwritten log. The length of time for which the malt is ground is crucial and the procedure is carefully supervised. The grist, which is part flour and part solids, is placed in a container known as a mash tun, and boiling water

starts to ferment immediately and the mixture begins to give off carbon dioxide and foam. The wash will rise in temperature during the final fermentation to about 89·6°F (32°C). The aim, however, is to maintain a slow fermentation so that the alcohol is as pure as possible. Scottish malt distillers use covered washbacks with lids that incorporate a rotating blade, and this stops the foam from pouring over the sides. The sugars are converted into alcohol and after some 48 hours, a warm sweet peaty beer with an alcoholic content of around 7·5 percent is achieved.

Washbacks vary considerably in size from 264 gallons (1,000 liters) to over 15,850 (60,000). Washbacks are traditionally made of Oregon pine, although today many are made of stainless steel. Oregon pine is still seen by many distillers as the perfect raw material. Recently Bowmore distillery took out its stainless steel washbacks and reinstalled wooden ones. Large washbacks make excellent swimming pools and they were used for this purpose during the war at Highland Park Distillery in the Orkney Isles.

is added. Distillery managers jealously guard their water supplies, which help to give each malt whisky its particular flavor and aroma. The shape and size of the mash tuns vary but they are normally of copper and usually have a lid. The boiling water dissolves the flour and releases the sugars in the barley. The resultant liquid, known as wort, is drawn off from the base of the mash tun through the finely-slotted bottom,

cooled, and passed into fermentation vessels, or washbacks. The solids or draff (as they are known in Scotland) are removed from the mash tun and used as cattle feed.

Fermentation

Yeast is added in either liquid or solid form to the liquid wort, which has been cooled to around 68°F (20°C) in the large wooden washbacks. The yeast

Distillation

The fermented wort, or wash, is then piped to the still room. Traditionally, stills in a Scottish malt whisky distillery are made of copper. All spirit stills are handmade and every distillery has stills of a different shape and size. Some are pot bellied, some have long thin necks, others have bulbous necks, some are thin, some are tall and others are squat. Experience has shown that only by replacing them with identical stills can the quality, flavor and aroma of the malt whisky be assured. The size and shape of the still and the skill of the stillman contribute to the quality of the final spirit.

One of the companies involved in making and repairing stills is A. Forsyth & Sons of Speyside. Their managing director Richard Forsyth described repairing stills in the account of the history of Ballantine's whisky, "Distillers used to be almost paranoid about keeping the size and shape exactly the same, especially distilleries with individual owners. If a still had a dent or a bash in it, they insisted on [replacing it with] something identical."

The first and largest still is the wash still, where the wash is boiled so that it breaks down into its constituent parts and the alcohol can be drawn off. The boiling point of alcohol (173°F/78°C) is lower than that of water (212°F/100°C), so the liquor is the first vapor to rise up the neck of the still. Alcohol has various chemical constituents and some of the first to rise up the still are crude alcoholic vapors, which the stillman discards. The vapor produced by the still is passed into a condenser – a series of pipe coils running through cold water. The angle of the pipe, or lyne arm, connecting the still to the condenser affects the quality and speed of condensation.

From the condenser the liquid, now called low wines, is collected in the low wines receiver. The low wines contain

All pictures: Copper stills are different in size and shape at every distillery. Some have very long lyne arms and at others the condensors are inside the still room. These stills are from the Blair Athol and Glenfiddich distilleries.

approximately 30 percent alcohol and must be distilled again in a spirit still, since they are unpalatable. Spirit stills are usually smaller than wash stills. The second distillation, which produces the pure spirit, is a carefully orchestrated and very precise procedure. Spirit produced in the spirit still will pass via the spirit safe – for it is here that the involvement of the British Customs and Excise begins and, indeed, that of governments the world over. All spirits are subject to customs duty and production is strictly controlled to ensure that the correct amount is paid. Locks are fitted to the spirit safe by a customs representative and measurements are taken of the amount

of spirit produced. The spirit safe contains several glass bowls into which the spirit can be directed using external faucets by the stillman.

The stillman or woman starts to test the spirit as soon as the rising vapors are condensed and pass through the spirit safe. He or she directs the first liquid, which is known as foreshots, to the glass bowls, which drain off into a collecting tank at the back of the stillroom. Foreshots turn cloudy when they come into contact with water because they are still impure. The stillman or woman can test the spirit in the spirit safe by adding water at regular intervals and checking the specific gravity.

As soon as the spirit starts to run

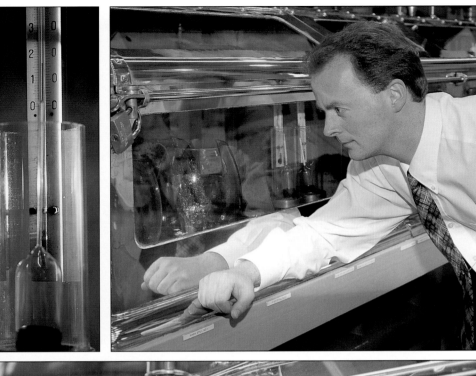

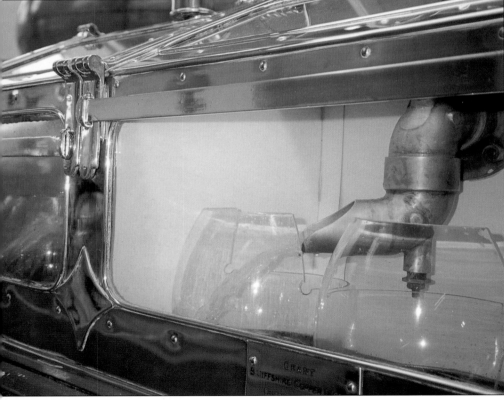

clear, the faucets are opened on the outside of the spirit safe and directs the spirit so that it flows into the spirit receiver. To ensure the clarity and purity of the spirit the speed of distillation is normally reduced at this stage. After several hours most of the alcohol will have been distilled and what remains is a mixture of impure compounds which would spoil the whisky. This weakened spirit, or feints, is diverted back to the low wines and feints-collecting tank.

In some distilleries, notably Bushmills in Northern Ireland and Auchentoshan in the Lowland region of Scotland, the spirit passes through a third or intermediate still to produce a lighter whisky. This is known as triple distillation.

A watery residue remains in the still once the feints have been collected. This residue is called spent lees and is normally discharged into the sewer after treatment. At Royal Lochnagar distillery the spent lees are sprayed over surrounding farmland. The foreshots and feints are added to the next wash for distillation, when the process is repeated.

Maturation

The pure spirit is pumped from the spirit receiver to a vat where water is added to reduce the alcoholic content from around 70 percent to 63·5 percent (111° proof) before it is transferred to casks. Some distilleries do not in fact add water at this stage, but Denis Nicol of Allied Distillers feels that "water actually promotes maturation and enhances the process." The casks are weighed empty and then again when filled, so that the distillery manager can calculate the amount of spirit in each cask. This measure is recorded so that Customs and Excise have an idea of how much whisky is in each barrel, but this amount changes during maturation. The spirit is colorless, crude and fiery – at this stage it has some of

Right: Filling barrels at Blair Athol Distillery.

Top left: Hydrometer inside the spirit safe to check the strength.

Top right: Graham Eunson, distillery manager at Glenmorangie, checks the quality of spirit flowing through the safe.

Above: The spirit safe at Glenturret Distillery.

the characteristics of whisky but certainly none of its final elegance. It now has to mature in barrels for three years before it can legally be called whisky in Scotland. During this time the spirit will become softer and start to turn color as the character of the new oak wood or the residues of bourbon, sherry, or port in the wood casks it is stored in are absorbed.

Maturation is a slow process and a cool, wet temperate climate such as that in many parts of Scotland seems to be the best. As the whisky slowly seeps into the oak barrels it starts to absorb some of the elements in the wood, notably lignin which is composed of wood sugars, lactones and vanillins. The

WHISKY HUMOR

The following stories are from *A Little Book of Wit and Humor* (1918). "A Highlander was once asked what he would wish to have, in case of some kind divinity purposing to give him the three things he liked best. For the first, he said, he should ask for 'a Loch Lomond o' gude whisky'. 'And waht for the second?' inquired his friend. 'A Ben Lomond o'gude sneeshin', replied Donald. 'And what for the third?' He hesitated a long time at this; but at last, after his face had assumed many contortive expressions of thought, he answered: 'Oo, just another Loch Lomond o' gude whisky.'"

"Archie Campbell, a city officer of Edinburgh, a noted celebrity, had the misfortune to lose his mother; and, in order to gratify her last wish, he had her body conveyed to the Highlands, in a hearse, for interment. He returned, it was rumored, with the hearse full of smuggled whisky. A friend, one day, began to tease him on the subject. 'Wow, man,' replied Archie, 'there's nae harm done. I only carried awa' the body and brought back the speerit.'"

wood also acts as a filter and because it is permeable some of the whisky will evaporate; most distillery managers quaintly describe this lost liquid as "the angels' share." This amounts to about one to two percent per year. With the angels' share go many of the harsher elements of the whisky. At the same time the air surrounding the barrel seeps in so that whisky stored in bonded warehouses by the sea, for example, absorb the salty tang of seaweed and spray.

Where whisky is subject to extreme changes in temperature it matures at a different rate, often quicker, and tastes quite different than a single malt. This explains why many bourbons and whiskies produced in countries such as India are deemed to have reached their maturity at a far younger age than Scottish single malts.

The barrels are stored for at least eight and probably for between 10 and 15 years if the whiskies are to be used for a single malt or for a deluxe blend. The longer a malt whisky is left to mature in the barrel, the more changes will take place, which is why malts of varying ages from the same distillery are so different. Also, the longer a malt matures, the more spirit is lost (to the angels) so the quantity that finally emerges is lower than the number logged when the cask was first filled.

From time to time the barrels are tapped to check that all is well. A firm, resonant sound means that the barrel is intact and the whisky is maturing well. A leaking or broken barrel produces a dull sound and the distillery manager knows that it must be inspected and probably replaced. He or she draws a small amount from the barrel and pours it into a nosing glass, then noses (smells) the whisky and swirls it around in the glass. A "string of pearls" around the surface of the

liquid indicates that the whisky is maturing satisfactorily, in which case the spirit is returned to the barrel.

Whisky barrels are traditionally stored in single-story buildings with casks stacked three high, but now barrels are being piled 12 high on racking. Denis Nicol of Allied Distillers believes that "in a warehouse where casks are stacked 12 high you can get what we call 'altitude.'

Above: Sampling the maturing whisky in the Laphroaig warehouse.

Left: Whisky slowly and silently maturing for at least 8 years at the Glenturret Distillery.

There will be a subtle difference between spirit matured at the top of the warehouse and that matured at the bottom. Some warehouses give a more mellow rounded flavor than others. The best are those built for the traditional three layers of casks, but they are not always economic in today's terms."

In the past, distillery workers were given old casks in which whisky had matured for many years. The casks were filled with hot water and steam and then rolled down the street. This produced several gallons of spirit. Unfortunately for today's distillery workers, the practice is no longer legal.

All casks used for the maturation of whisky are made from oak. The type of cask chosen by the distillery manager is very important and has a very direct influence on the final color and flavor of the single malt. As already mentioned the casks can be made from new wood, which are known as first-fill casks or they could have previously contained whisky, bourbon, sherry or port. Legislation was introduced in the U.S. to protect the American timber industry, stating that bourbon whisky can only be matured in new barrels. This means

Above: Whisky maturing at the Arran Distillery.

Right: Taking a sample at Highland Park Distillery.

there is a continuing supply of second-fill casks available to the Scotch whisky distiller and, indeed, those producing in other countries, such as Japan. It is interesting to note that new oak really complements the stronger, more pungent whiskies which are produced in the U.S. from rye, corn and other grains. In Scotland it is unlikely that a distillery would only use new casks, as malted barley produces a lighter spirit, which the vanillins and tannins present in new oak would overwhelm.

Typically a distillery manager will purchase his oak casks from the same source each year. This will ensure that the finished single malt is of a consistent quality. For example some will insist on casks made from American white oak from the Ozark mountains in Missouri, others will insist that the casks have been used to mature Oloroso sherry from a particular bodega in southern Spain before taking delivery.

Distilleries have experimented with different types of cask, and, for example, at The Glendronach distillery some whisky is matured in a mixture of seasoned oak and sherry and some is matured entirely in sherry casks. At the Nikka Whisky Distilling Co. Ltd's Hokkaido distillery in Japan, Yoichi single malt is matured in a mix of sherry, bourbon, refill and new barrels. At Laphroaig distillery on the Isle of Islay the distillery manager insists that this distinctive peaty single malt is matured only in American first-fill bourbon barrels. This is different than Bowmore distillery, also on Islay, where the whisky is matured in a mixture of ex-bourbon and sherry

casks. While it is difficult, as already mentioned at the very beginning of this chapter, to determine what makes one single malt distinct from another, it is easy to see how this final maturation in different casks could affect these two Islay whiskies.

At Glentauchers distillery essentially refill whisky casks are used and the result is a light, easy-going malt with a soft, dry finish, which you are more likely to find as the component part of a blend than as a single malt whisky. Traditionally certain single malt Scotch whiskies have been matured in old sherry casks. The most famous of these is The Macallan, which has a light, fragrant sherry nose and a full-bodied

taste with hints of vanilla and fruit. The Macallan is available at various ages and it is probably true to say that the longer it matures the more sherry features can be identified in the whisky. Other distilleries have matured their single malts in two or more different types of wood. One such is The Balvenie Double Wood, which is matured for 12 years in traditional oak and sherry casks. This distillery has also recently launched The Balvenie, aged 21 years matured in Port Wood.

In recent years many of the distilleries in Scotland have been experimenting with final maturation in different types of casks. The first company to do this was Glenmorangie plc; in 1996 the company introduced a range of Wood Finished Single Highland malt whiskies. These whiskies are first matured in American oak casks for at least 12 years and are then transferred to casks which were previously used for port, Madeira, or sherry for final maturation. This special second maturation is known as finishing and is used to give additional attributes to the single malts without masking their unique characteristics. As one would expect Glenmorangie finished in port casks is colored slightly ruby red and is typically slightly sweeter and warmer. Glenmorangie Madeira Wood Finish has picked up some of the cookie-type, slightly citrus features of this fortified wine and is golder in color than the traditional Glenmorangie.

The Classic Malts range from United Distillers, which includes such famous single malts as Talisker, Dalwhinnie and Glenkinchie has recently been extended to become The Distillers Edition. All of the Classic Malts are finished in different casks, which are said to add something special to the original whiskies. A typical example is Glenkinchie, a Lowland single malt, which was originally distilled in 1986 and finished in Amontillado cask-wood. As a Classic Malt Glenkinchie at 10 years old is a light slightly sweet Lowland malt with orange blossom and honey on the nose. The Amontillado finish adds extra sweetness to the flavor of the whisky and a dryness to the finish.

The Glenfiddich distillery has also been experimenting with finishing and launched their Solera reserve in 1998. This is produced in a large solera vat, which is used traditionally to make sherry in Jerez in southern Spain. In the solera vat Glenfiddich can marry single malt whiskies together which have been matured for at least 15 years in different wood casks – new wood, ex-bourbon and ex-sherry. This marrying and final finishing lends a complexity and richness to the single malt.

More recently, the Glen Moray distillery has been looking at finishing in Chardonnay and Chenin Blanc wine barrels. The Chardonnay comes from the Loire region of France and adds a hint of mellowness to this traditional Speyside single malt. After six to 10 years matured in ex-bourbon casks the malt is finished for six months in the Chardonnay barrels. At the time of writing, there are three finishes available and the 12 year old Glen Moray finished in Chenin Blanc barrels is really something different and well worth trying. It will be interesting to see where the whisky industry looks next for finishing inspiration.

Whether you will like these finished single malts is a matter of personal taste. What has to be said is that finishing adds different aromas and flavors to single malts and some are very successful. There are two interesting things to note about finished single malts. The first is that in the main the extra finishing appears to extend the aftertaste or finish of the whisky. The second is that in my opinion one or two of the single malts lose much of their additional features when water is added – often the traditional way of drinking a single malt.

The question of when the art of maturation was discovered has never been satisfactorily answered. Some say that it was discovered by accident, when smugglers left their whisky hidden in barrels for some time to evade the excisemen and, on their return, discovered the product was much smoother and more to their customers' liking. Certainly by the beginning of the 19th century early blenders such as George Ballantine had realized that matured whisky enhanced the quality of their blends and increased demand.

Distilling grain whisky

The distillation of grain whisky should technically be addressed alongside the distillation of single malt whisky, since of course barley is a grain. The distinction lies in the fact that grain distilleries can produce large quantities of whisky continuously and not in small batches. Grain whisky can be made from all types of grain: barley – malted or unmalted, rye, corn or wheat. A grain distillery is a large building and the inside bears a closer resemblance to a chemical plant than to the traditional image of a whisky distillery.

Aenas Coffey is credited with perfecting the continuous still and he patented his design in 1830. An earlier design had been invented by Robert Stein of Fife in Scotland. The design of the still in a grain distillery remains basically the same as Coffey's original. The first patent still was a tall wooden column, inside of which were copper plates over which the wash or beer passed. The wash boiled under steam pressure and the vapor produced rose through holes in the plates to the top of the column still. Today stills are made from copper instead of wood and the number of horizontal plates inside is determined by the individual distillery. For example, at Dumbarton there are about half as many plates again as there are in a traditional Coffey still, since this produces a finer spirit. Continuous distillation produces purer alcohol and at a higher strength, 90 percent as opposed to 67 percent, than that made in a pot still. Once the grain whisky has been produced it is usually mixed with malt whiskies to produce blended whisky. Several distilleries produce a single grain whisky, most notably Cameronbrig and Invergordon.

Top left: Inside the Dumbarton grain distillery.

Above: This modern steel structure is William Grant's Girvan grain distillery.

Blended whisky

Blended whiskies account for 95 percent of whisky sales worldwide. Blended whiskies are the result of a marriage between a carefully chosen selection of single malts and grain whisky. To produce a blend in Scotland, single malts come from a variety of distilleries, each of which imparts its own special flavor and aroma to the final mixture. These are then mixed with grain whiskies usually produced at the company's own distillery. In Ireland, blends, which form the greater part of whiskies sold, are usually made from grain and pot still whiskies produced at the same distillery.

When writing about blends in *The Whisky Distilleries of the United Kingdom*, Alfred Barnard said, "Very many persons think they can blend whisky, and that it is just a matter of throwing a few brands together. The manipulation of whiskies requires as much care as the most delicate wines. Mountain air, peat moss of the richest quality, pure water from the hills and the best Scotch malt are absolute requirements for the manufacture of Highland whisky, in order to ensure the pronounced characteristics so highly valued by the experienced blender; and it is the development of these by age which gives bouquet and relish to a fine blend."

Below: White oak barrels, stored in the cellar of the Yamazaki Distillery.

Blends with a high percentage of malt whiskies are known as premium blends. The higher malt content gives the blend a fuller flavor and is reflected in their additional cost. Master blenders work closely with the malt whisky distillers, from the earliest stage of checking that the barley used will produce the right flavor, to the final testing of each barrel before selecting those to be included in the final blend. Blenders test by smell – their noses are as finely tuned as those of master perfumers. Apart from the fact that by nosing they can distinguish far more than by actually tasting the whiskies (our sense of smell is more refined than our sense of taste), to sample all the different barrels would not only be imprudent but take a considerable amount of time. The task is to ensure that the constituent malts, together with the chosen grains, produce the right taste and sensory notes for the blends to guarantee consistency.

Blending takes place in huge vats up to 30,000 gallons in size. Compressed air is passed through the vessel to ensure that the individual whiskies are properly mixed. The blend is then put into casks for six months to a year to mature. Sometimes the grain whisky is added at this stage, in other cases it is not included until bottling. Water is added to the whisky to achieve the required strength; in the U.K. this is usually 40 percent for the domestic market and 43 percent for overseas sales. A little caramel may also be included to maintain a consistent color, and the whisky is filtered.

Bottling

In Scotland, whiskies are usually bottled at large commercial bottling plants. There are two single malt Scotch whisky distillers who bottle on site, The Glenfiddich and Springbank. Throughout the world distillers predominately bottle on site.

In the past whisky was stored in stone jars. Many whisky companies have used replica china special editions to promote their brands. The earlier whisky bottles had corks, which had to be removed with a corkscrew, and were sealed with wax and metal foil. The cork was superseded by the current stoppered cork.

Both pictures: The Allied Domecq bottling plant at Kilmalid – which one is yours?

Making whiskies in North America

I t is not surprising that whisky production spread so quickly throughout North America. The continent had all the major ingredients for making whisky – large open spaces on which to grow plentiful supplies of grain, pure water sources and forests to provide timber for the barrels.

In addition, the early producers found they had an ever growing customer base as more and more immigrants flocked to the New World to seek their fortunes. As railroads and steamships were built whisky found its way from the distillers in the north, particularly those in Canada, to the south of the continent.

North American whiskies are grouped by type and by geographical situation. Essentially there are Canadian whiskies, which predominately use rye and grain spirit and are usually sold as blends. Then there are American bourbons and Tennessee whiskies and rye whiskies made in places as far apart as Bardstown, Kentucky, Weston, Missouri and San Francisco, California. This wide geographical spread means that varying types of grain are used, including maize or corn, and that the whisky matures at very different temperatures. These differences will be looked at in more detail as we discover how American whiskies are made.

In Canada, the whisky distillers spent a considerable amount of time trying to improve production methods and the final quality of the spirit. By the late 1920s, two of the great whisky dynasties had been founded – Seagram's and Hiram Walker. Seagram's headquarters are still in Canada and Hiram Walker is linked with the Allied Domecq group.

Samuel Bronfman of Seagram's built his first new La Salle distillery near Montreal, Canada, in 1924. This was linked with the family's original Waterloo, Ontario, distillery which dated back to 1857. Writing in the 1970s Bronfman described how the company's fortunes spread geographically to include the Gimli Distillery, which is placed almost in the middle of Canada on the shores of Lake Winnipeg. By spreading his distilleries across Canada, he was able to provide whisky to a vast sector of the population and indeed by Word War II Seagram's was the largest alcoholic distiller in North America.

Samuel believed that whisky should be enjoyed by everyone and an early advertisement read. "We who make whisky say Drink Moderately". "The real enjoyment whisky can add to the pleasure of gracious living is possible only to the man who drinks good whisky and drinks moderately. Whisky cannot take the place of milk, bread or meat. The pleasure which good whisky offers is definitely a luxury."

Hiram Walker started distilling in Canada at Windsor, Ontario, in 1856 and much of his life story is described on page 158 of this book. Hiram was a great innovator and experimented with whisky filtration using charcoal and

Left: Watching the wort turn into alcohol.

Below: Maple planks being burnt to produce charcoal for the filtration process.

other materials to ensure that the whisky he produced was as pure as possible. By 1930 the company he founded had crossed the Atlantic and purchased several distilleries, and by the end of 1936 they had purchased George Ballantine and Sons of Dumbarton, owners of the prestigious Ballantines blended whisky. His legacy of producing grain whiskies in multiple-column stills lives on in Dumbarton at the Allied Domecq grain distillery.

Most North American whiskies start in large fermentation vessels known as fermenters, which are usually made from stainless steel (this seems perverse considering that the pine used for the wooden washbacks in Scotland comes from Oregon!). They are usually first distilled in large beer stills or in column stills, although there are some using pot stills in broadly the same way as described for single malts, though the scale is far greater than that of the average single malt whisky distillery.

There are other differences, mostly dictated by the grain and raw materials available. Some whiskies are made from rye only, others from maize or Indian corn, while others can include a mix of rye, corn and malted barley.

Bourbon whisky must by law contain at least 51 percent Indian corn. This is a very important ingredient and helps to make Bourbon richer and sweeter than other whiskeys. Added to the corn, a little rye gives the whisky a bit of a bite. Usually the proportions are around 70 percent corn, 20 percent rye with perhaps a little wheat and malted barley. The starch in malted barley breaks down and assists fermentation.

Bourbon whisky-makers have a vocabulary all their own. While the first distillation is usually in a continuous column still, the second takes place in a "doubler" or "thumper" still. In a doubler, as with single malt whisky, the vapor is condensed back into liquid before the second distillation. However with a thumper the vapor is transferred straightaway without being condensed.

Sour mash whisky is made using a proportion of barley which has already been used in a previous fermentation and from which the natural sugars have been removed. A large proportion of North American whiskies use a percentage of sour mash in the mix.

Apart from the different grains used, what sets Tennessee whisky apart is the charcoal filtration effected after

distillation and before the whisky is put into barrels. This differs from Scotch whisky which is filtered after maturation before bottling – though not all Scotch whisky is filtered.

Filtration is achieved through charcoal, which is made on site and for visitors on a tour of the Jack Daniel distillery often forms part of the entertainment. A pile of some 1,500 maple planks is stacked under a canopy. By stacking the wood under a canopy, smoke is retained in the charcoal, and this is said to add flavor to the spirit, much as peat smoke is retained in Scotch single malts. The maple is set alight and a close eye is kept on the burning planks until such time as they

Left: Charring the inside of barrels helps to give American whiskies their characteristic flavor.

Right: Patiently waiting for the whisky to mature.

are almost burned through. A hose is then turned on and the smoldering wood or charcoal is collected to be broken into small pieces in a large grinder. The charcoal is then heaped to a depth of 10 feet (3 meters) in large wooden mellowing vessels which are lined with a wool blanket and sunk into the ground. Perforated copper pipes run across the top of the charcoal and the new spirit drips slowly through the holes over a period of 10 days.

Bourbon and rye whiskies must be matured in new oak casks, which are charred inside: by law they can be used only once. The tradition of charring in the U.S. is believed to have been started by one producer who had bought

barrels which had previously been used to store herrings. He used charring to remove the fishy odor.

The continental climate means that the whisky is subjected to extremes in temperature at many distilleries, particularly in Kentucky. As a result the whisky matures more quickly and the final spirit tastes very different than a Scotch single malt. Many distillers have taken advantage of these climatic changes to produce distinctive whiskies. At Maker's Mark in Kentucky, the whisky is matured in new charred-oak casks which are first placed on the upper and thus the hottest floors in the warehouses. After a couple of years' maturation in the heat the casks are moved down to lower,

cooler parts of the warehouses to continue their maturation.

North American distilleries distill using several different recipes as well as producing small batch distillations and single barrel whiskies. This means that at any one distillery whiskies are bottled under many different names. Often these recipes are preserved to keep old brand names alive. For example at Jim Beam you can find among others Knob Creek, Old Crow, Old Taylor and Booker's.

Some companies, such as Maker's Mark, still use sealing wax to seal their bottles and this is featured in their promotional campaigns as something that sets them apart from other whisky producers.

The Geography of Whisky

THE FIRST THING TO DO IS TO DISPEL THE VIEW THAT WHISKY IS PRODUCED ONLY IN SCOTLAND. SINGLE MALTS ARE MADE IN OTHER COUNTRIES: THEY ARE DIFFERENT, SOME ARE VERY GOOD IN THEIR OWN RIGHT, BUT MANY BEAR ONLY A PASSING RESEMBLANCE TO SINGLE MALT SCOTCH WHISKIES. SIMILARLY, WHILE MANY SINGLE MALTS DISTILLED IN SCOTLAND ARE SENSATIONAL, SOME ARE JUST GOOD AND SOME REALLY AREN'T THAT GOOD AT ALL. WHEN LOOKING AT WHISKIES OF THE WORLD ONE SHOULDN'T SEEK TO FIND SOMETHING SIMILAR TO THOSE PRODUCED IN SCOTLAND, BUT RATHER SEEK TO DISCOVER THOSE WHICH REFLECT THE DIFFERENT ENVIRONMENTS IN WHICH THEY ARE MADE AND THE DEMANDS OF THE LOCAL COMMUNITIES. THIS CAN BE JUST AS REWARDING AS A TASTING OF FINE SINGLE MALTS FROM SCOTLAND.

Why did whisky-making spread around the world?

Whisky is made on every continent. There are distilleries in Brazil, Uruguay and Argentina in South America; in India and Pakistan in Southeast Asia; in Spain, Italy and Turkey in Europe and in Australia and New Zealand, as well as in countries better known for their whisky such as the United States, Japan and Canada. While Scotland still has by far the most working single malt distilleries (well over 100) the surprise is that the country with the most working malt distilleries after Scotland is India – not, as many would imagine, the United States, Japan or maybe Canada. In India there are some 15 distilleries.

Single malts do not constitute the whole story. Whisky is made from grain, rye, corn and unmalted barley – and some of it is exceptionally good.

Trying to identify how many grain distilleries there are worldwide is not quite so easy. If a list were drawn up ranking countries by their number of grain distilleries, Japan would probably be near the top. The sheer size of grain distilleries, both in Scotland and overseas, defies description. Few even remotely resemble the small, almost farmhouse-style, single malt distilleries that can still be found in Scotland. Without grain whisky, however, distillers would be unable to produce the wide range of wonderful blended whiskies that is available throughout the world.

Above: Hokkaido in Japan.

All over the globe people saw the production of spirits as a logical way of using surplus cereals. Most countries developed the knowledge to distill spirits, initially for medicines and then as a way of producing an alcoholic beverage, from an excess of corn, wheat, barley, rye or potatoes to name but five possible raw ingredients. The quantity and quality of the spirits produced in those early days varied considerably from place to place – often the results were positively detrimental to the drinker's health.

Gradually, the specific process that led to the creation of a different spirit (which by the 1500s was already known as "uisgue beatha" or whisky) was disseminated around the world. Emigration in one form or another

seems to have been one of the key factors; emigration to North America from the British Isles is one example. By the time the Pilgrim Fathers landed in 1620 to found the first British colony in what was to become the United States, distilling was certainly well known in Scotland and Ireland. On the east coast, barley or wheat grew satisfactorily, but further south and west the land and climate of the vast continent changed and barley failed to grow. The settlers turned to the indigenous crops they discovered, particularly rye and corn or maize, as the staple for bread, fodder for their animals and ultimately the ingredient for their own spirits and home-brews. There is no evidence to show that the native population already had a tradition for producing spirits.

Indeed history would appear to affirm the reverse, since the introduction of strong drink had a dreadful effect on the Native Americans' way of life. So it seems safe to say that the settlers brought their distilling knowledge with them.

In the late 18th century other factors were to increase the number of people who left the British Isles. The East India Company, which was incorporated by Queen Elizabeth I in 1600, had grown considerably and British influence was being felt throughout Southeast Asia. The first British Governor of India, Warren Hastings, was appointed in 1774. The creation of the British Empire and establishment of new cities with their own industries worldwide meant that many traveled abroad to seek their fortunes. The time when half the world was "colored pink," representing its

Above: Inchgower distillery – railroads opened up new distilleries in Scotland and helped companies to distribute whisky around the world.

allegiance to the British crown, has long gone. Yet the expansion of whisky and other spirits' production worldwide is closely linked to the spread of British colonialism. The Dutch also spread the word on distilling spirits and set up distilleries for gin and rum in their colonies. Today the visitor to a distillery overseas may see equipment from Scotland which has been in use for well over 100 years. The copper stills at the Mount Gay Rum distillery in Barbados, for example, were produced in Edinburgh, Scotland in the 1880s.

The advent of railroads and the demand overseas for railroad systems, bridges and other construction projects created opportunities for engineers. Many of these came from Scotland and it is not illogical to assume that some of them hankered after their tot of whisky.

The heyday for railroad building in the British Isles was during the period 1846–50, during which one and a half million tons of iron went into railroads: over a quarter of the British iron output at that time was destined for overseas lines.

The creation of the East India Railway Company in 1850 coincided with the building of the first distillery at Kasuali – the mash tun (mashing cask) is dated 1855. James Andrew Broun Ramsay, the First Marquess of Dalhousie, a prominent Scot who had been involved with the growth of railroads at home, was Governor General of India. By 1850 Dalhousie was responsible for the creation of the East India Railway Company, whose track when completed stretched further than any other line in the world at that time.

As shipping companies started to build larger vessels that could travel longer distances at greater speeds with increased reliability, overseas markets were opened up by the Scottish and Irish whiskey distillers. Not only could they send bulk whisky but they could also despatch stills and other distilling equipment to sites abroad. To this day, whisky is sent around the world in huge bulk carriers to supply blending plants in countries such as Japan, India and the United States.

Can whisky be produced anywhere?

I t is perfectly possible to produce whisky from grain in a column still anywhere in the world. It would be wrong, however, to assume that settlers built distilleries indiscriminately to produce whisky wherever they went. Building a distillery is one thing; producing decent whisky is quite another. By this time it was known, for example, that to produce a single malt required a continuous supply of clean water, good-quality grain and a cool temperate climate so that the spirit could mature slowly. So it is no accident that malt distilleries were built in areas that have similar geographical and climatic conditions to those in Scotland – thus distilleries can now be found in Northern India, Canada, Japan and Tasmania.

Yet there are many exceptions. The most notable malt whisky exception is Mitchell's in Goa, India, an environment seemingly quite remote from a cold mountainous landscape. Goa is a semi-tropical, palm-fringed beach paradise and does not immediately conjure images of a single malt distillery. Nevertheless the visitor is greeted by the traditional pagoda nestling in the hills, and the single malt produced is well worth tasting.

Other whiskies, in particular those produced in North America, are distilled in column stills using local ingredients. Here, although the basic method of production is the same, there are differences and the spirit matures faster because the climate is warmer, helping to give it a distinctive flavor.

Top: Distilling whisky in the snow on Hokkaido, Japan.

Below: A tour of the Jack Daniel Distillery.

Whiskies of the world

The following examples have been chosen to reflect the different styles of whisky produced throughout the world. They are listed in order of production, with the largest producers coming first. Not every country is included because space doesn't permit an in-depth study of them.

SCOTLAND

Just as the wines of France are grouped according to their region of origin, so too are the malt whiskies of Scotland. Traditionally, malts are defined by a regional classification. Defining malt whiskies too rigidly, however, suggests uniformity; it would be inaccurate to say that all Islay malts have a strong peaty taste – Bunnahabhain, for example, does not. These regional classifications can assist when choosing a whisky.
The major regions are Campbeltown, Highland, Islay and Lowland. To these I have added Orkney and Speyside because they too produce distinctive styles. The stories, locations and the single malts produced by the following distilleries provide a short guided tour of Scotland and its unique distilling legacy.

Campbeltown

Campbeltown is situated on the Mull of Kintyre and was once called the whisky capital of Scotland. In 1794 the Statistical Account of Scotland noted

that there were 22 distilleries in the town and another 10 on the outskirts. The Reverend John Smith was responsible for the report on Campbeltown and he wrote "Next to the fishing of herrings, the business most attended to in Campbeltown is the distilling of whisky..." Campbeltown whiskies used a little peat in the malting of their barley and this, together with the distinctive tang from the salt-laden sea air, sets them apart from the blander Lowland whiskies available at that time. When Alfred Barnard visited Campbeltown in 1887, he saw 21 distilleries and annual production was nearly two million gallons. Campbeltown owed its growth to the availability of coal, its accessibility to Glasgow and the huge demand from blenders for malts.

A century ago a visitor to Campbeltown would probably have arrived by boat. As the boat turned into Campbeltown Loch, the town and surrounding area came into view and nearly 30 distillery chimneys would have been silhouetted against the skyline. Unfortunately, many Campbeltown distillers allowed quality to suffer as the quantity they produced increased. This together with the Depression, the loss of the American market in the 1920s due to Prohibition and the closing of the coal-mine in the 1930s led to the demise of many distilleries. Names such as Benmore, Glenside, Kinloch and

Below: Highland cattle still roam distillery farms such as The Glendronach.

Lochruan are now simply the stuff of history books, for of the 21 distilleries Barnard visited only two remain: Springbank and Glen Scotia.

Campbeltown, Argyll – Springbank Distillery

Springbank distillery is still family owned with a unique past and a very special range of single malts and blended whiskies. It was built in Campbeltown in 1828 by brothers Archibald and Hugh Mitchell on the site of their father's illegal still. Today the distillery is right in the heart of the town. It is believed that the Mitchells had been distilling for at least 100 years before this which, if true, would make Springbank one of the oldest distilleries in Scotland. By 1872 they owned four distilleries in the area – Toberanrigh, Drumore, Glengyle and Springbank. During the heady 1890s, distillery owners made large profits since local barley and coal were cheap and readily available. Unfortunately, many of

them couldn't resist making extra profits as demand for Campbeltown whisky increased during the early 1900s. Happily for us, while other distillers cut corners to meet the huge demand for whisky for blending, the high standard of single malt produced by the Mitchells never wavered and Springbank distillery survived. The present managing director is a direct descendant of Archibald Mitchell.

Production of single malt at Springbank is entirely self-contained. From the very first stage of malting barley in the traditional way on malting floors to the final step of bottling, everything is undertaken on site. Springbank is one of only two distilleries to bottle at source – the other is Glenfiddich. Springbank single malts are not chill-filtered nor is any color

added. The result of all this individual care is a highly-prized malt with a rounded taste and rich aroma.

At Springbank, Longrow single malt is also produced. This has a heritage as old as Springbank itself. A fine malt of this name was produced in 1824 but the distillery, built next door to Springbank, was closed in 1896. The recipe for this peaty malt remained in the family and in 1973 a distillation was produced at Springbank, bottles of which can be found at specialty retailers. From time to time new distillations are produced.

Springbank has long been considered one of the best single malts. In a blind tasting held by *The Times* newspaper, London, in 1983 Springbank came first and was described as the "Premier Grand Cru Classé" of malt whiskies. Springbank single malt Scotch whisky is normally available at 12 and 21 years old with two blends, Campbeltown Loch and Mitchell's 12 years old. From time to time special malts are available such as Springbank CV bottled at 46 percent and Springbank 1966 Local Barley, bottled at cask strength. Springbank also offers single malts matured in a choice of woods in cask.

Highlands

The road north of the Speyside region, where distilleries are less common, passes the site of the now dismantled Glen Albyn distillery and the distilleries of Glen Ord, Teaninch, Dalmore, Glenmorangie, Balblair, Clynelish and finally, near Wick, Pulteney. These distilleries are referred to as being in the Northern Highlands region. This is a mountainous and spectacularly beautiful part of Scotland where streams tumbling over granite, heather hills, and green glens introduce interesting flavors and aromas to the malt whiskies. The Highlands stretch on the mainland from Pulteney in the northeast to Oban in the west, to Tullibardine in the south. Each whisky is different than its neighbor and its characteristics owe much to the local topography and water supply. In common with other regions, its isolation meant that few visitors made the journey down narrow lanes to the farmhouses, so illegal distilling was relatively easy. Most of the distilleries that produce whisky today, however, were constructed in the early 1800s. Only Balblair claims to have been built before distilling was legalized in 1790.

Tain, Ross-shire – Glenmorangie Distillery

The road from Inverness to the northernmost tip of Scotland passes the distilleries of Ord, Dalmore and Teaninch before reaching the town of Tain. The road out of Tain to the southern shore of the Dornoch Firth leads to the home of Glenmorangie, perhaps one of the best-known single malt Scotch whiskies in the world.

Glenmorangie belongs to Macdonald & Muir Limited, a company founded in Leith, the old port of Edinburgh, in 1893. Descendants of the original family are still actively involved in the company,

which also owns Glen Moray, Speyside, Ardbeg, and Islay distilleries as well as marketing Highland Queen, Muirheads, Bailie Nicol Jarvie and James Martin WO blends.

Glenmorangie was first licensed in 1843 to William Mathieson and the first spirit was distilled in 1849. The original site was a brewery run by McKenzie & Gallie reputedly from 1738, making this one of the oldest locations in Scotland for the continuous production of alcohol. The first overseas sales of Glenmorangie were made in 1880 – the *Inverness Advertiser* noted: "We observed the other day, en route for Rome, a cask of whisky from the Glenmorangie Distillery, likewise several casks destined for San Francisco." In 1887 the company was reconstructed as the Glenmorangie Distillery Co. Ltd and in 1920 was purchased by Macdonald and Muir.

Glenmorangie is Gaelic for the "Glen of Tranquillity," which aptly describes the situation of the distillery. Water comes from the Tarlogie Springs, the distillery's own source, and where possible the distillery uses local barley, some of which is grown at the home farm, Cadboll. Glenmorangie is matured in traditional, low stone warehouses in American oak casks. The company once used the byline The Sixteen Men of Tain for a celebrated advertising campaign which focused on the care and commitment of its workforce to produce its special range of single malts.

Glenmorangie 10 and 18 year old single malt Scotch whiskies are known the world over. In 1996 the firm launched a range of Wood Finished Malt Whiskies. These are single malts that have been matured for a minimum of 12 years in American oak casks and then finished in casks which were previously used for port, Madeira or sherry. The new range was launched by Glenmorangie at

a special presentation to celebrate the 80th birthday of former British Prime Minister, Sir Edward Heath. These special whiskies also commemorate the fact that Macdonald and Muir traded in sherry, port, Madeira and claret right into the 1960s. This finishing imparts special flavors and aromas to each single malt and they are well worth seeking out.

Above right: Glenmorangie Distillery was the first to launch a range of Single Malts finished in port, sherry or Madeira casks.

GLENMORANGIE
SINGLE HIGHLAND MALT SCOTCH WHISKY

ESTABLISHED 1843   PRODUCE OF SCOTLAND

TEN YEARS OLD

The GLENMORANGIE
DISTILLERY COY, TAIN, ROSS-SHIRE
BOTTLED IN SCOTLAND

GLENMORANGIE
SINGLE HIGHLAND RARE MALT SCOTCH WHISKY

ESTABLISHED 1843   PRODUCE OF SCOTLAND

THIS SPECIALLY AGED, RARE MALT SCOTCH WHISKY, IS MATURED FOR
EIGHTEEN UNHURRIED YEARS IN MOUNTAIN OAK CASKS PRODUCING
A MALT OF RICH BOUQUET AND FULL, ROUNDED FLAVOUR.

YEARS 18 OLD

The GLENMORANGIE
DISTILLERY COY, TAIN, ROSS-SHIRE
BOTTLED IN SCOTLAND

Glenmorangie Ten Year Old Single Malt Scotch Whisky

A pale golden malt.

Nose: A light, slightly yeasty aroma.

Taste: At first deceptively simple then fuller flowery notes are detected with some nut and spice. A fresh, clean finish.

Glenmorangie Port Wood Finish Single Highland Malt Scotch Whisky

The finishing in port wood gives the single malt's golden color a pale blackcurrant hue.

Nose: Warm caramel yet fresh.

Taste: Gloriously full and smooth on the mouth with hints of citrus and spice. A delicious after-dinner drink.

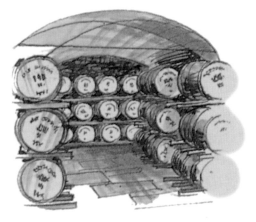

Above: Almost like an old diving bell – the unique onion shaped still at Old Pulteney.

Opposite: Old Pulteney celebrates the town of Wick's fishing heritage.

Wick, Caithness – Old Pulteney Distillery

The road north from Glenmorangie winds past Balblair and Clynelish distilleries, then the scenery changes as it follows the coastline toward Wick, the home of Scotland's most northerly mainland distillery. (There are two distilleries on the Orkney Islands which are further north.) The rocky, windswept coastline close to Wick provides a fine setting for Old Pulteney distillery, which sits on the outskirts of the town.

The distillery was built in 1826 by James Henderson when Wick was a thriving herring fishing port. Unfortunately drunkenness and lawlessness also thrived in the town to the extent that magistrates decided to introduce local Prohibition and Wick became in effect a "dry town" (though Old Pulteney continued to distill whisky throughout this period). Prohibition remained until 1947. Old Pulteney distillery was purchased by Inver House Distillers in 1996 from Allied Distillers and in 1997 the company celebrated the golden anniversary of the local repeal with a new bottling.

The copper stills at Old Pulteney are unique in shape. Although new, they faithfully replicate the original stills and should help to ensure that the single malt retains its original distinctive flavor.

Inver House Distillers is an independent company owning four other distilleries in Scotland: Speyburn, Knockdhu (bottled under its Gaelic name An Cnoc), Balblair and Balmenach. The company has won HM Queen's Award for Export since over 95 percent of its production is sold overseas. In addition to single malts, Inver House markets a range of blended Scotch whiskies including Hankey Bannister, Catto's and Pinwinnie.

Old Pulteney is marketed as a 12 year old single malt and also as a 15 year old cask-strength matured in a single sherry cask. The label on both bottlings bears a picture of a traditional Wick herring drifter.

Old Pulteney 12 year old Single Malt Scotch Whisky

This is a lovely malt and another personal favorite. The color is deep amber with flashes of copper.

Nose: A dry, salty, slightly sweet aroma.

Taste: The proximity of the distillery to the sea is palpable in the initial salty taste, but this is quickly replaced by hints of peat, allspice and soft caramel. A short, crisp finish.

Old Pulteney Sherry Wood 15 year Cask-Strength Single Malt Scotch Whisky

The long maturation in old sherry casks gives the malt a deeper rich color.

Nose: The dry, salty aroma again, with sherry overtones.

Taste: Full-bodied malt. The sherry adds smoothness to the smoke and spice.

Islay

To a whisky connoisseur, "Islay" immediately suggests peaty flavored single malts and names such as Laphroaig, Lagavulin and Ardbeg.

The island of Islay is situated on the west coast of Scotland off the Mull of Kintyre. Islay is the most fertile of the Hebridean Islands which run along the west coast of Scotland. It is diamond-shaped, has a deep inlet – Loch Indaal – on the southwest coast, and is steeped in history. Standing stones from the Bronze Age, old Celtic crosses dating from AD 800 at Kidalton, an old medieval chapel at Kilnave, and numerous tales of illegal whisky distilling all add color to Islay's intriguing past. The journey by boat from Kennacraig on the mainland takes some two hours and, before air travel, the citizens of Islay were often cut off from the rest of the world, so it is not surprising that whisky distilling started on Islay way back in the sixteenth century.

Islay is a beautiful, though often windswept, island with rugged hills. The highest peak is Beinn Bheigeir, which rises to 1,450 feet (442 meters) above sea level. Deep wooded valleys punctuate miles of open moorland and rolling agricultural countryside. With its isolated position, ready source of peat fuel, unlimited water and local barley, Islay was a natural place to start whisky distillation. The seven distilleries on the island produce very different malt whiskies, from the light Bunnahabhain and Caol Ila to the stronger, aromatic Laphroaig and Ardbeg. The other distilleries are the well-known Lagavulin and Bowmore and also Bruichladdich – at the time of writing the last is silent, but its fine single malt can be obtained from specialty retailers.

Cool, clear water bubbles out of the ground, over rocks, into lonely hillside pools and then down to the sea. Barley grows in the fertile fields and peat is dug from the moorland. Malted barley dried over a peat fire in Islay has a taste and an aroma all of its own. Islay malts are known for their peatiness and several distilleries produce whiskies with a pungent peaty smell. Peat bogs cover much of Islay and the main road from Port Ellen to the capital Bowmore literally floats on the peat in certain spots, making the surface unexpectedly bumpy.

All the distilleries in Islay are built close to the sea to facilitate the whisky's transportation to the mainland. The island was served by small coastal steamers, known as puffers, which transported barley, coal and empty casks from Glasgow and returned with full casks. The seas between Islay and the mainland are often turbulent and landing could be very difficult. Iain Maclean, a distillery worker at Laphroaig for 54 years, described how goods were taken ashore: "There were two big iron rings in the rocks, one on each side of the bay. A rope ran from each and was tied to the boat to hold it steady. The distillery had a farm where they grew turnips, corn and potatoes and kept four horses. The horses waded into the sea pulling carts to meet flat-bottomed boats bringing coal in from the puffer. Once the carts were fully loaded, they had to haul them out of the water and up the slipway to the distillery. It was deep out there and long, heavy work for the horses."

Port Ellen – Laphroaig Distillery

"Laphroaig no half measures" is one of this distillery's advertising slogans which almost acknowledges that you will either love it or hate it. There is no doubt that with its strong phenolic aroma and taste, Laphroaig is very distinctive and as such not one for the faint-hearted. It epitomizes peaty Islay as do its other Kidalton neighbors, Ardbeg and Lagavulin. This stretch of coastline on the southeast coast is closely associated with whisky distillation and for many years there were distilleries operating from secret hideaways in the rocky coastline. At one time there were five licensed distilleries, although Ardenistiel, close to Laphroaig, could never have been deemed a commercial success because its manager seemed more interested in

Left: Islay to the west of the Mull of Kintyre is home to really special peaty malts.

Left: Bowmore's round church sits proudly at the top of the town's main street overlooking Loch Indaal.

Above: Love it or hate it – you will immediately recognise this distinctive single malt.

breeding pigs than distilling whisky. Port Ellen distillery is now closed and operates as commercial maltings for many malt whisky distilleries.

Laphroaig means "the beautiful hollow by the broad bay" in Gaelic and is perhaps best viewed from the sea, apparently clinging to the shoreline. Laphroaig distillery was founded in 1815 by Alexander and Donald Johnston, who started farming there around 1810. The first recorded distillery listing for Donald Johnston dates back to 1826. He died in June 1847 after falling into a vat of burnt ale. This unprecedented accident left Laphroaig with no one to take over the reins since Donald's son, Dougald, was only 11 at the time. The trustees appointed Walter Graham, a distiller at Lagavulin, manager until such time as Dougald could take over. Dougald took control in 1858 by which time Graham had increased production considerably. When Alfred Barnard visited Laphroaig in 1887, during his tour around the U.K. whisky distilleries, he wrote "The whisky made at Laphroaig is of exceptional character... the distilling is greatly aided by circumstances that cannot be accounted for, and even the most experienced distillers are unable to change its character, which is largely influenced by accidents of locality, water and position."

Right: Bessie Williamson, who came to Laphroaig for three months and stayed for 40 years.

Below: Laphroaig's magnificant copper stills.

Far right and below: Laphroaig distillery hugs the shore on the east coast of Islay.

The distillery, which boasts the world's shortest railroad track (20 yards or 18 meters linking the peat store to the malt house) remained in the Johnston family's hands until 1954 when the then owner, Ian Hunter, died and left the distillery to a Bessie Williamson. Ian, who was an engineer by training, took over the distillery in 1908. He sought to expand its production and started to sell the single malt, which had been traditionally used for blending, in bottles. He opened up overseas markets such as Scandinavia and Latin America and successfully negotiated the legal sale of Laphroaig in the United States during Prohibition by promoting its medicinal smell and taste.

While he traveled the world, Bessie Williamson, who had joined the distillery as a temporary office manager in 1932, looked after Laphroaig. She was to take over much of the traveling from Hunter when he suffered a stroke while visiting an old Islay distiller, Thomas Sherriff, in Jamaica. During World War II, Laphroaig went out of production and the Army took over the distillery. When production started again Bessie took over as distillery manager, for Ian was now permanently disabled. On inheriting Laphroaig, she was to become one of the first women to own and manage a distillery and she continued to do so until her retirement in 1972.

Today Laphroaig is part of the Allied Domecq malt whisky portfolio and its leading single malt brand. An invitation to own a square foot of land adjacent to the distillery is currently enclosed in bottles of Laphroaig. There are now thousands of proud owners, each of whom is offered an annual payment of a tot of Laphroaig provided that they come to the distillery to claim it. Some have taken their ownership very seriously, including one young man who proposed to his girlfriend on his square foot, and a Japanese barman who, after being photographed by the distillery manager, Iain Henderson, carefully cut the grass on his plot to take home with him.

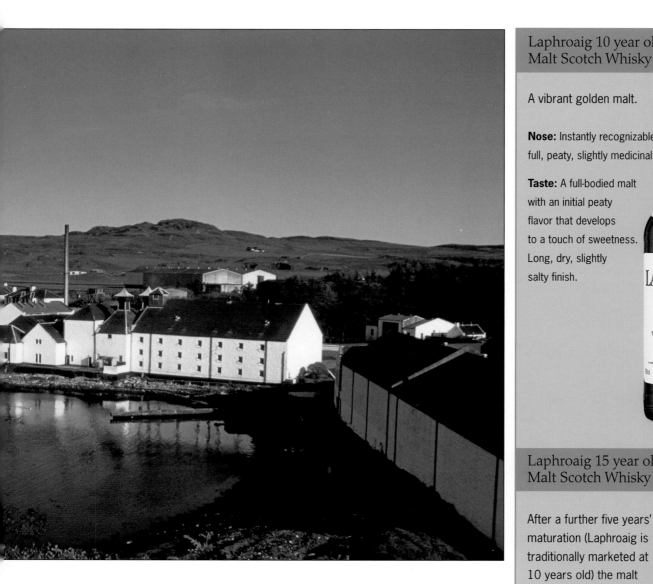

Laphroaig 10 year old Single Malt Scotch Whisky

A vibrant golden malt.

Nose: Instantly recognizable, full, peaty, slightly medicinal.

Taste: A full-bodied malt with an initial peaty flavor that develops to a touch of sweetness. Long, dry, slightly salty finish.

Laphroaig 15 year old Single Malt Scotch Whisky

After a further five years' maturation (Laphroaig is traditionally marketed at 10 years old) the malt has gained in color, flavor and taste. A dark gold single malt.

Nose: A light smoky aroma with hints of summer harvests and sugar cane fields.

Taste: Smoky with a hint of the sea on the tongue plus caramel, mace, crisp hazelnuts and a long, warm finish.

Above and right: Auchentoshan produces a triple distilled single malt on the site of an old monastery brewery.

Lowland

The undulating countryside of the Scottish Lowlands is less immediately identified with Scotch whisky production than mountains and tumbling streams. In this part of Scotland there are few granite hills and very few peat bogs. There is, however, a ready supply of fine barley and pure water. Lowland malts have a sweeter, mellower flavor than those from other regions, which owes much to the inherent qualities of the malted barley. Lowland malts also benefit from a slightly warmer and more equable climate. It is said that this contributes to faster maturation and Lowland malts are often sold at 10 or even eight years old. Most Lowland malts are produced with very little peat, though Glenkinchie, a slightly dry, smoky malt, is a notable exception.

In the late 19th century there were far more malt whisky distilleries in this region than there are today. Historically the Lowland region, which lies south of an imaginary line linking the Clyde and Tay rivers, produced whisky in large stills to meet the insatiable demands of the big cities. It had none of the delicacy or flavor of the Highland malts. While Lowland malts had the advantage of large local markets, they also suffered because these were more accessible to the excisemen, loath as they were to venture into the inhospitable Highlands.

Within the Lowland region are Scotland's two major cities, Edinburgh and Glasgow, plus the great shipping highway of the River Clyde. The Clyde gave distilleries easy access to overseas markets, and ships loaded with illegal and legal stocks of whisky were a common sight. The Clyde shipyards built such famous ships as The Queen Mary and Queen Elizabeth I and II. South of the industrial area of the Clyde the landscape becomes agricultural with fields of cereals, and sheep grazing on the low hillsides. It is also home to Scottish cashmere and has many knitwear mills.

There are now only two fully operational Lowland distilleries, and these are Glenkinchie and Auchentoshan. Glenkinchie, which is on the eastern side of Scotland, was founded in 1837 and is now part of the Diageo whisky portfolio. Colorful characters in Glenkinchie's history include the distillery manager, W. J. McPherson, who was probably more interested in cattle than whisky. He farmed the land himself and fed his cattle on spent grain from the mash. His cattle won the Supreme Champion's Prize three years running at Birmingham, Edinburgh and also at Smithfield agricultural shows. Glenkinchie was also a "summer holiday" home for the Clydesdale Dray Horses who carted whisky to the train station and brought back coal and barley to the distillery.

Above: The three pot stills at Auchentoshan and the range of single malts produced.

Dalmuir, Dunbartonshire – Auchentoshan Distillery

The Lowland region has much in common with Northern Ireland, the home of Bushmills. The proximity of Northern Ireland to this Scottish region led to an interchange of skills and it is believed that the Auchentoshan distillery was founded with assistance from Irish monks. One principal common characteristic of Irish whiskey and the malt produced at Auchentoshan is that it is triple distilled. Triple distillation probably started in the Lowland region because the sheer size of the stills meant that the spirit at the bottom effectively burnt and had to be distilled one further time to remove the burnt taste. This extra distillation also produced a far stronger spirit and removed more of its compounds, producing an exceptionally pure whisky. A purer spirit matures more quickly too, so that although the initial cost of

distillation is high, the spirit does not need to be held in bond for such a long period of time.

Auchentoshan means "the corner of the field" in Gaelic. The site overlooks the Clyde River close to the Erskine bridge and sits at the foot of the Kilpatrick Hills. A monastery was built on the distillery site in 1649 and the monks were reputed to brew ale and probably later distilled whisky. The present distillery was built in 1823 and the first recorded owner is John Hart in 1830. Auchentoshan then passed through many hands until 1969 when it was purchased by Eadie Cairns who re-equipped the distillery. In 1984 it was purchased by the present owners Morrison-Bowmore Distillers.

Auchentoshan, with its associate distillery Bowmore, was awarded the title Distiller of the Year by the International Wines & Spirits Competition (IWSC) in 1995/96. Auchentoshan 21 year old won the IWSC Gold Medal in 1992 and 1994.

Auchentoshan produces single malts from the unaged Select, through 10, 21, 22, 25 to 31 years old. They have recently been experimenting with an Auchentoshan three wood where the whisky is matured for 10 years in bourbon first-fill, then spends a year in Oloroso sherry first- and second-fill barrels and finally six months in barrels which contained Pedro Ximénez sherry.

Auchentoshan 10 year old Single Malt Scotch Whisky

Visitors to the northern edges of Glasgow can catch a glimpse of the Auchentoshan Distillery which sits on the banks of the River Clyde. This is the home of a traditional triple distilled Lowland malt.

Nose: A fresh aroma with citrus and raisins.

Taste: Soft sweetness with a hint of oak and lemon and a long, round aftertaste.

The Orkney Isles

At the northernmost tip of Scotland lie the Orkney Isles, a group of islands with the Atlantic Ocean to the west and the North Sea to the east. The Orkney Isles are nearer to Oslo, Norway than to London and it is no surprise to find many Norse influences here.

Standing stones and burial chambers from the Bronze Age can be seen at Skara Brae and Maes Howe. More recent history can be seen in the waters of Scapa Flow where wrecks of the German naval fleet lie, scuttled in 1919 to stop the boats from falling into Allied hands. Across the Churchill Barriers, which were built to protect Scapa Flow in World War II, is the Italian chapel on Lamb Holm. Inside are beautiful murals painted by Italian prisoners of war.

Standing on the Main Island, the largest of the Orkney group, it is difficult to say where the sky ends and the sea begins, for the fertile countryside is principally flat and treeless. On Hoy the land is more rugged and rises to some 1,400 feet (427 meters) above sea level. The coastal cliffs are a birdwatcher's paradise, accommodating among others curlews, kittiwakes, guillemots, puffins and sometimes the great skua. The meadows are covered in wildflowers, and the moorland and low hills are a blaze of purple when the heather comes into bloom.

The isolated location of these islands, together with their natural resources – plentiful water, fertile soil for growing barley, and large supplies of peat – allowed whisky distillation to continue virtually undiscovered. Records show that several distilleries were built here. In 1805 excisemen destroyed a large number of distilleries on the outlying islands. Now only two remain, Scapa, which is currently out of production, and Highland Park. Neither is situated on the Main Island.

Orkney whiskies smell of sea air, which seeps into the wooden barrels as they mature in warehouses close to the shore. Peat on the island, which is used to dry the malted barley, is made from heather and this imparts a honey flavor to the whisky.

Far right and below: The stills at Highland Park Distillery and its imposing gateway.

Right: Highland Park a glorious single malt from Orkney.

Kirkwall – Highland Park Distillery

Highland Park was founded in 1798 and its origins are closely linked with the notorious smuggler Magnus Eunson (*see* Chapter 1). Eunson was finally caught in 1813 although he doesn't seem to have ever gone to trial for illicit distilling. The distillery was reputed to have been taken over by a John or David Robertson, one of Eunson's arresting officers. Its early history is unclear and the distillery may have passed through various hands until 1825 when the stills, a malt barn and other buildings were purchased by Robert Borwick, who may have been in partnership with Robertson earlier on.

By the time Borwick died in 1840 the distillery had gained considerably in size. Highland Park passed to his son George, who was not interested in the business. George died in 1868 leaving the distillery to his brother James, a churchman in Fife, who also rejected the life and put Highland Park on the market. In 1876 Stuart and Mackay purchased the distillery and started to regain its fortunes. Soon it was selling its fine single malts to many of the new blenders including Chivas Brothers, John Dewar and Son, and George Ballantine. In 1898 the number of stills was increased from two to four to meet increased demand.

In 1935 the distillery became part of Highland Distillers. The group also owns other distilleries including Bunnahabhain, a subtle, fresh single malt from Islay with just a hint of peat; The Macallan, a unique Speyside malt matured in sherry casks, and Glenturret in the Southern Highlands. Highland Distillers are also well-known for their blends, particularly The Famous Grouse. The drinks portfolio also includes Gloag's dry gin.

Like all Orkney distilleries, Highland Park benefits from its own water supply. The distillery was built on a source of crystal-clear water emerging from two springs fed by a pool at Cattie Maggie's. It continues to produce single malt using traditional methods including malting its own barley on floor maltings and using peat cut from the distillery's own supplies at Hobbister.

An audiovisual presentation at Highland Park's visitor center shows images of Orkney interwoven with the production of whisky: Highland Park's own peat bogs, the standing stones of Maes Howe, the malting floors and the waters of Scapa Flow which are now contained by the Churchill Barrier.

Highland Park 12 year old Single Malt Scotch Whisky

A glorious gold with a flavor enhanced by the distillery's own maltings over peat smoke, and the salt-laden air.

Nose: Rich, smoky with a hint of honey.

Taste: A glorious rounded malt in the mouth with heathery, peaty and warm nutty overtones. A dry, yet sweet aftertaste. A perfectly delicious after-dinner malt.

Highland Park 25 year old Single Malt Scotch Whisky 53·5 percent

The additional maturation adds sweetness and body to the single malt which is a clear gold in color with copper hues.

Nose: Warm, smoke, oak, and peat; very full and aromatic.

Taste: A full-bodied malt with light caramel, orange and warm spice, and a long, honeyed finish.

Speyside

The Speyside whisky region sits in the Highlands of Scotland. The River Spey flows between the Ladder and Cromdale Hills into the Grampian Hills. Numerous waters flow down to the River Spey, notably the Rivers Avon and Livet. There are now only two distilleries along the Valley of the River Livet: The Glenlivet and Tamnavulin. This mountainous region was virtually inaccessible during the 17th and early 18th centuries so illegal distilling was a favorite pastime. With its abundant fresh water, easy access to barley, and peat on the moorland hills, Speyside had everything necessary.

Many distilleries in this region use underground springs. The purity of the water, which has come from deep in the hillsides and flows over granite in this part of Scotland, imparts a crispness and a unique flavor to the whisky. Having been made far from the sea and the influence of salt-laden winds, no salt is perceptible in the final product which tastes cleaner, sweeter, perhaps simpler than a complex Islay single malt such as Laphroaig.

The individual distilleries throughout Speyside produce different malts, but most of them have a characteristic balance and sweetness. The region's long history of distilling led to distilleries producing exceptionally fine malts. This area has the highest density of malt whisky distilleries per square mile – there are about 40 in all, and could arguably be designated as part of the Highland area. In spite of the number of distilleries which incorporate the word Speyside into their names, very few of them are actually built on the River Spey.

The 1860s saw an increase in the number of Speyside distilleries as well as the expansion of the railroads. Railroads provided easy access to the region at a time when roads were still under-developed. Cragganmore distillery, for example, was built in 1869 alongside the Strathspey railroad. The Distillers Company Limited had its own "coal line" carrying anthracite from the Welsh coalfields to the Speyside distilleries. In 1889 the Keith & Dufftown railroad opened to serve the many distilleries in this part of Speyside including The Macallan, Glenfiddich, Balvenie, Glen Grant and Strathisla. Trains delivered coal and empty barrels and returned south with barrels full of fine single malt whiskies. The railroad closed along with many others in 1968, but was purchased by a group of enthusiasts in 1992 and should be carrying passengers again in 2000. In 1897 Glendullan distillery was built and shared a private siding off the Great North of Scotland Railway with its neighbor the Mortlach distillery. Dailuaine distillery was served by a railroad link for over 100 years.

Ballindalloch, Banffshire – The Glenlivet Distillery

Most farmers produced some whisky for their own consumption, and this was accepted by the authorities. Trouble came when farmers started to sell whisky and the government decided that such stocks should be taxed. Most farmers refused to pay. However, as described in Chapter 1, one landowner, the Duke of Gordon, worked with others to introduce the legalisation of

whisky distillation. One of his own tenants, George Smith, applied for the first license to distill whisky in 1824 at his farm at Upper Drumin.

Smith was a colorful character. His decision to "go legal" did not meet with universal approval. His neighbors, who were continuing to distill illicitly, saw that he would put them out of business and decided on sabotage. George remembered the times vividly several years later, "I was warned before I began by my civil neighbors that they meant to burn my new distillery to the ground, and me in the heart of it." George did not take this threat lightly for several other distillers had lost their distilleries through attacks by groups of smugglers. "The Laird of Aberlour had

Below: The Glenlivet Distillery sits on the Livet valley with the Highlands on every side.

Marquis de Custine (1790–1857)

Travelers to Scotland have written many books on the subject, the most celebrated perhaps being Alfred Barnard who journeyed around the distilleries of the United Kingdom. A lesser-known traveler was the Marquis de Custine (1790–1857) who visited Scotland in 1822. This was a particularly interesting time for whisky, because King George IV had just been to Edinburgh and had called attention to the distillery industry by asking for a dram on his arrival. Custine appears to have found the Scots far more convivial than the English for he wrote: "I swear an intellectual interest in that everything in Scotland attracts me, delights me, whilst in England everything repels me..." The Marquis doesn't seem to have been particularly enthralled by the sound of the pipes, but he did enjoy tasting whisky. His exploits were republished, in French, by Francis Bourin in 1995 as *Le Marquis de Custine, Memoires et Voyages*. Another French writer was Necker de Saussure who took a trip to the Hebrides in 1822. "We frequently quitted the coast in order to go through the villages, built on tops of hills which bound it; the inhabitants, little accustomed to see strangers, took us for custom-house officers; thus we saw them flying before us, and shutting up, at our approach, all their huts in which they had established private distilleries of whisky, which are prohibited by law.

"Arriving at the foot of the rocks, at a distance from all habitation, we stumbled by accident on the depot of all the contraband. In a small cavern, the entrance into which was covered with briars, were ranged thirty or forty casks of whisky, destined to be transported during the night on board a vessel anchored at a little distance. Some very ancient iron lances were lying at the mouth of the grotto; they were the arms used by the smugglers in case of attack. Raising our eyes, we perceived, on the top of the rocks a troop of men who, with eager looks, were attentively watching all our movements. These were the proprietors of the whisky. We hastened to calm their uneasiness, by retiring without touching the depot; but no doubt these unfortunate people, seeing their enterprise discovered, expected their casks to be seized before the close of the day."

Do we look
INFLUENCED
by trends?

One place.   One whisky.

The
GLENLIVET
AGED 12 YEARS
Pure Single Malt
Scotch Whisky
PRODUCT OF SCOTLAND

presented me with a pair of hair trigger pistols worth ten guineas, and they were never out of my belt for years. I got together two or three stout fellows for servants, armed them with pistols and let it be known everywhere that I would fight for my place to the last shot. I had a good character as a man of my word and, through watching by turns every night for years, we contrived to save the distillery from the fate so freely predicted for it. But I often, both at kirk [church] and market had rough times of it among the glen people. "His pair of hair trigger pistols are proudly displayed in The Glenlivet reception center.

The Glenlivet distillery is situated about 700 feet (213 meters) above sea-level in an area with ready supplies of peat from the Faemussach Moss, and cool clear water. The valley floor of the River Livet is quite wide, but it narrows sharply as the valley rises into the hills. The distillery's isolated position in the Glen meant that it was cut off from the outside world and to this day the old smugglers' trails can be identified as narrow pathways which climb the surrounding hills.

George expanded his farming interests, taking over Castleton in 1838, Nevie in 1839 and Minmore in 1840. In 1859 he built a new distillery at Minmore close to the original site at Upper Drumin. In 1862 he had over 600 acres, thus owning one of the biggest farms in the area. At Minmore he had 150 West Highland and Shorthorn Cattle and had 15 men working for him. This robust growth continued when George's son took over in 1871.

In 1863 the Strathspey Railway came to Ballindalloch which was eight miles from Minmore. George Smith built a coal store at the station and in 1889 John Gordon Smith built a warehouse

Left: Captain Bill Smith, owner of The Glenlivet until his death in 1975.

to store barley. The railroad was used to receive coal and fuel and to take whisky from the distillery. Plans to construct a railroad link were abandoned because of the high costs involved.

Many distilleries incorporated the word "Glenlivet" in their whisky to let the consumer know that it came from this part of Speyside. This led to problems of recognition and in 1880 the Smiths took others to court to stop them from using "The Glenlivet." The judgment was found in the Smiths' favor and now distilleries can use "Glenlivet" only by adding the word to their own name – for example, Tomintoul Glenlivet. Only one distillery can call itself "The Glenlivet."

In 1891 John Gordon Smith purchased the Delnabo estate and in 1899 the Auchintoul estate. In 1901 he died and the estate was inherited by his nephew Colonel George Smith Grant. He was more interested in farming and left the business in the hands of his manager Peter Mackenzie. He died in 1911 but his eldest son John was just 18 and could not inherit the distillery, so Peter Mackenzie continued to run it. John died in 1918 in France during World War I and his brother Bill took over.

In 1952 the distillery joined forces with J. & J. Grant of Glen Grant and The Glenlivet & Glen Grant Distilleries Company was formed. In 1970 the company further expanded with the addition of the Longmorn distillery and the blending and bottling concern of Hill Thomson. The company then continued to trade as The Glenlivet Distillers Ltd. The Glenlivet remained in the hands of the Smith family until 1975 when the owner, Captain Bill Smith, died. In 1977 it was purchased by The Seagram Company Limited. Seagram's had previously bought the blenders Chivas Brothers and Strathisla distillery and in 1957 built Glen Keith distillery.

The Glenlivet 12 year old Single Malt Scotch Whisky

A pale golden color and one of the world's favorite single malts.

Nose: A fragrant malt with hints of fruit.

Taste: A medium-bodied malt with a sweet, slightly sherry taste and a long finish.

The Glenlivet 15 year old Single Malt Scotch Whisky

One of the whiskies chosen by The Glenlivet distillery managers for their own archive bottlings.

Nose: Full fruit and summer floral notes.

Taste: A mellow whisky with a long slightly sweet finish.

The Glenlivet 18 year old Single Malt Scotch Whisky

The additional maturation enhances the flavor and aroma of this single malt with a deep rich color.

Nose: A rich aroma with caramel and peat.

Taste: A gloriously rich malt, yet dry, with fruit, peat, and a spicy, sweet finish.

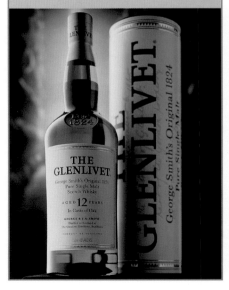

Isle of Skye

The beautiful Isle of Skye, where visitors are never far from the sea and where peat abounds and water flows from mountain springs, is probably one of Scotland's best-known Western Isles. Flora MacDonald carried Bonnie Prince Charlie "Over the sea to Skye." Climbers associate the island with the Cuillins mountains which offer spectacular rock faces such as the Storr and Quiraing and 11 mountains over 3,000 feet (914 meters).

Skye – Talisker Distillery

Talisker is the only distillery on the Isle of Skye and was built in 1830 on the edge of Loch Harport by Hugh and Kenneth MacAskill. The MacAskills already had a reputation on the island, principally for driving tenant farmers off the land so that Hugh could breed Cheviot sheep, and had acquired land around the Minginish peninsula, including Talisker House.

Talisker is set in a sheltered glen on the west coast of the island and draws its water from Hawk Hill beside the distillery. Hawk Hill is a favorite spot for some of the few golden eagles still to be found in Scotland. The water used to make Talisker is rich in iodine and this gives the single malt a distinctive flavor.

Talisker is part of the United Distillers whisky portfolio, a member of the Diageo group and is marketed as part of their Classic Malt range. Recently the company launched The Distillers Edition which offers whisky connoisseurs double-matured single malts. Talisker's second maturation is in cask wood that previously contained Amoroso (a style of Oloroso sherry) which adds sweetness to the single malt's traditional peppery character.

Talisker 10 year old Single Malt Scotch Whisky

Robert Louis Stevenson spoke of Talisker as "a regal drink." It is full of character and instantly recognizable.

Nose: full, sweet yet peaty.

Taste: a well-rounded, full-flavored malt with peat and honey and a lingering finish.

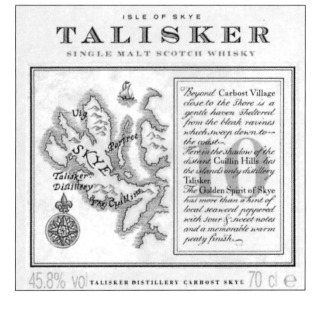

Right: Talisker is the only distillery on the Isle of Skye – a whisky full of the sea and peat.

Kentucky

There are now 11 working distilleries left in Kentucky, reduced from a reputed 2,000 in 1838, although not all of these would have distilled whisky. Many have closed in the last few years. In 1996 the Lawrenceburg, Ohio Distillery belonging to Seagram closed, at present the Weston distillery in Missouri is silent. But the news is not all bad: there are some very good whiskies still being produced in Kentucky. One obvious brand name, Maker's Mark at Loretto, is not listed here but features in Chapter 4 under the Samuels' family.

Heaven Hill, Willett, and Barton distilleries are in Bardstown, the home of the annual Bourbon Festival and the whisky museum. Heaven Hill distillery and much of its whisky stock was destroyed in a fire on November 7, 1996. At present distillation has been transferred to the Early Times distillery in Louisville using Heaven Hill's own recipe, and plans are going ahead to rebuild the original distillery.

At the Willett distillery several special whiskies are produced including Johnny Drum and Noah's Mill. These were distilled at the original Willett distillery which closed in 1980 and has since been rebuilt. Distilling has just started again. Old stocks of Johnny Drum and Noah's Mill can be found and are worth seeking out if only to discover what an old American pot still whisky probably tasted like.

Barton distillery was owned by Oscar Getz who was responsible for the opening of the whisky museum. Barton produce several whiskies including Colonel Lee Kentucky Straight Bourbon and Very Old Barton.

Below: Fine Bourbons are made from a mixture of corn, rye and barley - the distilling process is very similar to Scotch malt whisky.

Right: New barrels are essential to give Bourbon its distinctive flavor.

Clermont, Beam – Jim Beam Bourbon

Jim Beam Kentucky Straight Bourbon Whiskey is probably the best-known Bourbon outside the United States. Jim Beam White Label four year old is the best-selling brand and one of the world's 20 top-selling spirits.

In the 1700s a Mr Bohm emigrated to Maryland from Germany, when the name was changed to Beam. The first distiller was Jacob Beam of Washington County who started distilling in 1795. In the 1800s, David Beam built a distillery at Clear Springs, which is just along the road from the current distillery founded just after the end of Prohibition at Clermont in Bullit County. The company owes its name to Jacob Beam's grandson, who founded the James B. Beam Distilling Company in 1935 and who revived the fortunes of the company once Prohibition had ended. The fame of Jim Beam grew under the management of Jim Beam's grandson, Booker Noe, one of the legends of Kentucky whiskies. Members of the family are still involved with Jim Beam and whiskies are still being produced by members of this dynasty at other distilleries such as Early Times and Heaven Hill.

The Clermont distillery is still there, close to the Baptist Church, although the old oak-timbered distillery was rebuilt in the 1970s. The Beam family did not stop at one distillery, however, and a further one was built a few miles away at Boston, which is now referred to by the company as Beam, Kentucky. Most bottle labels now show the address as Clermont, Beam, Kentucky; a combination of the two sites. Distilling for all Jim Beam brands takes place at both distilleries.

Jim Beam brands include Jacob's Well, Old Crow and Sunny Brook, while small-batch bourbons include Booker's

Above: Booker Noe, Jim Beam's great, great grandson no longer works at the distillery but keeps an eye on its fine batch Bourbons.

and Knob Creek. Jim Beam is available as a bourbon at varying ages using different grain mixes. For collectors of special editions Jim Beam Straight Bourbon Whiskey offers a set of about a dozen ceramic decanters. Designs have included American buildings, fire trucks and trains complete with wagons and animals.

Frankfort

Frankfort was one of the major centers for distilling in Kentucky. The area was named for Stephen Frank who had been killed by Native Americans on the banks of the Kentucky River. There are now only two distilleries in the neighborhood, Leestown Distilling and Labrot and Graham.

Leestown Distilling Company is situated just outside Frankfort at Leestown. The Blanton family started distilling here in 1860. By the time Prohibition was enforced, the distillery

Jim Beam Kentucky Straight Bourbon

Matured for a minimum of four years.

Nose: Light and flowery with a hint of oak.

Taste: Rounded, mellow yet light on the tongue with an oak finish.

belonged to a Captain George Stagg, one of the few distillers to be given a license to continue to produce whisky for medicinal purposes. Stagg saw no merit in running the distillery for such limited production and it was closed down. It re-opened after Prohibition and grew, rather haphazardly it would seem, from the collection of brick red painted buildings that fill the site today, set in the midst of gardens and woodland. A life-size statue of Colonel Blanton, leaning on a stick, looks as though it might be about to stroll around the distillery to ensure that everything is still being done as it should be.

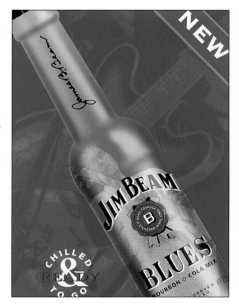

This page: From cask to bottling line, Jim Beam is America's best known Bourbon.

Several of the whiskies produced by the distillery bear the names of the managers who have worked there, including Colonel Blanton and Elmer T. Lee (the manager between 1952 and 1980). The distillery has built a reputation for producing exceptionally fine single-barrel whiskies. Perhaps the most famous name to come from this distillery is Ancient Age. Maturing whisky in Kentucky isn't always an easy task since the very hot summers subject the barrels to extreme changes of temperature. Whiskies tend to mature early and many to my taste have just too much oak, but try Ancient Age at 10 years old and I believe you will agree it is a very good Bourbon indeed.

Millville – Labrot and Graham Distillery

Founded in 1838 as the Old Oscar Pepper distillery, it became Labrot and Graham in 1878. The Oscar Pepper family started distilling at Old Crow probably at the end of the 18th century. The distillery continued to produce whiskies until it closed in 1971. For 25 years the buildings lay empty until in 1995 the owners Brown-Forman took the unusual step of deciding to start again. By this time much of the land had been sold off and everything needed to be rebuilt.

Brown-Forman wanted to reproduce whiskies similar to those originally distilled in Kentucky. To do this the firm commissioned Forsyths of Speyside, Scotland to produce three new copper stills. The first new spirit was distilled in 1995 and it will be ready to taste in 2001. All we have to do is wait and see.

Lawrenceburg – Wild Turkey Distillery

As many distilleries in Scotland are set in dramatic natural landscapes, so is Wild Turkey, not among mountains and streams but above the winding Kentucky River etching its way into the limestone escarpment. Wild Turkey sits on a cliff above the river which is crossed by a single-track railroad bridge. This railroad line once brought supplies to and from the distillery, but like branch lines the world over it is closed now and the bridge is unsafe to cross.

Wild Turkey owes its origins to the Austin Nichol Company, a firm of grocers and wine and spirit merchants founded in 1855, which mainly imported goods from Britain. During World War II the company was unable to obtain stocks from either Scotland or Ireland, so decided to try to source a local whisky for its customers. Wild Turkey was made for Austin Nichol by various distilleries until 1971 when it decided to buy its own. The distillery it bought had been founded by the Ripy family, who had started distilling on a different site in the 1850s and were one of the distillers to supply Wild Turkey whiskey.

Earlier Wild Turkey whiskeys were a marriage of the distillery's own with others such as Ancient Age. Today the distillery belongs to Groupe Pernod Ricard and the whiskey is wholly produced at Wild Turkey. Wild Turkey produces a range of whiskey at various ages as well as Kentucky Legend and Kentucky Spirit and, in duty free outlets, the 1855 Reserve. Austin Nichol's Wild Turkey is widely available at eight years old and 101° proof .

Right and below: The Wild Turkey distillery.

Louisville

Louisville, Kentucky has a ring about it and the name was once synonymous with whisky. Louisville distilled gallons of the stuff when the railroad came to Kentucky's largest city, which lies close to the Ohio River and the border with the state of Indiana. Just a century ago there were 21 whisky distilleries; today there are only two.

Wild Turkey eight years old Straight Kentucky Bourbon

At 8 years old Wild Turkey is aged longer than most Bourbons. The whiskey reflects this longer maturation and has a smooth rich taste. Most readily available at 101 proof, which also sets Wild Turkey apart from the rest.

Nose: Toffee and caramel with hints of oak.

Taste: Full bodied and rounded on the tongue; a warm whiskey with a smooth long finish.

Old Forester Kentucky Straight Bourbon Whisky

This is a whisky, not a whiskey, which featured in many Raymond Chandler stories as the favorite drink of gumshoes and hoodlums alike. Old Forester contains more rye than many whiskies and has a full bodied slightly sharp flavor which distinguishes it from traditional Bourbons.

Nose: Spicy with hints of rye and sugar.

Taste: A full bodied whisky with plenty of flavor and a nutty finish.

Louisville – Early Times Distillery

The present distillery was built in 1935 and started life as the Old Kentucky Distillery. It was purchased by Brown-Forman in 1940 who largely rebuilt it. Early Times is however a much older whisky and distillation started around 1893 in Bardstown. Before Prohibition Early Times had gained in stature and was one of the largest-selling brands in America. By the time Prohibition had ended Early Times had moved again and production finally settled in Louisville.

The distillery sits behind a row of trees not far from the Churchill Downs racecourse. As the owner of a leg of a racehorse, I enjoy a day at the races; perhaps I might be invited one day to watch the Kentucky Derby and enjoy a glass of Old Forester or Early Times at the same time.

Brown-Forman produce both Old Forester, whose original home was near the present distillery, and Early Times. The original Old Forester was a vatted bourbon and started life in 1870 when it was marketed by a second-generation American, George Brown, whose family originally came from Scotland. Old Forester joined Early Times in 1979.

Much of the Early Times produced is destined for distillers in Canada, where it is mixed with local distillations. The recipe is predominately corn with a little rye and malt. Old Forester has a higher rye content and less of this brand is made each year at the distillery, which is a pity because it is full of character and a very distinctive drink.

Above: Jimmy Bedford, Jack Daniel's master blender says he has the best job in the world.

Right: Jack Daniel, founder of the oldest registered distillery in America.

Tennessee

Tennessee shares the same limestone escarpment as Kentucky and its early whiskies had much in common with those of Kentucky. The whiskies now produced there by just two distillers, Jack Daniel and George Dickel, are not Bourbons but true Tennessee Whiskies. Tennessee is mountainous, with plenty of well-hidden valleys and ample supplies of fresh water. In addition to the 700 or so legal distilleries operating about century ago there were also many illicit stills.

Lynchburg – Jack Daniel Distillery

The Jack Daniel distillery was first established in the 1830s. The name was registered in 1866 and it is the oldest registered distillery in the United States. Jack Daniel was born Jasper Newton Daniel and after running away from home at the age of six he settled with Mr Dan Call of Lynchburg, a Lutheran minister and whiskey-maker. In time Dan Call decided to give up whiskey-making for full-time preaching and sold his business to Jack, who moved the operation to a permanent iron-free water source from a cave spring. Jack was clearly a

colorful individual and he sold his whiskey to both sides during the American Civil War. In 1904 the distillery won a gold medal at the St Louis World's Fair. One day in 1905 Jack had difficulty opening his safe; he kicked it in a fit of temper, gangrene set into the wound and he died six years later on October 10, 1911. He never married and the distillery was inherited by his nephew Lem Motlow, whose name still appears on every bottle of Jack Daniel's whiskey. The distillery was sold to Brown-Forman in 1956.

Jack Daniel still uses water from the Cave Spring which flows through the

Above: Jack Daniel built the office in 1865 and his statue still watches over the distillery.

This is the home of the George Dickel Distillery which is some 16 miles from Jack Daniel's. It is set in a "dry" county and was only recently permitted to sell its whiskey to visitors. The distillery is certainly worth visiting, but take a packed lunch with you and a good map – I understand it is not easy to find!

Dickel's whiskies are not nearly as well known as those of their near neighbor, but are highly recommended, particularly Dickel No. 12.

Jack Daniel's Old No. 7 Tennessee Whiskey

Tradition has it that Jack Daniel's was Frank Sinatra's favorite whiskey and he is reputed to have said when asked whether he believed in God that he would vote for anything which helped him get through the night - a prayer, a tranquilizer, or a bottle of Jack Daniel's.

Nose: Mellow with honey, apricots and rye

Taste: Caramel, spice and a little rye sharpness; a medium-bodied whiskey with a warm finish.

limestone escarpment. The distillery produces a range of whiskies, all from a mix of corn, rye and barley malt. The whiskey is made using the sour mash process described in Chapter 2. Once the sour mash has fermented, the wash, known as stiller's beer, is produced which is then distilled. These distillations include Jack Daniel's Single Barrel Tennessee Whiskey, Jack Daniel's Old No. 7 Black Label Tennessee Whiskey and a Green Label, and Gentleman Jack Rare Tennessee Whiskey. They are matured in new oak barrels which are charred inside and filtered slowly through 10 feet (3 meters) of hard sugar maple charcoal

before maturation. Jack Daniel's whiskey is subjected to extreme temperature changes during the year. As the spirit expands it seeps into the oak; as it contracts it draws away from the sides of the barrel. As with other American whiskies, Jack Daniel's matures relatively quickly and the distillery bottles at four and six years.

Today the master distiller at Jack Daniel is Jimmy Bedford. He says, "It is funny to see the reaction I get from people when I tell them what I do. Most people find it hard to believe at first, but when they realize I'm telling the truth, most of them will ask for my autograph."

Southern Comfort

And then there is Southern Comfort. Clearly not a whisky, Southern Comfort typifies a way of life of southern belles, paddle steamers and long, hot summers.

In 1860 a young barman, M. W. Heron of La Rue Bourbon in New Orleans, created a drink that he believed embraced the true spirit of the South. He initially designed it to balance the harsh whiskies, which were often of dubious quality and were commonly served straight from the barrel. In 1889 Heron moved to Memphis, Tennessee and opened up a bar where he served his drink and gained such a reputation that by 1890 he was selling Southern Comfort in sealed glass bottles. In 1979 Southern Comfort was purchased by Brown-Forman. Today the company markets the drink simply as a liqueur.

California

One further whisky to look out for is the new Old Potrero Rye Whiskey single malt from the Anchor distillery in San Francisco, California. Fritz Maytag, the owner, has spent a long time carrying out trials for this whiskey. The first batches were made in 1994 and 1995. I haven't tasted it yet, but would still like to raise a cheer for someone who is trying to revive the kind of whiskies that the first immigrants probably would have drunk.

Right: They take it easy in Jack Daniel's country.

Left: Southern Comfort a mixture of spirit, peach and lemon matured in oak barrels.

IRELAND

As described in Chapter 1, Ireland has played a fundamental part in the development of whisky. Whether whisky distilling started in Ireland or Scotland will probably never be known. The proximity of Northern Ireland to Scotland has encouraged the belief that whisky distilling was brought to Scotland from Northern Ireland in the early 1400s. However recent research on the Island of Rhum, Scotland, situated south of the Isle of Skye, has indicated that distilling could have started in Scotland some 4,000 years ago. If this is proved true, then the accepted history of whisky may have to be rewritten.

Irish whiskey today is the story of one large company, the Irish Distillers Group, and of one independent distiller, Cooley and Connemara. The Irish Distillers Group was formed in 1966 when three distillers, Jameson, Powers and Cork Distilleries, got together. Because of its location in County Antrim in Northern Ireland, Bushmills joined the group in 1972 (see under Northern Ireland for more detail). All these companies now form part of the Groupe Pernod Ricard, which incidentally has other whiskies in its portfolio such as Aberlour from Scotland as well as Austin Nichols and Wild Turkey from Kentucky, U.S.

Irish whiskey is produced slightly differently than Scottish whisky. Barley is dried in closed kilns without smoke, so that the final taste is of pure malt. Irish whiskey is usually made with a mixture of malted and unmalted barley and is for the most part triple distilled. By distilling the whiskey for a third time it is said that the final product is very smooth and pure. The tradition of triple distilling in Ireland probably dates only from the end of Prohibition when the Irish sought to attract back

American drinkers by producing something lighter than traditional Scotch whiskies. Irish whiskies are married before bottling, so that different flavors combine to make the final version. In the case of key blends some of the whiskey used is made in a pot still and added to the traditional grain whiskies.

Right: Millars, established in Dublin in 1843.

Below: The mountains of Ireland with their hidden locations were perfect for illicit distilling.

Cork Distilleries is the home of all whiskey production for the Irish Distillers Group except that produced at Bushmills.

One of the delightful advantages of visiting distilleries, wherever they are in the world, is that many are set in very beautiful places. Cork is one of them. It is not an idyllic spot in the middle of the countryside, but a city with pleasant streets, fine buildings and churches built alongside the River Lee. Today, however, no whiskey is distilled in Cork at such famous distilleries as North Mall or The Watercourse. To find the nearest whiskey distillery, you have to take the country road to the town of Midleton and the former James Murphy's distillery. Midleton, now a modern distillery built alongside the original one, is not open to the public, but you can walk around the old distillery and see its stupendous pot still which held 38,009 gallons. Midleton started life as a textile mill, as did other distilleries such as Deanston at Doune in Scotland. Textiles and whisky have a common requirement for clean running water, and the River Dungourney was able to provide this as well as the power to run the distillery.

Midleton was purchased, along with other members of the Cork Distillers Company, in 1966 to become part of the new Irish Distillers Company. In July 1975 the new distillery was opened and with it a new era. Midleton distillery incorporates both continuous and pot stills for making grain whiskies and also makes three different styles of malt. One of the key whiskies produced is Midleton Very Rare, which was launched in 1984. Because it uses some of the oldest whiskies in the company's portfolio, each year's bottling is numbered and the company keeps a register with the names and signatures of all purchasers. Another key whiskey is Paddy. Paddy is

Right: The River Awberg, in County Cork, Ireland.

Below right: The waterwheel at Midleton Distillary, County Cork.

Paddy Old Irish Whiskey

This is a light blended whiskey which has long been a favorite in Ireland. Originally sold with the rather boring name of Cork Distilleries Co. Whiskey it was renamed Paddy's in 1930.

Nose: A light, warm malty aroma.

Taste: Light on the tongue with hints of malt and toasted hazelnuts, and a light finish.

named for Paddy Flaherty, who was Cork Distillers Company's most successful salesman in Munster, the southern province of Ireland. (Ireland is divided into four provinces: Ulster, Leinster, Connacht and Munster, which are all depicted on the front label of a Paddy Old Irish Whiskey bottle.) He used to cover his round on a bicycle and his arrival was an excuse to join him at the local inn where he was known for his generosity at the bar.

Tullamore Dew (at 12 years old this interesting blend merits some attention) is another brand produced at Midleton: this is now owned by Allied Domecq.

The most famous whiskies produced at Midleton are marketed under the name of Jameson.

Founded by John Jameson in Dublin in 1780, Jameson is perhaps the best-known Irish whiskey in the world today. Because written records are not available, it is not certain whether Jameson actually started the distillery or took over an existing one. It would appear that the original John Jameson came to Ireland from Alloa in Scotland and that his wife was a member of the Scottish Haig whisky family. He had two sons, John junior and William. By 1810 John Jameson senior was producing pot still whiskey with a 1,508 gallon still from his premises in Bow Street. This distillery was taken over by his son John, while brother William worked at another distillery at Marrowbone Lane with a distiller called John Stein. John Stein seems to have had an interest in both distilleries, but by the late 1800s the Jameson brothers appear to have been in control. They were to found the biggest Irish distilling company. By 1880 the company employed around 300 people and distilled about 1.2 million gallons of whiskey a year. The stills were huge – the wash still had a capacity of 28,824 gallons and the two low wines stills some 16,800 and 15,600 gallons each. They were fired by coal and used internal steam coils. The practice of using large stills is similar to that of the large Lowland distilleries of Scotland and the effect of the huge coal fires underneath was to "cook" the spirit, particularly at the base of the still. This could explain why triple distillation was introduced, but no one knows the real reason. Today those huge distilleries are silent.

Jameson's whiskey was traditionally sold by the cask and wasn't actually bottled until as late as 1968. For many years it was sold by other companies, who purchased casks and then bottled the contents under their own brand names. Crested Ten and Red Seal were the first brands to be bottled by Jameson's themselves. The standard Jameson bottling still bears the red seal on the front and neck labels. Most whiskies produced at Jameson's are blends or marriages, each with a unique recipe of different whiskies. These include Jameson 1780, a 12 year old which is matured for some time in sherry wood; Jameson 12 Year Old, produced for the Far East; Jameson Gold, a blend of traditional pot still and older grain whiskies, and Crested Ten. The company also markets Redbreast Pure Pot Still Whiskey, which has been triple distilled and matured for at least 12 years. This promotion of a wide brand range is similar to American marketing methods.

Above: John Jameson, the founder of perhaps the best known Irish whiskey in the world.

Jameson Gold

Until the 1960s Jameson's finest whiskies were destined for other bottlers. The company had long been famous for maturing when most whiskies were sold young. Jameson Gold is one of a wide range made from a mixture of pot still and grain whiskeys.

Nose: Delicate, sweet with oak.

Taste: Smooth, honey flavored with ripe fruit on the tongue and a warm long finish.

Dublin – Powers Distillery

James Power started his distillery in Dublin in 1791. His son John was the first whiskey distiller to produce a miniature bottle known as the "Baby Powers." Before he could sell it though, an Act of Parliament had to be passed. Powers is a triple distilled whiskey and is the bestselling brand in Ireland. Irish Distillers Group recommend its "robust and full flavor." Powers is the perfect whiskey for making a Hot Irish Whiskey. For those who would like to try it, their recipe is as follows. "... First heat the glass by rinsing with boiling water (remember to keep a spoon in the glass). Then add one and a half teaspoons of demerara or brown sugar and a slice of lemon studded with cloves. Pour in a measure and a half of boiling water. Stir. Add one measure Power's Irish Whiskey. Stir again. Then sit back and enjoy the warmth." This sounds like good advice.

Below: Powers whiskey being bottled in John's Lane Distillery in 1897.

Left: John Power in 1820.

Far left: The Irish Whiskey Corner museum, Dublin.

Cooley – Cooley Distilleries

In 1970 John Teeling, an Irish business-man, was studying at Harvard Business School. One of the topics he covered was the Irish whiskey business and he investigated whether it would be possible to revive its fortunes. He was joined in his musings by Willie McCarter who was studying at the Massachusetts Institute of Technology. It wasn't until 1987 that the two of them, together with Paul Power, managed to raise £3 million to purchase a former alcohol plant in Cooley. They converted this into two distilleries – one with a pot still for making single malt whiskies and the other with a patent still to make grain whiskies. Cooley Distillery plc was formed. In 1988 the company purchased the old Lockes distillery from its owner, Lee Mallaghan, who joined the board of Cooley. Lockes was one of the oldest licensed distilleries in the world, dating back to 1757.

Whiskey manufactured at Cooley is taken to Lockes distillery in Kilbeggan to mature for a minimum of three years before it is bottled. The first matured cask of Lockes Single Malt was fittingly tapped by the granddaughter of the last John Locke. Since then the distillery has relaunched one old brand and produced several new ones. Tyrconnel Single Malt made a reappearance in 1993 after 50 years. Kilbeggan blended whiskey and Lockes premium blend, which has a high percentage of malt, were introduced in 1994 and then the company launched several new brands in 1996: Connemara peated single malt, Inishowen, a slightly peaty blend, and Millars Special Reserve blend.

It is encouraging to see a new whiskey distiller in Ireland reviving some of the old brands. Cooley won the Irish Exporter of the Year Award in 1998; key markets are France, Holland and the U.K. with new sales campaigns recently launched in Asia and South America. Cooley also won two gold medals and a trophy at the International Wine and Spirits Competition in 1998, so things are certainly looking good for the future.

Left and above: Tyrconnell and Connemara are single malts from Cooley Distillery where the whiskies are matured at the old Locke Distillery nearby.

Tyrconnell Pure Pot Still Single Malt Irish Whiskey

An Irish malt whiskey, which is only distilled twice from unpeated barley. This was a best seller in the United States before Prohibition and is named after a very successful racehorse owned by the Watt family who produced the whiskey at that time.

Nose: Fresh, malty bouquet.

Taste: Warm and sweet, full in the mouth with a smooth dry finish.

Connemara Pure Pot Still Connemara Irish Whiskey

Unusually for an Irish whiskey, Connemara uses barley which has been dried using peat smoke.

Nose: Peaty.

Taste: In spite of its relatively young age a full-bodied whiskey with hints of honey and smoke and a warm finish.

CANADA

Canada encompasses a huge area stretching from the Pacific to the Atlantic and northward past the Arctic circle, with huge forests, mountains, prairies and lakes, and settled by English- and French-speaking peoples plus original native populations. Canada, like the U.S., grew out of the immigration movement initially from Europe, and has welcomed immigrants from around the globe, yet it is still one of the world's least populated countries. As with all continental countries, Canada experiences great changes in temperature from hot summers to freezing cold winters, as well as huge variations in rainfall.

Trying to discover when whisky distilling started in Canada is, as usual, very difficult. Written records are rare, although it is said that the first distillery for rum was licensed in 1769. The first recorded spirits were probably a mixture of cereals and sugar – a type of whiskrum that didn't appear to have a beneficial effect on those who drank it! William Henry, a fur trapper in southern Manitoba wrote in his diary that after drinking "two gallons of high wine" an old lady was murdered in her tent and that Native Canadians "quarreled."

The influx of settlers from Ireland and

Left: Alberta Distillery, situated on the outskirts of Calgary.

Bottom left: The mash house at Glemora Distillery.

Scotland led by the 1830s to whisky being produced from surplus grain. The oldest Canadian distillery still in existence (although its days appear to be numbered) is Gooderham and Worts near Toronto, which was founded in 1837. Whisky-making stopped in 1957 and rum-making in 1990. The neighboring maltings, which were erected in 1863, were relatively unchanged in 1997. There are nine distilleries for the different brands still operational in Canada.

Problems arose when the authorities tried to tax whisky distillers and many small enterprises went out of business. Larger companies survived, essentially by producing whisky in a wooden version of the continuous still. To this day there are very few Canadian distillers producing whisky in batches in traditional pot stills.

Governmental concern for the welfare of Canadians, and efforts to prevent the "whiskey-sodden American brigands" who sold the spirit from entering Canada, led to the foundation of the Royal Canadian Mounted Police in 1874. The Mounted Police were most successful in their efforts and soon very little American whisky was available in Canada. This had the effect of increasing home-based production and when Prohibition was enforced in the United States, Canadian distillers were ready with their own whisky to meet, albeit illegally, the demands of their neighbors.

Canadian whisky uses rye as its main cereal. Because of the inherent sharpness of rye, most Canadian whiskies are a blend of rye and grain spirit which gives a lighter taste. As with blended whiskies in Scotland, there was much discussion as to whether these really constituted whisky. The U.S. authorities confiscated 6,000 cases of Canadian whisky in 1906, saying that it wasn't true whisky. After much deliberation a presidential commission declared that it could be called whisky, as did the U.K. government around the same time.

Left and below: Large lakes of pure clear water and wide open spaces contrast with mountains and streams – both environments well suited to making whisky in Canada.

Lethbridge, Alberta – Lethbridge Distillery

Lethbridge distillery sits in the middle of the vast plains of Alberta. Alberta has spectacular geographical features which contribute the raw ingredients for whisky – the Rockies' water, the rolling farmland rye, wheat and maize.

Lethbridge is where Smirnoff vodka is distilled. The current distillery is new, but its history dates back to 1939. The first distillation was also its last for some time because of the outbreak of World War II, but in 1945 production started again and by 1951 a fine whisky was being made. Sales grew and in 1973 the new Lethbridge distillery was built and the old one closed down. Key brands produced at Lethbridge include Triple Crown and Red Feather Saloon.

Kelowna, British Columbia – Okanagan Distillery

This distillery was closed by its owners, Hiram Walker, in 1995 and with it went almost the last of whisky-making in British Columbia. But not quite ... for a small amount of Potter's whisky is made each year at a brewery in Kelowna. Never destined to be a single malt, the whisky spirit is blended with whiskies from elsewhere and ultimately, after maturating for some eight to 10 years, is bottled under various guises: Royal Canadian Whisky for the Taiwanese market, Potter Bush Pilot and Potter's Old Special.

Gimli, Manitoba – Gimli Distillery

Lake Manitoba provides the pure cool water for Gimli distillery. The large distillery site is near Lake Winnipeg in the middle of the prairies. Gimli belongs to Seagram's and produces the well-known Crown Royal brand. It is the last working distillery in the

Right: The low outline of Palliser Distillery merges into the Alberta plains.

Below: Seagram's Gimli distillery spreads across the Manitoba countryside.

Seagram's portfolio in Canada. Others such as their first Waterloo distillery, established in Ontario in 1857, La Salle in Montreal dating from 1920 and Beaupré in Quebec are closed. When they were producing at full capacity in the 1960s, Seagram's achieved sales of nearly 40 percent of total Canadian consumption. This in fact accounted for only seven percent of the company's total worldwide sales.

La Salle continues as the base for the company's blenders – and boasts a Coffey still making grain whisky for Seagram's blends. Seagram's blends are produced from a mixture of old whiskies from these defunct distilleries as well as new distillations from Gimli. Using the accumulated knowledge of many years, the company is seeking to replicate some of these old whiskies.

The Seagram's portfolio is a large one with specialist blends made for various markets, such as Lord Calvert at three years old for Scandinavia and four years old Seagram's Five Star and Canadian Hunter. But the blends which reinforce the notion that Canada can produce some really good whiskies sold the world over include Seagram's VO, Seagram's Crown Royal and Crown Royal Special Edition.

Seagram's VO

A blended whisky which is sold throughout the world. The blend, which was first produced in 1912, is made of 6 year old whiskies

Nose: Warm, scented with oak.

Taste: A rounded whisky with plenty of vanilla and oak on the tongue.

Cape Breton Island, Nova Scotia – Glenora Distillery

The location of the Glenora distillery, on Cape Breton Island in northeast Nova Scotia, bears more than a passing resemblance to a Scottish whisky distillery. Visitors reach Glenora along a winding road which clings to the shoreline. It is this scenery that gives Nova Scotia its name, for the first settlers felt themselves almost at home though they were thousands of miles away. And it isn't just the scenery that is reminiscent of Scotland, for many of the inhabitants still talk with a faint lilt. However whisky distilling is relatively new and the first settlers seemed to have preferred rum or moonshine made from a mixture of malted barley and sugar.

Glenora was set up in 1986 by Bruce Jardine of Scots descent. Working closely with Harry Cockburn, who was at the time with Morrison Bowmore, he selected the position for the distillery beside the MacLelland Brook whose waters are clean and pure. The choice of Nova Scotia as the home of a whisky distillery would seem at first sight an obvious one, but in fact the climate is not as temperate as it is in Scotland. Water freezes in winter and the summer temperatures rise to 90°F (32·2°C), so whisky can be distilled only in fall. Maturation in such a changeable climate should affect the final product.

Glenora was designed by David Forsyth, the late Scottish architect. The buildings were completed in 1990 and are similar to the Scottish traditional farmhouse style distillery with long, low buildings and a pagoda-style chimney. Starting a new whisky distillery from scratch is an expensive undertaking and Glenora has had a checkered career, going into receivership in 1991 and bankrupt in 1993. New investors led by Lauchie MacLean stepped in, and with increased local industry and government support, the company produces an average 2,640 gallons (30,000 liters) a year. The company also adopted a scheme of selling certificates at 15 Canadian dollars each which entitle the owner to a bottle of Glenora 10 year old in the year 2000.

The first whisky sold by Glenora came from Bowmore, because the first distillations could not be used. Kenloch is a special bottling of five year old Bowmore. Unaged single malt from Glenora is also available under the brand name of Liquid Silver. The first blended whisky to incorporate Glenora was launched early in 1998. Called Breton's Hand and Seal it is a blend of

Above and below: Canada's most easterly distillery, Glenora on Cape Breton Island.

for the brand. The distillery now belongs to Brown Forman who are perhaps best known for Jack Daniel's, of which more later. Canadian Mist is still the best-selling blend in the United States ahead of both Seagram's VO and Canadian Club by at least a million cases a year.

Canadian Mist is a good example of a whisky produced for a particular market using different distilling methods. It is made from corn and malted barley, unusually in stainless steel column stills. It is perhaps difficult to believe that a whisky made without copper and with water straight from the faucet, with whatever chlorine or other chemicals the local waterworks has chosen to add, will taste good at all, but the results – especially when Canadian Mist is bottled at eight years old – are really worth trying. To give the blend the characteristic Canadian "rye" flavor, a little rye whiskey from Early Times distillery in Louisville, Kentucky, together with a hint of bourbon from the same distillery, is added. Canadian Mist sold in the United States is usually a three year old, while in Canada it is more than likely to be a four year old whisky.

four 8 to 12 year old whiskies made in Canada and its own single malt. Glenora uses lightly peated malted barley and is made in the traditional way using three wooden washbacks made in Scotland and two small pot stills made in Rothes, Scotland.

As with many distilleries, Glenora has attracted its fair share of tourists, and chalets are to be built to accommodate people visiting the distilleries and attending gatherings, tastings and conferences. Glenora distillery has secured a key role in the local community, having a restaurant and a pub serving a wide range of single malts, and has increased interest in all things Scottish – concerts and *ceilidhs* (traditional Gaelic gatherings for music, dancing, story and song) are often held.

Collingwood, Ontario Distillery – Canadian Mist Distillery

The Canadian Mist was built in 1967 at the time when Canadian whisky was enjoying success worldwide and demand outstripped production. Canadian Mist had been distilled by Melchers for Barton Brands for two years before they took the decision to build their own distillery. The site was chosen because of its proximity to the United States, which was the key market

Canadian Mist

Canadian Mist is the best selling Canadian whisky in the United States. Brown Forman produced a special bottling in 1995 to celebrate the completion of the Canadian Pacific Railroad in 1895.

Nose: Unmistakably rye with honey.

Taste: A full-flavored whisky with perhaps a rather harsh finish.

Hiram Walker founded an empire in Walkerville. The first distillery was built in 1858 and in 1884 he bottled his first six year old Canadian Club whisky produced in continuous wooden stills. Canadian Club is produced from a mixture of grains: the highest proportion is corn with a little rye, malted barley and oats. During Prohibition it must have been particularly galling for the Americans living in Detroit to look across the river to the distillery legally making whisky in Canada when they could no longer produce it themselves.

The growth of Walkerville was phenomenal and in 1894 Hiram Walker celebrated the opening of new corporate headquarters, inviting 1,500 people. This building, with carved oak paneling, wrought iron gateways and marble columns, provided the company with an imposing place from which to control its whisky production. The company expanded its interests into other areas, including transport.

History is replicated every time whisky is made in Walkerville, because the yeast used in the highly-flavored rye whiskies is the same strain as that perfected in 1858. Today's distillery dates from 1930 and has many similarities with the Dumbarton grain distillery built in Scotland at the same time. At Dumbarton, whisky is still matured in warehouses nearby, whereas Walkerville's barrels are matured at Pike Creek some eight miles distant. Much of the equipment used dates from 1930 and there is a happy marriage of the most up-to-date pressure cookers for mashing the corn and fermentation vessels installed in the 1950s.

At Walkerville, as with all Canadian distilleries, a wide range of whiskies is produced. Some, such as Wisers 10 years, are destined purely for the local market. Canadian Club is bottled at various ages and for some the younger blends are just that bit too young. However, a tasting of the older styles such as the eight and 15 year olds should persuade any skeptics that Canadian whisky is worthy of consideration.

Canadian Club 12 year old

This blended whisky was first bottled in 1884. The whiskies are blended together before being aged in barrels for at least 6 years.

Nose: Slightly smoky with rye and sugar.

Taste: Caramel and rye; a mixture of sweet and dry on the tongue with a short, light smoke finish.

NORTHERN IRELAND

There are many links between Northern Ireland and Scotland. They share a common language – Gaelic (which has developed differently in the two countries) – and the landscapes are similar with large lakes, tumbling streams, peat bogs, rolling agricultural countryside and mountains. Indeed, legend has it that the Giant's Causeway off the north coast of County Antrim was a footpath to Scotland.

Northern Ireland is the home of Bushmills, the oldest recorded licensed distillery in the United Kingdom. A license was granted in 1608 to Sir Thomas Phillips by King James I to establish a place for the production of whiskey "... within the countie of Colrane, otherwise called O Cahanes country or within the territorie called the Rowte in County Antrim" – which describes a large part of Ireland. It is probably impossible to prove whether or not Bushmills' foundation dates from the same time as this license, but all bottles show this as the date when the distillery was established. The current distillery's history perhaps dates only from 1784. Bushmills was owned by Irish Distillers Ltd until 1988, when the group was acquired by Groupe Pernod Ricard.

Not far from Bushmills, St Columb's Rill, the distillery's water source, rises from the peat bog and flows into the River Bush. As early as 1276 there were stories of the spirit being produced in the area and by the 1600s there were many mills with distilleries alongside the river. Distilling had become part of the town's everyday life. The distillery still occupies a waterside site and its twin pagoda-shape malting towers are a prominent feature of the town.

As in Scotland, making whiskey here was a logical extension of a farmer's life and a means of using surplus grain. The copious pure water and peat for fuel ensured a steady supply of the raw ingredients. At Bushmills, as at Auchentoshan and Rosebank in Scotland and Midleton in Ireland, the whiskey is triple distilled. As a result the final spirit is simpler than whisky that is distilled only twice, since fewer constituent ingredients remain in the spirit. It is difficult to pinpoint what makes one whiskey different than another, but apart from the triple distilling Bushmills is very slightly further south than most distilleries in Scotland and therefore warmer, which could affect maturation in the barrels. There is no doubt that Bushmills, a firm favorite, is a distinctive whiskey with a full flavor.

Bushmills 10 year old single malt

The ubiquitous Irish single malt, Bushmills 10 year old is justifiably world renowned and a mellow, corn-colored whiskey.

Nose: Warm, honey with sherry and spice.

Taste: A smooth malt, warm on the tongue with full flavors of sweetness and spice and a dry, slightly diminished finish.

Right: Bushmills Distillery alongside the Bush River.

Japanese whisky owes much of its origins to Scotland. The first distillers were trained in Scotland and took their newfound knowledge to traditional *sake* distilleries in Japan. The landscape of the northern island, Hokkaido, is very similar to that of the highlands of Scotland, having peat bogs, mountains, and cool, fresh streams which flow over granite rocks. The peat produces a less intense aroma than Scottish peat. Most whisky distilleries in Japan are not on Hokkaido but on the main island of Honshu.

The largest company, Suntory, has large grain distilling capacity and also distills pure malt at three distilleries: Yamazaki near Osaka; Hakushu; and Hakushu Higashi near Yamanashi on the main Honshu island. Suntory produces most of its whisky for home consumption, with about three per cent exported, principally to the Pacific. The company produces a range of blended whiskies including the premium blended Hibiki.

The second-biggest company is Nikka, which produces two single malt whiskies, Miyagikyo Sendai and Yoichi. Nikka also has a grain distillery at Nichinmoya where a pot still whisky is produced using malted barley. Nikka predominately markets blends produced from specially selected whiskies which are married together for at least six months before bottling. Brands include Memorial 50, which was produced to celebrate the company's 50th anniversary, and Special-age. It is only recently that Nikka has started to bottle its single malts, Yoichi and Sendai.

Other major distillers are Sanraku Ocean, with two distilleries, and Seagram's Kirin distillery near Gotemba not far from Mount Fuji.

Above: Nasetaka Taketsuru, the founder of the Nikka distilling company.

Top: Fine whisky is distilled at Yoichi.

Okkaido Island – Nikka Yoichi Distillery

Nikka Yoichi produces a single malt whisky, unusual in Japan where for the most part whiskies are known as pure malt and are not produced in the same way as they are in Scotland. The Nikka Whisky Distilling Co. Ltd is different, for its founder, Masataka Taketsuru, learned his craft in Scotland. He was a student at Glasgow University in 1918 and worked at Hazelburn in Campbeltown as well as at Lagavulin on Islay, where he learned to love its peaty style. While in Scotland he met and married his wife Jessie and returned home with her to work for Suntory. He left Suntory in 1934 and set up his first distillery at Yoichi on Hokkaido Island. The spot he chose, surrounded by mountains on three sides and the ocean on the fourth, was ideal for whisky distillation, having a steady supply of pure water from underground springs rising through peat bogs.

The first spirit ran from the stills in 1940, but the war years meant that the distillery could not obtain barley and was forced to produce alcohol for the government instead. Distilling began again slowly after the war and alcohol was produced from fruit as well as from grain.

Yoichi produces a range of single malts varying from the very peaty 12 year olds to 10 year olds matured in sherry casks. Regrettably few of Nikka's single malts are available outside Japan, but you may be lucky enough to find an example of their 12 year old Yoichi.

Left: Natural forest around the Hakushu Distillery.

Far left: Copper stills at the Hakushu Distillery.

Below left: A keen sense of taste and smell is used by the blenders at Suntory.

Yoichi Single Malt Whisky
12 years

A deep, vibrant copper-colored single malt.

Nose: Peaty with a hint of sherry.

Taste: Full-bodied with a peaty taste and a long finish.

Yamazaki – Suntory Distilleries

Shinjiro Torii founded the first whisky distillery in Japan in 1923 in the Yamazaki Valley on the outskirts of Kyoto. The first whisky produced by the company was Suntory Shirofuda in 1929 – this is still available as Suntory White. The company specialized in blend, following Shirofuda with Kakubin in 1937 and Old in 1940.

Suntory built a second distillery further north in 1973 at Hakushu Valley in the Japanese Alps and a third, Hakushuk Higashi, was constructed alongside in 1981. The more northerly distilleries produce some whiskies with a peat influence, while the whiskies from Yamazaki tend to be softer. The company still concentrates on blends.

Suntory Pure Malt Whisky
12 years

This single malt is produced at the first distillery founded by Shinjiro Torii in 1923.

Nose: Light, slightly sweet with malt.

Taste: A medium-bodied malt with hints of fruit on the tongue and a sweet, long finish.

SPAIN

The Iberian peninsula – Spain and Portugal – is for most people synonymous with fine wines, port and sherry, but also produces a considerable amount of fine whisky at a malt whisky distillery in Segovia. Visitors to Spain will already know that away from the sunny tourist beaches there is a rich diversity of landscape – from the green-clad mountains of the north to the hot, dry central plains. So perhaps it shouldn't be such a surprise that all the natural ingredients for producing whisky are available.

Segovia – Destilerias y Crianza del Whisky SA

Destilerias y Crianza del Whisky SA (DYC) was founded in February 1959 by Nicomedes Garcia to produce whisky for the home market. The company's headquarters are at the Distilerio Molino del Arco – the "distillery of the mill by the arch" – which sits at the foot of the

Above and right: The cloistered Moorish courtyard and large distillery complex with the snow-clad mountains behind. The cultural mix which produces DYC whiskies.

Sierra de Guadarrama, an imposing range of snow-clad mountains outside the city of Segovia. Segovia is an old walled city with an aqueduct built by the Romans some 2,000 years ago to pipe water from the mountains.

DYC distills 5·1 million gallons (20 million liters) a year and the distillery occupies a large site with 18 whisky warehouses storing 200,000 barrels of whisky. As you round the bend toward the distillery the first thing you notice is the pagoda, which looks more Scottish than Spanish. The distillery malts all of its own barley in Saladin maltings similar to those at Tamdhu in Scotland. It has seven stills, all different in style. The striking thing about DYC is that even though it produces all this single malt it does not market any of it as such. DYC is a major player in the blended whisky market selling over two million cases in Spain each year.

In 1968 DYC purchased Lochside distillery in Montrose, which has subsequently closed, since the malts produced were used in the company's blends. In 1990 the company was purchased by Pedro Domecq and is now part of the Allied Domecq group.

DYC Blended Whisky

Sold principally in Spain since 1963 this blend is distilled with peat-dried malt and matured in old Bourbon barrels. For many years the blend has been number 25 in the world list of top selling whiskies.

Nose: Malt and oak.

Taste: A lot of malt and sweetness on the tongue with a hint of oak and smoke.

Dunedin in New Zealand is the most southerly distillery in the world, as opposed to Highland Park on the Orkney Isles in Scotland, which is the most northerly. It is no accident that Dunedin is the home of a distillery, for this is a Scottish town in all but location. Scottish settlers chose the South Island to live on and set about turning it into a "home from home."

New Zealand had its first whisky distillers by 1867 when the New Zealand distillery opened in Cumberland Street, Dunedin, closely followed by the Crown Distillery in Auckland. Unfortunately both these were short-lived: they were closed by 1873. The government was under pressure from the Scotch whisky distillers back home to close these new enterprises and was offered financial support for its railroad-building program as an incentive to do so. Not for the first time did a government respond to such demands by imposing heavy taxes on the distillers, and so legal distilling came to a temporary halt. This did not stop the distillers, particularly those who had been operating illicitly in the Hokonui region of South Island, which is very similar to the Highlands of Scotland. Illegal distilleries were set up and bars sold a mixture of Scotch and local whiskies.

The Wilson Malt Extract Company was founded in 1926 and for the first 60 years of its life brewed a range of beers. In 1969 the company started to distill its first whisky, but in stills of stainless steel, not of copper as with the traditional single malt pot stills. The resulting whisky certainly showed the difference. Happily for Wilson's, Seagram's bought the distillery and installed a copper condenser, which immediately changed the style of the whisky for the better.

Lammerlaw Single Malt was named for the Lammerlaw Mountains from which the distillery obtains its water supply. At the time of writing, the distillery is not in production, but Seagram's assures me that this will soon change. However, supplies of Lammerlaw Single Malt and Wilson's blended whisky, which has a high percentage of single malt, are available.

Above: Teacher's whisky arrives in New Zealand in the early 1900s.

Right: Lammerlaw single malt from Dunedin.

Lammerlaw 10 year old Single Malt

From Dunedin where the first Scots settled in New Zealand. The whisky was produced using a single pot still and is aged in American oak barrels.

Nose: Strong and peaty.

Taste: A full-bodied peaty mouthful with hints of honey and citrus.

AUSTRALIA

There are two distilleries in Australia, both on the island of Tasmania whose geography has much in common with Scotland. There were earlier whisky distilleries started by immigrants in much the same way as distilleries developed in the United States, but these are long gone.

At the Gasworks distillery in Hobart the stills are run every two weeks to produce a single malt in an old alembic style along the lines of an 1861 design. The first whisky was produced in 1995 and I have yet to taste the company's Sullivan's Cove Single Malt Australian Whisky.

Andrew Morrison, a farmer of Scots descent who lives on the island of Tasmania, has started to produce a single malt whisky at Cradle Mountain distillery. A barrel of his first distillation has found its way to Scotland and is currently maturing in the warehouses of J. & A. Mitchell. It will be interesting to taste the mature whisky when it is ready. In an interview in The Observer newspaper on November 17, 1997 Andrew said, "With an ideal climate and great raw ingredients, our dram will stand up to anything the Scots can produce." We shall have to wait and see.

DENMARK

Denmark doesn't naturally spring to mind as a whisky-distilling country, and indeed none is produced there today, but for some time Cloc whisky was available. Production started in a factory belonging to the Danish Spirit Factories in the town of Roskilde on the outskirts of Copenhagen in 1947. The company, established in 1921, also produced gin and vodka. In 1924 it was joined by a Mr R. M. Macdougall who examined the possibility of producing whisky. The company was allowed to continue

distilling by the Minister of Trade during World War II. The first Cloc whisky was bottled on September 1, 1952 in both 74cl and 37cl bottles. The company followed this five year old whisky with a seven year old. In 1974 they stopped selling whisky, reputedly because legislation meant that they had to change the bottle size from 74cl to 70cl. I am indebted to Jens Tholstrup who is investigating this distillery and describes Cloc as a fairly peaty whisky.

GERMANY

Whisky distilling would be a thing of the past in Germany were it not for one small remaining distillery. From the basement of his shop, the Blue Mouse, in Neues Eggelsheim, Robert Fleischman distills one or two casks of Glen Blue and Glen Mouse whiskies every year. I have yet to try them but I understand they are pretty good.

INDIA

I have visited India several times, and lately have had the good fortune to taste some of the really good single malts and blends.

The first I tried was the malt whisky made at the Kasuali distillery which is perched up in the Himalayas. It was built by Edward Dyer, a Scotsman, in 1855 and is run along traditional lines by the current owner Rakesh Mohan. Production never meets demand, but the distillery doesn't make any profit and I wonder how long Rakesh will continue before economics confound his aim to preserve the local industry.

A most surprising distillery is McDowells, which is situated in the southern state of Goa. Here a pure, pot still malt whisky is produced just a short distance away from the blue sun-kissed beaches. As with all distilleries in warmer

climates, McDowells matures relatively quickly. In Goa the humidity is high, which also influences the maturation process. At two years old McDowells may seem too young to drink, but it is quite acceptable and has much in common with whisky from Scotland. As the whisky ages its characteristics also change: a four year old is very different than the two year old. I have never brought any home, but have the feeling that like many drinks enjoyed on holiday, when you bring them back they can taste disappointingly different.

PAKISTAN

Considering that Pakistan was once part of the British Empire, the presence of a distillery there should not be a surprise – except that it is operating in a Muslim country. The distillery survives only because when the state of Pakistan was created the rights of the non-Muslim minority were protected, and this included distilling and drinking alcohol.

Murree distillery is owned by the Murree Brewery Company and was founded in 1850 to supply the British who missed the beer and whisky they were used to at home. Much of the distillery was damaged in a fire during Partition, but remnants of the original buildings still exist. It has wash stills built outside in the open air and cellars beneath the ground where the whisky matures. Underground cellars prevent the hot weather from accelerating maturation, so Muree whisky can be left in the barrels for a relatively long time. Murree whisky is usually bottled at eight years old although sometimes it is left to mature for a further four years. Murree is not available outside Pakistan but at eight years Murree's Malt Whisky Classic is a good whisky, light on the nose and with a well-rounded crispness on the tongue.

The Culture of Whisky

COLLINS ENGLISH DICTIONARY DESCRIBES CULTURE AS, AMONG OTHER THINGS, "THE ARTISTIC AND SOCIAL PURSUITS, EXPRESSION, AND TASTES VALUED BY A SOCIETY OR CLASS, AS IN THE ARTS, MANNERS, DRESS, ETC." IT IS THIS PART OF THE DEFINITION THAT BEST DESCRIBES THE THRUST OF THIS CHAPTER, WHICH EXAMINES HOW WHISKY IS REPRESENTED IN ADVERTISING AND LITERATURE, WHISKY PERSONALITIES PAST AND PRESENT, AND WHISKY FAMILIES.

Advertising, promotional campaigns and sponsorship

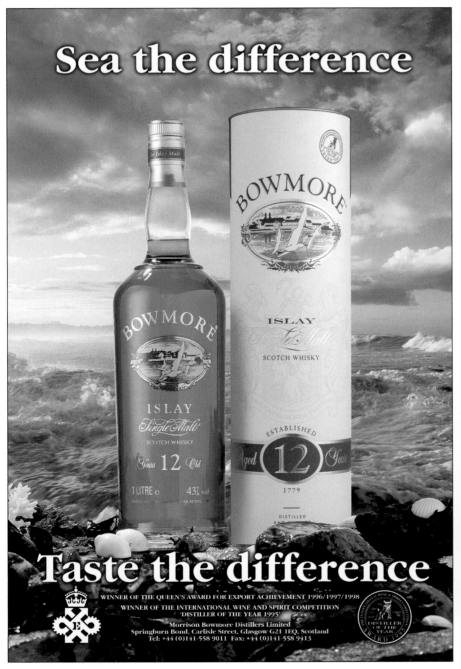

Whisky advertising and promotional campaigns have long reflected the tastes, pursuits and peculiarities of individual markets. What is designed to be effective for one country does not necessarily work in another, which is why some brands are better known in some countries than in others.

By the time the first blended whiskies were being marketed in the late 19th century, the poster was a respected advertising medium. Whisky companies' posters could be seen on many a street corner and on the sides of city buses.

Left: Bowmore advertising from 1995.

Below: Suntory advertising from 1976.

An international blended whisky brand

The development of the Cutty Sark blend was closely associated with its marketing. The company made a bold decision at the very beginning by commissioning a well-known designer, James McBey, to design its bottle and front and back labels.

Cutty Sark was launched by Berry Bros & Rudd in 1923 during Prohibition in the United States. Since that time the brand has grown in international renown. It is marketed throughout the

Below: Cutty Sark 1988 – those in the fast stream "Live a Cutty Above."

Left: In 1970 Cutty Sark was still the best-selling blended Scotch in the U.S.

world, and its advertising reflects the markets in which the brand is promoted.

The following examples include three from the United States dated 1970, 1988 and 1991 and from Greece 1997. It is interesting to see how advertising has changed in the past 20 years.

The early 1970 advertisement for the United States is a traditional one. The bottle of Cutty Sark – America's No. 1 Selling Scotch Whisky – is strategically placed in front of the tea clipper the *Cutty Sark*. The more sophisticated 1988 advertisement tries a play on words. The dinner-jacketed businessmen are looking at a new high-rise development with a glass of Cutty Sark in their hands and the caption reads "Live a Cutty Above." Then in 1991 we have a simpler advertisement which carries the exclusivity of Cutty Sark a step further, asserting "If you are the sort of person who thinks caviar tastes better when it costs $120 an ounce, you'd probably like Cutty Sark better if it cost $120 a bottle. Let us know. Our price tag can be easily changed."

The image on a Korean advertisement of 1997 is similar in style to the earlier American one but shows the clipper racing under full sail, presumably straight into the nearest Korean port, laden with Cutty Sark whisky. The aircraft overhead creates an interesting juxtaposition of old and new forms of transport, reinforcing the idea of the blended whisky's long pedigree.

If you're the type of person who thinks caviar tastes better when it costs $120 an ounce, you'd probably like Cutty Sark better if it cost $120 a bottle. Let us know. Our price tag can be easily changed.

CUTTY SARK®
SCOTS WHISKY
UNCOMMONLY SMOOTH

FOLLOW THE HEART OF CUTTY SARK

Top: Sophisticated whisky drinkers know the value of a fine Scotch blend.

Right: A Greek advertisement for Cutty Sark 1997.

GLENMORANGIE

"The Sixteen Men of Tain"

U nusually, this campaign was successful in the United Kingdom but also appealed to overseas whisky aficionados. The advertisements were simple black and white woodcuts reflecting the style of the bottle labels. The campaign revolved around those involved with the making of Glenmorangie Single Highland Malt Scotch Whisky in Tain, Ross-shire, hence the title of the campaign. Tasks such as maturation and distilling were illustrated, as were more unexpected operations such as Kenny White leaving the cooperage every year to clear the weeds from the Tarlogie Springs, Glenmorangie's water source.

I. KENNY WHITE leaves the Cooperage every year to tame the whins and broom that sprout around the Tarlogie Springs *(whose hard waters, rich in mineral content, are the source of Glenmorangie).* With the leaves turning and the sea-breeze gusting from the Dornoch Firth, the scything marks the true beginning of the "malt whisky season."

Handcrafted by the Men of Tain.

Right: Tradition is very much part of the Glenmorangie's worldwide image.

DYC

"People without complexes."

This is the headline accompanying an advertising campaign for DYC whisky in Spain. Just over five gallons (20 million liters) of whisky are produced at the company's distillery in Segovia. The campaign reflects the universality of the DYC brand, suggesting that everyone can belong to the club.

Left and below: Old or young, eccentric or contrary, DYC whisky is everyone's favorite in Spain.

GLENLIVET

"One place. One whisky."

This is the theme for The Glenlivet campaign launched in New York on August 27, 1998. It emphasizes the "Scottishness" of The Glenlivet, focusing on the landscape, the remoteness of the distillery and the brand's heritage.

As with most successful advertising, the theme reflects current preoccupations – in this case the concern of religious communities in the United Kingdom that so many people now work on Sunday, traditionally the day of rest. Hence the headline "Sometimes we find ourselves here on Sunday Morning. Somehow we think the Lord will understand." And many will sympathize with the sentiments of this advertisement, "Located in the same remote highland glen for nearly 200 years. Great for making whisky. Not so good for meeting women."

This is very different in style than two other Glenlivet campaigns, dating from 1977: The "The" Glenlivet campaign focused on the fact that only one whisky has the right to call itself "The Glenlivet". The second campaign, used by The Glenlivet Distillers Limited to publicize other whiskies in their portfolio, referred to Scotland's other important asset, North Sea oil.

Above: Part of the 1998 advertising campaign, this image reflects the traditions and location of the company.

Right: The Glenlivet and Glen Grant are just two of the fine single malts used in blends such as Something Special and Queen Anne.

Left and above:
Only one whisky can call itself "The Glenlivet." 1998 – The Glenlivet advertising captures the image of a small distillery in the Highlands of Scotland away from it all.

Sometimes we find ourselves here on SUNDAY MORNING. Somehow we think the LORD will understand.

One place. One whisky.

"The Right Spirit Boys"

In 1926 a *Sunday Pictorial* photographer took a picture of two little boys playing cricket in a London street with a wicket made of three empty bottles. One of the wickets was an empty Teacher's whisky bottle. The directors of Teacher's saw the photograph and thought it would make a good advertisement for their brand. Teacher's decided to find out who the two boys were and discovered they were Charlie and Frank Smith. At the time of the photograph Charlie was six and his younger brother was four. Teacher's contacted the boys' mother in Brixton, London, and agreed to pay her an annual allowance of £5 to help her bring up the two boys. So began a long association with the boys' family and a highly successful advertising campaign.

Left: This puts "an apple for the teacher" in the shade!

Far right: Charlie and Frank Smith playing cricket in London in 1926.

An extract from an old Teacher's magazine reports that; "In one of the annual letters, dated June 22, 1939 – just before World War II – a Teacher's director wrote: 'We take pleasure again in sending you £10 which we hope will enable you to take a holiday with your family.' The £10 in those days would have been more than enough for a holiday, when the price of a bottle of Teacher's Highland Cream retailed at around three shillings and sixpence. The correspondence is a fascinating history lesson. A 1940 letter revealed Frank had just celebrated his 18th birthday while the younger children had been evacuated to Sussex for safety during the war... "

"In 1945 Teacher's sent one of their London-based representatives to see Mrs Smith. Now aged 60, she earned thirty shillings [£1.50 in today's coinage] a week from her cleaning job, plus a widow's pension of ten shillings [50p] and an allowance of seven shillings [35p] from one of her sons in the army. With a total weekly income of £2.35 the allowance from Teacher's was well received."

Teacher's kept in touch with Mrs Smith, even sending her flowers when she was unwell, until she died in December 1978, aged 92.

The boys' photographs were used in a series of advertisements and promotional material. Their faces could be seen on the outside of the wooden cases in which whisky was delivered. In 1930 the boys appeared in an advertisement to celebrate Teacher's 100th birthday. Here the boys are giving their teacher, complete with black gown and mortarboard, a case of Teacher's whisky. Today such advertising – effectively using young people to promote alcohol – would not be countenanced. They are truly advertisements of their time and as such give a snapshot of a bygone age.

TEACHER'S WHISKY

The Right Spirit

CHIVAS REGAL
Old and new

Chivas Regal is another blended Scotch whisky that has a considerable reputation, particularly in the United States. The first advertisements designed for the American market focused on traditional Scottish elements, such as the old banqueting hall decorated for Christmas with a family servant carrying in the Yule log (used in the 1950s). The Scotland's Prince of Whiskies advertisement refers to the fact that Chivas Brothers had carefully laid down stocks of whisky so that the superiority of the blend could be assured after the end of World War II. Again this draws on traditional images of Scotland.

Later the company used cartoons to illustrate how special Chivas Regal was to its consumers. Here a woman is speaking to her friend, or maybe her husband, on the telephone: "They took some of the gems... most of the Van Goghs... and all the Chivas."

Left and right: Traditional or modern, the advertising message is the same; Chivas Regal is a special blended Scotch whisky.

Scotland's Prince of Whiskies
A MESSAGE OF ASSURANCE
Most pre-war Scotch whisky was used up during the war shortage. With determination and foresight Chivas Brothers laid down a limited amount for superior ageing.
Like all luxuries Chivas Regal 12 year old Scotch is rare rather than prohibitively expensive, and many discerning people want it.
Please do not be disappointed if you can not get it every time you order it. But, while limited, the supply is continuous. Only time can increase it...for you will always find its quality worthy of the name—"Scotland's Prince of Whiskies."
Scotch Whisky
PRODUCE OF SCOTLAND
THIS WHISKY IS 12 YEARS OLD
CHIVAS REGAL
FOUNDED 1801
BLENDED SCOTCH
WHISKY
PRODUCE OF SCOTLAND
4/5 QUART
100% SCOTCH WHISKIES BLENDED AND BOTTLED BY CHIVAS BROTHERS LTD. DISTILLERS ABERDEEN SCOTLAND
86 PROOF
CHIVAS BROTHERS LTD. of Aberdeen, Scotland—Established 1801. By Appointment Purveyors of Provisions and Scotch Whisky to the late King George VI.
CHIVAS REGAL
12 YEAR OLD SCOTCH WHISKY

Holidays, changing lifestyles and tradition

Japanese whisky advertising also reflects changing lifestyles. The first advertisement shown dates from the 1960s and focuses on a sweepstake which offered the chance to visit Hawaii. The headline "Drink Torys Whisky... Go Hawaii" would have appealed to the Japanese who at that time rarely traveled abroad and for whom Hawaii was regarded the dream destination. I understand the message in this advertisement only too well: in the late 1960s I worked with successful businessman Shogo Moriyama who went to Hawaii on vacation, much to the disgust of all his staff who couldn't possibly afford such a trip.

The second advertisement, used during the 1970s, promoted a very daring concept. Up until then Japanese people drank *sake* or *shochu* in their local sushi bars and restaurants. Whisky was gaining in popularity but was drunk only in hotels, bars or Western-style restaurants. Suntory's advertising campaign successfully established that whisky could be drunk anywhere – even in your local sushi bar. It shows a sushi bar-owner sitting enjoying a glass of Suntory Whisky Old at the end of a busy day.

In the 1980s Suntory launched two new campaigns. The first was designed around the Suntory Royal blend and illustrates the work of Arthur Rimbaud, a surrealist French poet (1854–91) whose work influenced the writers, painters and thinkers of his day. The question posed by the advertisement is: Who will be the poetic genius to influence us at the end of the twentieth century?

The second advertisement focuses again on the Suntory Whisky Old brand and is designed to illustrate that Old can become new, and as such is always desirable.

Both pages: Suntory whisky capturing the mood of the age with its trendsetting advertising. Examples from Japan in the 1960s (top left), 1970s (far left) and 1980s (left and above).

JOHN WALKER & SONS

"The first truly global brand."

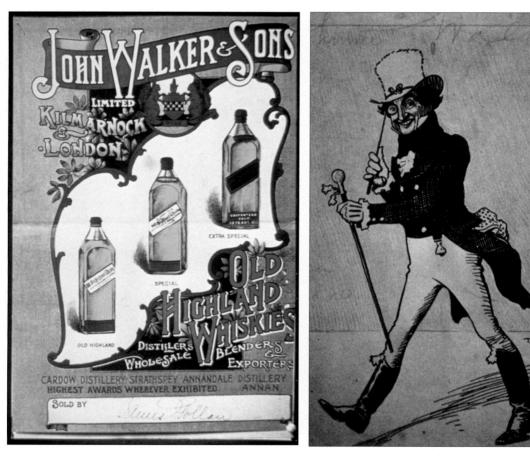

Far left: A early advertisement for Johnnie Walker.

Left: Johnnie Walker's Striding Man – perhaps the first whisky logo.

T his is the claim made by Johnnie Walker Red Label. In the early 1920s Johnnie Walker Red Label was selling in over 120 markets. The growth of the brand was masterminded by Alexander Walker, grandson of John Walker who had established his grocery business in 1820. John's business sold teas, wines and spirits from his shop in Kilmarnock, Scotland.

Several marketing statements set the Johnnie Walker brand apart. The first was the square bottle, which was developed in the 1870s, with its slanting label. The second was the Striding Man figure, which was drawn by Tom Browne, a well-known contemporary cartoonist, in 1909. The original sketch was made during lunch with Alexander's brother, George Walker, and several colleagues. Browne's designs

were familiar throughout the United Kingdom and United States.

At this stage advertising was restricted to show cards and posters at railroad stations or on street corners, so choosing a striking image such as this made a considerable impact. Since then the design has been redrawn by various artists including Basil Partridge, Clive Upton and the latest version is the work of Michael Peters.

Today the Johnnie Walker range includes Black Label, Gold Label, Blue Label, Swing Superior and Premier blends.

Stocks and shares from The Famous Grouse

In 1987 the public relations company I worked for conceived the first bottle collar campaign for The Famous Grouse blended whisky. Purchasers were offered the chance to win £25,000 in stocks and shares and there were also 100 monthly prizes of £100 cash, making a total prize fund of £55,000.

Using a bottle collar to promote a competition was a relatively new thing and had not been tried before since distillers felt it would stop their bottling lines – they were right, it did! Though the first design was unsuitable I am happy to say that the eventual promotion was a great success and led the way to a variety of competitions on bottle collars by other brands.

Left: The Famous Grouse launched one of the first bottle collar competitions in 1987.

Above: The Famous Grouse guide.

TEACHER'S
Whisky and sport

Whisky companies are always looking at new ways of attracting new customers. For many years whisky brands have been actively promoting golf matches – Bells, The Famous Grouse and Teacher's have all sponsored major competitions. Teacher's started sponsoring golf in the United States in 1954, working with the United States Professional Golfers Association to promote a Senior Championship. The old Teacher's Highland Cream Scotch Whisky advertisement shown right illustrates the company's support for this sport.

This "interaction" of life and public relations is reflected in 1999's The Balvenie Alternative Season. The Balvenie is a fine single malt distilled by William Grant. The Alternative Season offers unconventional activities as alternatives to traditional pastimes. For example, instead of recovering quietly from your hangover on New Year's Day, you could enter the Lothian Health Triathlon in Edinburgh by swimming 400 meters (about 0.25 miles), cycling 11 miles (17.5 km) and running 3·3 miles (5.3 km) in succession. Or in July you could have taken yourself to Congham Cricket Club, Norfolk where the World Snail Racing Championship was taking place –the perfect leisurely pursuit while sipping a dram?

Right: Teacher's have been sponsoring golf in the US since 1954.

IN GOLF...
EXPERIENCE IS THE GREAT TEACHER

IN SCOTCH...
TEACHER'S
IS THE GREAT EXPERIENCE

Paul Runyan, the 1962 holder of The Teacher Trophy for the PGA Seniors' Championship.

In Teacher's Highland Cream you have the end result of 130 years of experience in doing just one thing to perfection: creating a Scotch with unmistakable flavour and character. Making Teacher's has been a <u>family</u> craft since 1830 and its distinctive formula is strictly adhered to by William Teacher's three great-great grandsons.

See PGA Seniors in action in a free (loaned) 16mm sound film. Have your Entertainment Chairman name a date for showing by writing to Modern, Dept. PG, 3 East 54th St., New York 22, N.Y.

It's the flavour ... unmistakable
TEACHER'S
HIGHLAND CREAM SCOTCH WHISKY
BOTTLED IN SCOTLAND

BLENDED SCOTCH WHISKY / 86 PROOF / SCHIEFFELIN & CO., NEW YORK

TEACHER'S

CITY SCRIBBLERS
AWARDS 1991

Whisky and medicine

It has been suggested that a glass of whisky a day is good for you, particularly if you are a heart patient. I am not qualified to argue the case one way or the other, but I do know that whisky and medical fund-raising go hand in hand. For years, Teacher's whisky has been supporting The Bart's City Life Saver Scheme, which is run by St Bartholomew's Hospital in the center of London. The scheme has successfully taught many thousands of city people to recognize the symptoms of a heart attack. The training course teaches basic cardiac life support, which is crucial if a victim is to stay alive until the ambulance arrives. Many people working in the City of London owe their lives to trainees' swift reactions. As a way of drawing attention to the project and recruiting more members, Teacher's launched The City Scribblers Competition in 1989. This ran for three years and the standard of limericks and cartoons submitted by members of the public – as well as some well-known figures – was particularly high. Sir Bob Reid, who was then chairman of British Rail and responsible for the management of the railroad system in the United Kingdom wrote:

When a broker succeeds yet again
Celebrates, and at length 'feels no
   pain'
Keep him safe and alive
Tell him 'Don't drink and drive
Down your Teacher's and travel by
   train!

Lord Marshall, Chairman of British Airways, submitted an entry reading:

An analyst living in Bow
Said 'Here is the one thing I know:
My advice makes no sense
But when traffic is dense
It's faster by Tube to Heathrow.

Diageo, owner of such famous whisky brands as Johnnie Walker and brewers of Guinness stout, has like most large companies its own charitable foundation working with local communities and funding research projects. One of the most interesting projects is looking into sickle-cell anemia, an hereditary disease that particularly affects people of African or Caribbean origin.

Top: Fund raising and creativity go hand in hand in this Teacher's competition of 1989.

A WHISKY FOR YOUR PAINS

The taking of a glass at breakfast for medicinal purposes was not uncommon in the U.K. at the turn of the century. Sir Archibald Geike who was traveling in the Isle of Skye while on a geological trip wrote in his *Scottish Reminiscences* of 1904: "In a few moments the eldest daughter of the house entered bearing a tray laden with bottles and glasses which she brought up to my bedside, in order that, as she said, I might 'taste something before I got up'. Not being used to such a matutinal habit, I declined her offer with my best thanks. But she grew quite serious over my refusal, assuring me that my tasting would give me an appetite. In vain I maintained that at breakfast time she would see that I stood no need of any help of that kind. She only the more ran over the choice of good appetizing things she had brought me. 'Some whusky nate? some whusky and wahtter? some whusky and milk? some acetates?' This last I conjectured to be a decoction of bitter roots in whisky, often to be found on Highland sideboards in the morning."

Perhaps we should follow the advice of W.C. Fields who is reported to have said: "I gargle with whisky several times a day and haven't had a cold in years." Indeed a cure for the common cold is recorded as, "Take your toddy to bed, put a bowler hat at the foot and drink until you see two."

Whisky families

L ooking at whisky families is rather like looking at stitches in a tapestry: they are the fabric of the industry and maintain an important role in holding it together. Many made significant contributions to the industry's development. George Ballantine worked with Andrew Usher to perfect blended whiskies. William Teacher researched his own blends, created a demand for whisky in his dram shops and introduced the self-opening bottle. The Glenfiddich distillery took the unusual step in 1961 of marketing its single malt on its own, not merely a constituent part of blended whisky.

In a world of growing international conglomerates, it is heartening to discover that many whiskies are still produced by the same families who founded the distilleries. While some of the family-owned companies highlighted in this section have been producing whisky for over a century, a few promising distilleries have also been founded in the last 10 years by enterprising families.

Allied to the family-run distilleries are several companies that have been marketing whiskies and other spirits for many years and that still belong to descendants of the people who founded them.

There is room in this book to mention only a few of the family-owned companies involved in the making and marketing of whisky, but the examples below illustrate the determination, enthusiasm and innovation of these special people.

Left: Tradition lives on at the sign of the Coffee Mill – the home of Berry Bros & Rudd.

Top left: The wedding of William Grant's daughter, Isabella, to Charles Gordon.

A NEW SINGLE MALT WHISKY
Arran

I n 1995 Harold Currie, who had been Managing Director of Chivas, opened a new distillery on the Isle of Arran. Arran has a history of distilling and the whisky produced always had a good reputation. The last distillery to operate here, the Lagg, had closed in 1837.

The new distillery, built to a traditional design in the village of Lochranza, lies in a valley bordered by hills, close to a 14th-century castle. The Eason Biorach stream runs alongside, providing a source of pure water. To create interest in Arran, the company launched a campaign inviting members of the public to purchase a bond entitling them to a case of Isle of Arran Founder's reserve single malt whisky in the year 2001. Bond holders are also members of the Isle of Arran Malt Whisky Society.

The first spirit ran from the stills in June 1995 and is now maturing in warehouses on site in sherry hogsheads. In 1997 the Distillery Visitor Center was opened by Her Majesty Queen Elizabeth II. The spirit was tasted officially for the first time on Saturday July 25, 1998. Everyone agreed that the whisky was making excellent progress and that it had matured beyond all expectations.

Top: The opening of the Arran Distillery Visitor Center by Her Majesty Queen Elizabeth II.

Above: The new distillery and visitor center on the Isle of Arran.

Lochranza Blended Whisky

This blend, sold in a blue bottle, contains some of the three year old Arran whisky.

Nose: Smoky on the nose with a hint of sweetness.

Taste: Medium-bodied, slightly dry, with a clean finish.

CUTTY SARK

The Story of Berry Bros & Rudd

No. 3 St James's Street in London's West End has been the home of one family or its close associates since the 1690s. The story of Berry Bros & Rudd, however, starts in 1731 when William Pickering leased these premises. The small square behind No. 3 St James's Street is to this day known as Pickering Place. The company traded as "Italian warehousemen" or grocers, and arms painting, and heraldic furnishing suppliers.

William Pickering died in 1734 and the company was taken over by his widow Elizabeth – not the first time that a woman had been involved in the running of a business on this site, for in 1698 the Widow Bourne had lived there and she too ran a grocer's shop. The sign representing a coffee mill which hangs outside Berry, Bros & Rudd dates from Widow Bourne's time. Elizabeth ran the company until 1737 when her two sons, John and William Jr, took over. The heraldic side of the business ceased trading soon after and little by little the grocery side of the business was developed with spices, tobacco, snuff, teas and coffees finding their way in clippers from across the seas to a shop which remains virtually unchanged today.

The fascinating history of this part of London is quite well recorded. In the cellars of No. 3 and in the oak beams on the wall in the passageway into Pickering Place, for example, are the remnants of an old royal tennis court. This was closed down during the time of Cromwell, because the Puritans were unimpressed by tennis courts and considered them "centres of idleness."

In 1754 John Pickering died; his children were very young and his brother William had no suitable heir. William decided he could not continue on his own and went into partnership with John Clarke. Christopher Berry Green, the current deputy chairman of the company, is directly descended from John Clarke. George Berry was John Clarke's grandson and he joined the business in 1803. He had to wait seven years until his name appeared above the door. The company continued in Berry hands and was run by two brothers Walter and Francis, until after World War I (1914–18) when they were joined by Major Hugh Rudd, who before the war had worked with his father in wine trading in Norwich.

The company has been supplying wines and spirits to the British royal family since 1760. A visit to Berry, Bros & Rudd's premises is like taking a walk through history. Old bottles can be seen on the shelves and prints, drawings and copies of old invoices and stock lists hang on the walls. The company also has a famous pair of scales and from 1765 many of the well-known visitors to the shop were weighed. Their weights are recorded in nine special volumes which make fascinating reading.

On the wall at the entrance to the narrow access from St James's Street into Pickering Place there is a plaque showing that from 1842 to 1845 the government of Texas set up a legation office at No. 3 St James's Street. At that time Texas was an independent state and could send ambassadors to the English Court. In 1845 Texas became a part of the United States of America and this peculiar arrangement ceased.

As the company's fame spread, the bias shifted toward wines and spirits and in particular the introduction of Cutty Sark blended whisky. By the beginning of the 20th century the company was selling its own brand Scotch whisky. In 1923 a group of people, including the partners and the Scottish artist, James McBey, found themselves sitting at a table in the company's dining room discussing the fact that Prohibition in the United States of America couldn't last forever and that when the market re-opened there would be increased demand for whisky. The company wanted to create an original whisky "finer than anything being sold" and the idea for a gentle, crisp whisky of a pale natural color was born. The choice of a pale color was deliberate for at that time many blends available to the North American market were colored by caramel.

The company chose the name Cutty Sark, because the famous tea clipper ship was much in the news and had just returned to England. Cutty Sark was a suitable name, since it comes from Robert Burns' poem "Tam O'Shanter" and refers to the short skirt of a good-looking woman. James McBey was asked to design the label, which is still in use today.

In spite of the fact that Prohibition continued for another seven years Cutty Sark achieved considerable sales. Berry, Bros & Rudd like many other whisky

Below: The inside of 3 St James's Street.

Right: The old cellars beneath St James's Street.

Below right: Old and new bottles showing the subtle changes in the label's design.

companies were loath to undermine Prohibition themselves by getting whisky into the United States, but were prepared to deliver cases to Nassau in the Bahamas without asking too many questions regarding their eventual destination. Their agent Captain William McCoy (*see* Chapter 1) was a bootlegger with an excellent reputation and from the beginning the pale blend with an exceptional taste was well received. The phrase "the real McCoy" was born and Berry Bros & Rudd's fortunes assured.

Berry Bros & Rudd also market The Glenrothes single malt, a fine Speyside whisky, at a variety of different ages. Details can be found in the directory at the back of the book.

Cutty Sark Scots Whisky

Cutty Sark Scots Whisky is made from grain whiskies and about 20 single malts, including such famous names as The Macallan, The Glenlivet, Tamdhu and The Glenrothes, chosen to create the slightly peated, sherried blend. The whiskies are blended and kept in casks for about six months before they are bottled.

Nose: Vanilla and oak with hints of sweetness.

Taste: Smooth on the tongue with hints of sherry and peat and a long crisp finish.

The Chivas Brothers

When James and John Chivas left their eight young brothers and sisters behind to walk the 20 miles from their home to Aberdeen, it is interesting to conjecture whether they had any idea of the dynasty they were about to found. John's first position was with a clothing warehouse and James worked in a grocery store on Castle Street belonging to a Mr William Edward. Mr Edward's business prospered and he moved to larger premises on King Street in 1839. In 1841 William Edward died and James Chivas took over the business with a partner, Charles Stewart. Thus, the wine and spirit merchants Stewart & Chivas was started, specializing in blending Scotch whiskies. James started researching single malts and laid down stocks of the finest he could find. His dream was to create the finest blended Scotch whisky.

In 1842 Queen Victoria visited Scotland for the first time and Stewart & Chivas made many deliveries to the royal household. In 1843 the company was appointed "Purveyor of Grocery to Her Majesty," the first of many royal warrants granted to the firm during the next 112 years. In 1857 James ended his partnership with Charles Stewart and persuaded his brother John to join him

Top: Strathisla, one of the fine malts laid down by the Chivas Brothers.

Right: Glenfarclas has been in the same family's hands since 1836.

forming Chivas Brothers, though John died in 1862. In 1879 a further shop was opened in the district of Aberdeen in Union Place. James' son Alexander took over the management of this branch. Blending continued and brands such as Royal Strathythan 10 years and Loch Nevis 20 years were shipped worldwide.

In 1886 James died leaving two sons, James junior who was the "black sheep" of the family and did not enjoy hard work, and Alexander, who took control at his father's death. He was particularly successful in exporting Chivas Brothers' blended whiskies and continued to lay down fine single malts. Alexander married in 1891, but sadly he died of a throat infection, aged only 37, in 1893. His wife died, reportedly of a broken heart, only three days later. The business was taken over by the company's clerk, Mr Alexander Smith, and his partner, Charles Stewart Howard. The two were determined to keep the company going and to produce a blend which would ensure that the name Chivas would be synonymous with excellence. So it was that in 1909 James' dream was realized with the launch of Chivas Regal.

The fame of the blend spread worldwide and survived both world wars and Prohibition. In 1949 Seagram's purchased Chivas Brothers and in 1950 obtained Strathisla distillery, a single malt that had long been at the heart of Chivas Regal.

Chivas Regal uses whiskies that have been matured for at least 12 years in oak casks. Colin Scott, Chivas Regal's master blender, describes the responsibilities of the job: "A good whisky blender knows intimately the character of all the whiskies he uses. They are as unique as people. Some are subtle, some are bolder. My job is to produce a distinctive blend of whisky of the highest possible quality which is consistent in flavor and bouquet from year to year. I would describe Chivas Regal as smooth, with a honeyed richness, round and full bodied, slightly smoky with a long, lingering finish, the classic, premium Scotch whisky."

THE HEART OF SINGLE MALT
Glenfarclas

T he Glenfarclas distillery was founded before Queen Victoria came to the British throne. It lies south of Inverness airport on the road that passes through the Highlands to Speyside. This is the heart of single malt whisky distilling in Scotland, boasting 52 distilleries. Not all are open to the public, but visitors to Glenfarclas are rewarded with an interesting glimpse into a family-owned whisky distillery.

Glenfarclas means "Glen of the green grassland," which would once have described the distillery's position. At first glance the buildings belie the fact that Glenfarclas was founded in 1836 for

(I hope the Grant family won't mind my saying so) they are neither particularly old nor attractive. Happily, inside the visitors' center there are some interesting things to see including the wooden paneling in the tasting room which came from the *Empress of Australia* (1913–52), a Canadian Pacific passenger liner that was dismantled at Rosyth shipyard.

A license was granted to Glenfarclas in 1836 just before Queen Victoria ascended the throne. The distillery was built at Rechlerich Farm that nestled at the foot of Ben Rinnes Mountain. In 1865 the lease passed to John Grant and the distillery quickly established itself as a favorite stopping point for drovers (cattle dealers) on their way to market.

John Grant and his son developed the distillery slowly and started to market their single malt. The company's records show that the owners were cautious, prudent men who knew that the production of a fine single malt needs time. This philosophy holds good today: Glenfarclas is still owned by the same family and is a truly independent distillery. The managing director, John L. S. Grant, is a fifth-generation member of the Grant family to be involved and his father George S. Grant is chairman of the company. The number of stills was increased from two to four in 1960 and again to six in 1976. The distillery has the largest stills and mash tun on Speyside.

Glenfarclas single malt

Glenfarclas single malt is bottled at 10, 12, 15, 21, 25 and 30 years old together with Glenfarclas 105, which is bottled at 105° proof (60 percent). The company also markets its own blend, The Glen Dowan, and special bottlings to celebrate events such as the bicentenary of the Johnstons Woollen Mills in Elgin.

Glenfarclas 105 60 percent

This cask-strength whisky is shown as unaged, but nothing is bottled at Glenfarclas until it is 10 years old. This is the only malt readily available at this strength and has a warm golden color.

Nose: A very pungent malt with a round, ripe aroma.

Taste: On the tongue a full sweet flavor with hints of caramel and a delicious aftertaste – not a malt for the faint-hearted.

Glenfarclas 25 year old

A deep golden malt.

Nose: Full of character and promise.

Taste: The maturity of this single malt is apparent immediately, myriad flavors develop in the mouth and it has a long, slightly dry finish with oak undertones.

GORDON & MacPHAIL
Estd. 1895

Gordon & MacPhail

The small Scottish city of Elgin had one of the finest cathedrals of the Middle Ages, known as "The Lantern of the North." Its remains still stand as a reminder of the city's turbulent past. The fine Victorian city which developed owed its prosperity to the farms and many distilleries – such as Corn Crain, Caul, Manbeen and Lesmurdie – in the surrounding area, though only a few, such as Linkwood and Miltonduff, remain.

The merchants of Elgin were quick to see that selling Scotch whisky could be profitable. On Friday May 24, 1895 Mr James Gordon and Mr John Alexander MacPhail started a partnership that was to create a new groceries and wine merchant. James Gordon, who had spent his early career traveling for a local wholesaler and building a reputation as a man of integrity, appears to have been the driving force. The company published the following advertisement in the local newspaper, the *Elgin Courant and Courier*, announcing their intention to start trading. "Gordon and MacPhail, Family Grocers, Tea, Wine and Spirit Merchants. Having secured a Lease of those New, Centrical and Commodious Premises, No's 38 and 40 South Street, Elgin… beg very respectfully to intimate that they will OPEN the same on Friday, the 24th May, 1895. Their stock being personally selected, the GROCERIES, WINES and SPIRITS are all High-Class Goods, and Customers favouring them with their Patronage may depend on getting a superior article at a popular price. All Departments under Person Supervision. G. & M. trust to be favoured with a share of the support of the public, who may feel assured that it will be their endeavour to give the utmost satisfaction."

As the company grew so too did the surrounding whisky industry with the building of new distilleries. Benriach and Glen Elgin were built in 1889, Longmorn opened in 1894, then Glenlossie was rebuilt and in 1897 Coleburn and Glen Moray were opened. This period of spectacular growth was colored by the collapse of the Pattison blending company which forced many distilleries and merchants to close. Gordon and MacPhail survived by continuing to supply groceries and fine single malts that had already been purchased.

In 1915 John MacPhail retired and his position was taken by John Urquhart who had been with the company for many years. Unfortunately only two weeks after the new partnership started, James Gordon died of a heart attack. Mrs Gordon carried on her husband's role as co-partner and John Urquhart set about developing the whisky side of the business. In the 1930s and 40s the company laid down considerable stocks of fine malts and the Connoisseurs Choice range of malt whiskies was launched even though the current fashion was for blended whiskies and very few distilleries were selling their single malts independently. The 1960s were to change all this with The Glenfiddich starting to market their

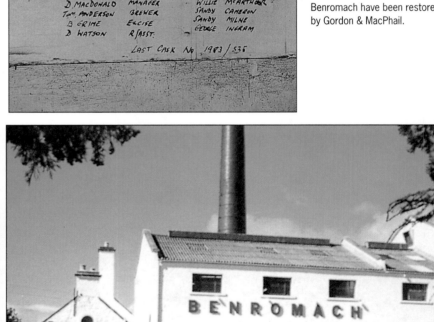

Left: Gordon & MacPhail family grocers and wine merchants of South Street, Elgin.

Below: The fortunes of Benromach have been restored by Gordon & MacPhail.

Above: The stills at Benromach are now producing spirit again.

Below: Special bottling to commemorate Benromach's centenary in 1998.

single malt and Gordon & MacPhail's range gaining worldwide recognition.

Today the company is run by John Urquhart's descendants. Though it retains the grocery business, it is best known for its wide range of fine whiskies. In addition to the original Connoisseurs Choice which covers distilleries long gone as well as those still in production, Gordon & MacPhail has a range of vatted malts which illustrate the style of each region, for example Pride of Islay and Pride of the Lowlands, and also sells a selection of cask strength and rare single malts.

In 1993 the company purchased Benromach distillery, which had closed in 1983. It had been built in 1898 by Charles Doig, the architect who designed the pagoda-style kiln chimney. At Benromach he designed a recycling process for the water taken from the Mosset Burn, so that it was cooled and returned unpolluted. The distillery was reopened on October 15, 1998 by HRH The Prince of Wales and the first trial production runs, following extensive refurbishment, started. New spirit will need to mature for at least 10 years before connoisseurs can taste it. Happily, stocks of Benromach survive and can be purchased direct from Gordon & MacPhail.

NEVER SAY WHEN

Whisky is usually served as an aperitif or after-dinner drink, although many people enjoy it as part of a cocktail. Generally speaking whisky can be drunk at any time, although we may not wish to emulate the people of the Hebrides, of whom John Stanhope, a Scottish businessman who traveled throughout Scotland, wrote in his diary of 1806: "...they still continue to take their streah, or glass of whisky, before breakfast, which, though by no means a palatable regiment to Englishmen seems at least to be a very wholesome one, if one may judge from the healthy appearance and ruddy skins of the natives – indeed, in such a wet climate, it is almost absolutely necessary to drink spirits in some degree. Additional streahs are never refused in the daytime."

Some two hundred years earlier Tobias Smollett (1721–71) wrote of a Highland breakfast: "One kit of boiled eggs; a second, full of butter; a third, full of cream; an entire cheese made from goat's milk; a large earthen pot, full of honey; the best part of a ham; a cold venison pasty; a bushel of oatmeal, made into thin cakes and bannocks; with a small wheaten loaf in the middle, for the strangers; a stone bottle of whisky." Such huge repasts can only have been presented at the richest tables.

Benromach Centenary Bottling

Three rare casks, used since 1886, 1895 and 1901 for the seasoning of sherries were filled with 15 year old Benromach. Two years later the single malt has been bottled to commemorate the distillery's centenary. The bottling is restricted to 3,500 units.

Benromach 12 year old single Speyside Malt Scotch Whisky

A more readily available and affordable example of Benromach. A clear gold malt.

Nose: Distinctive light, sweet, fresh.

Taste: A good rounded malt, light caramel with spice and a long, slightly strong finish.

William Grant & Sons Ltd

Many inventions, discoveries and business successes owe their origins to the determination of one individual. Glenfiddich Single Malt Scotch Whisky is one such example.

William Grant was born on December 19, 1839 in Dufftown. His father, also called William, was apprenticed as a tailor, but at the age of 23 he joined the fight against Napoleon and became a member of the 92nd Regiment of Foot, which later became the Gordon Highlanders. His last battle was against Napoleon in 1815 at Waterloo and in later life he was known as "Old Waterloo." He returned to Dufftown and started working again as a tailor. He had two wives, the second of whom, Elizabeth Reid, gave birth to William at the age of 26 when "Old Waterloo" was 55. Little is known of Elizabeth other than that she was reputedly a pipe smoker.

At the age of seven William started work as a herdsman, looking after cattle for a local farmer some six miles (9.6 km) from Dufftown. As a result his schooling was confined to the winter months. However, he seems to have been a dutiful scholar and records show that he was given extra lessons in mathematics by an older pupil. William was first apprenticed to a shoemaker, then in 1863 he started working as a clerk at the Tininver lime works at

Craichie just outside Dufftown. By then he was 24 and married with three children, one of whom died in the first year. After three years at the lime works, William moved on to become a bookkeeper at Mortlach distillery. By this time he had gained a reputation for hard work and for having an inquiring mind. After several years he was promoted to manager. He noted down as much as he could on the workings of this and other distilleries, for his ambition was to build one of his own which would distill the "best dram in the valley."

Above: William Grant.

Right: Glenfiddich were innovators when they started to market their single malt in the 1960s. Today they are still experimenting with new bottlings.

For many years he tramped the hills looking for the perfect site, which he eventually located in the valley of the Fiddich. The Robbie Dhu Springs provided a cool, clean, continuous source of water. William and his family, two daughters and six of his seven sons (the seventh was a schoolmaster and continued working to provide the family an income) started building the Glenfiddich distillery themselves, hiring just one qualified mason to assist them. The foundation stone was laid at the end of 1886. Many stories surround the building of the distillery: the concrete

Right and far right: Images of Glenfiddich Distillery from early horse drawn delivery to today's modern visitor center.

chimney, for example, was constructed using an old watering can with its spout and handle wrenched off as the mold for the inside, by building in layers and moving the can progressively upward.

The first spirit flowed from the stills of the new Glenfiddich distillery on Christmas Day, 1887. In 1892 a second distillery, The Balvenie, was built nearby to secure the rights to the water for the company. The company now owns 1,200 acres of land surrounding the Robbie Dhu Springs.

Since those early days the company has grown beyond William Grant's wildest dreams. A third single malt distillery, Kininvie, was added in 1990 in order, according to William's great-great-grandson, Glenn Gordon, to "guarantee an independent supply of high-quality malt for Grant's blend." The company's grain distillery at Girvan was built in 1963 and epitomizes the view of Sandy Grant Gordon, the great-grandson of the founder that "Tradition is worth nothing without innovation." For William Grant & Sons

market not only Glenfiddich and Balvenie single malts in different styles and at various ages, but also a wide range of blended whiskies including Grant's Family Reserve, Robbie Dhu 12 year old, Clan MacGregor and the Gordon Highlanders (named for Old Waterloo's regiment). The company also sells its own single grain whisky Black Barrel. With its own bottling plants and marketing companies worldwide William Grant & Sons is a truly remarkable family-owned and -managed business.

Both pages: The number one selling single malt in the world, The Glenfiddich is still family owned.

The story of William Grant & Sons isn't just the founding and development of a whisky company. It was William Grant & Sons' decision to start marketing Glenfiddich in 1963 in England and Wales that opened up the current worldwide interest in malt whiskies. At that time single malts were readily available only in Scotland.

Glenfiddich is the only Highland Scotch whisky to be distilled, matured and bottled at its own distillery. There is also a busy cooperage at Glenfiddich, a rarity at a distillery today.

Glenfiddich Special Old Reserve

In its distinctive green triangular bottle developed by the company in 1957, Glenfiddich Special Reserve can be found on liquor store and bar shelves the world over. Sales of Glenfiddich account for some 27 percent of single malt whisky sales worldwide. This one is produced unaged, but the youngest whisky is at least eight years old. The consistent Glenfiddich character is achieved by marrying casks together in large wooden marrying tuns for three to six months.

Nose: A delicate, fresh aroma with a hint of peat.

Taste: At first light, slightly dry, then a fuller flavor develops with sweet, subtle overtones. A good all-round malt, suitable for drinking at any time of day.

Glenfiddich Solera Reserve

A 15 year old single malt made using the solera system associated with sherry production. The system uses a solera vat to marry selected 15 year old single malt whiskies and is kept half full so that there is always a reserve of mature Glenfiddich Solera Reserve. This ensures consistent characteristics and flavor. The 15 year old whiskies include single malts matured in old bourbon and sherry casks and also whisky finished in new wood for three to four months.

Nose: Warm fruity spice with hints of sweetness and malt.

Taste: Soft and clean with hints of honey, spice and a long finish.

Glenfiddich Ancient Reserve 18 year old

The marriage of single malts which have been matured for at least 18 years in traditional oak casks and in Oloroso sherry casks. Both have been matured in cold, damp Dunage warehouses with stone walls, low ceilings and earthen floors. The Ancient Reserve has a more sherried finish than the Special.

Nose: A clean, smooth malt with a hint of oak.

Taste: Sweet and soft in the mouth with warm notes of fruit and vanilla and a dry finish.

William Grant & Sons have also introduced their own Glenfiddich Malt Whisky Liqueur.

Nose: Light, sweet, yet with a palpable whisky smell.

Taste: warm, honey with oranges and a hint of spice. William Grant & Sons recommend trying it with ice.

Maker's Mark

In 1894 William Samuels established a distillery next door to his mill. The present distillery dates from 1953 when Bill Samuels decided to start distilling again at the then silent Star Hill distillery, and set about creating Maker's Mark. It uses winter wheat, which is purchased from the convent of the Sisters of Loretta a few miles from the distillery. This wheat forms part of the grain mix which is normally 70 percent maize, 14 percent wheat and 16 percent malted barley. By using winter wheat instead of rye, Bill Samuels Sr felt that he could produce a smoother bourbon whiskey. The mark on each bottle is composed of an "S" (for Samuels naturally) IV for the fourth-generation Kentucky distiller Bill Samuels Sr, who devised the recipe in 1954, and a star representing the Star Hill Farm where Maker's Mark is distilled.

The distillery produces around 38 barrels a day and is the smallest commercial distillery in the United States. Maker's Mark is now part of the Allied Domecq group, but continues to be run by Bill Samuels Jr the way his father would have liked, producing just a small quantity of good whiskey each year. Supplies of Maker's Mark are not always readily available but as a good example of a Kentucky bourbon it is one that should be tried by all whisky drinkers. Every bottling comes from a batch of only 19 barrels and is usually bottled after six years at 50·5 percent (101° proof) or 45 percent (90° proof).

Maker's Mark

Originally the family made more from its timber business and were more interested in quality than quantity. Happily for us this continues and Maker's Mark is still produced in small batches.

Nose: Warm, rich with spice and oak.

Taste: Lighter on the palate than you might expect at first, then sweeter. A short, crisp finish.

Above: Bill Samuels Sr toasts us with a glass of Maker's Mark.

Left: Star Hill Distillery – early buildings at the home of Maker's Mark.

Wm Teacher & Sons Ltd

I n his book *Reminiscences 1893-1938* William Bergius describes his first day with the family firm, "When I found myself on Wednesday, 3rd August, 1893, in my uncle Adam Teacher's office at 14 St Enoch Square I felt very 'out of place.' It was the middle of my summer holidays, and I had always thought I was going to be an engineer! and I hadn't even thought of leaving school yet." It is a good thing that he did continue working for his uncle, for his reminiscences give us a clear idea of what it must have been like working in a company at the end of the 19th century. William talks of large gas jets lighting the area above his desk, of everyone chewing tobacco – and I thought this only happened in cowboy films – and squirting it into wastepaper baskets. Apart from his many clerical duties, William was often sent out for supplies of "thick black" (tobacco). He records his views on his fellow workmates, "The invoice clerk, Tommy Jenkins, sang comic songs in a splendid voice whenever the bosses were not about. Alexander Dumas was bookkeeper, a nice steady old chap, twenty five percent negro. Daniel Bartholomew McFarlane had got in through some influence, and was a bad lot. Finlayson was the son of an excise surveyor, and also bad." William's colleagues' opinions of him, as the boss' nephew, are not recorded!

William Bergius had joined a prestigious firm founded by his great-uncle William Teacher (1811-76). His father was a sailor who drowned at sea before his first birthday, so his early days were hard ones. His mother Margaret worked at a spinning mill near Glasgow and at the age of seven William started working there too. At eleven he was apprenticed to a tailor, Robert Barr. On completing his apprenticeship he went back to cotton spinning and appears to have been something of a revolutionary. These were troubled times: new government taxes had been put in place to recoup funds lost through the abolition of income tax in 1815. William got into trouble when, at the age of 17, he took part in a Reformist march and placed a flag on the mill roof. He was lucky to escape without a custodial sentence and seems to have taken whatever telling off he received from the magistrate to heart. By the time he was 18 we hear of a far more sober, well-dressed young William working in a Mrs McDonald's grocery shop and marrying her daughter Agnes.

In 1830, Mrs McDonald obtained a license to sell liquor in part of her shop and by the time William and Agnes were married in 1834 the wines and

Right: Teacher's bottles from the 1860s.

spirits were taking over from the traditional grocery sales. William had by then assumed the business and the next 25 years saw a steady growth in the business with 18 licenses being issued to Teacher's to sell liquor in Glasgow and the surrounding area.

The start of the famous Teacher's dram shops dates from around 1861 when William's son Alexander obtained a license to sell whisky at 136 New City Road in Glasgow. The first shops sold whisky only for customers to drink away

from the premises. With the growth of selling whisky to be drunk on the premises, paradoxically known as the "off-trade," William insisted that his customers follow strict guidelines. As described by Geoffrey Cousins in his book on the Teacher family, *A Family of Spirit*, "William Teacher... forbade smoking, and in addition, to prevent over-drinking on his premises, ensured that none of his whisky should add to the befuddled state of a man already the worse for liquor. Any would-be customer who had imbibed too freely elsewhere knew better than to enter a Teacher shop."

In the 1860s Teacher's started selling whisky wholesale, and, in 1876 an office in London was opened. William Teacher died on December 27, 1876 and his sons Adam and William took over the business. In around 1878 the company started exporting to New Zealand. In 1880 William Teacher Jr died and his son William Curtis joined the business. His arrival was to coincide with a period of growth for the company including the registration of the Highland Cream label in 1884. In 1898 the company built its first distillery, Ardmore at Kennethmont. This Speyside distillery produces an exceptionally fine malt, the bulk of which is destined for blended whisky, in particular Teacher's Highland

Above: Scotch and water are inseparable as typified by Teacher's advertising in the 1960s.

IN ART...
EXPERIENCE IS THE GREAT TEACHER

IN SCOTCH...
TEACHER'S
IS THE GREAT EXPERIENCE

Only experience could produce Scotch of such unvarying quality and good taste as Teacher's Highland Cream. Today, the fourth and fifth generations of the Teacher family still personally supervise the making of this famous product of Wm. Teacher & Sons, Ltd.

TEACHER'S HIGHLAND CREAM BLENDED SCOTCH WHISKY / 86 PROOF. SCHIEFFELIN® & CO., NEW YORK, N.Y.

Cream. Ardmore was the last distillery to use coal fires to heat its stills. At the same time the company opened its bottling and blending plant in King Street, Glasgow.

During the two world wars and Prohibition, Teacher's experienced some severe setbacks, but the company continued to grow and in 1960 added The Glendronach distillery to its portfolio. Teacher's saw this as an important acquisition since The Glendronach single malt had long been one of the whiskies used in Teacher's Highland Cream. This purchase coincided with the sale of the retail outlets. For years Teacher's have focused their promotional activities on the effect of mixing their whisky with water. In the United States a water theme campaign ran in the late 1960s including slogans on buses, "No Scotch improves the flavor of water like Teacher's." At around the same time in the United Kingdom a "50-50" campaign was launched, which was aimed at women and suggested that Teacher's whisky should be drunk 50:50 with water.

Teacher's Highland Cream is one of the world's best-selling blended whiskies. The company is now part of Allied Domecq and William F. Bergius, a fifth-generation Teacher, continues to work promoting Teacher's Highland Cream.

Below: William Teacher cut a striking figure in Glasgow in the 1860s.

Left: Part of the Teacher's advertising campaign, from the 1950s.

WHISKY in WRITING

The famous book *Whisky Galore* by Compton Mackenzie was based on a true story and was also made into a movie. In 1941 the boat the SS *Politician* ran into trouble off the island of Eriskay near Calvay. The crew were safely taken off the ship and while they were recuperating from their ordeal they let slip to the islanders that the cargo they were carrying was a rather special one – 24,000 cases of Scotch destined for the United States. The islanders decide to set the cargo free before the Home Guard seize it, and return with sufficient whisky to keep them going until the end of the war. The film, which was made in 1949 at the Ealing studios in England, altered the story slightly but captured the sense of danger and fun which surrounded the whole episode. From time to time bottles from the SS *Politician* come on the market, but alas most of them have long gone!

In *The Moon's A Balloon*, the late English actor David Niven wrote of his short stint as a salesman for Ballantine's whisky in America. "The first day at work, Kriendler (the boss of 21 Brands, Ballantine's agents in the States) sent me to F.B.I. headquarters to have my fingerprints taken and to be photographed with a number round my neck, and to this day at '21' is that picture of me: underneath is written – 'Our First and Worst Salesman'."

Perhaps the most recent novel written about whisky is *Proof* by Dick Francis (1984). In this gripping crime thriller the hero is a wine merchant who knows a lot about whisky and has an acute sense of taste. By using his specialist knowledge he assists in the detection of a great drinks scam. An interesting as well as a gripping read.

Hiram Walker

Reference has already been made elsewhere in this book to the contribution made to the growth of the whisky industry by the railroads. In Canada the reverse is probably true. For the introduction of the railroad meant that it was no longer necessary to make whisky in every town, as it could be easily shipped in from elsewhere. By the late 1860s the sight of long whisky trains was quite common. For example, Corby's special whisky train, which stretched to almost half a mile in length, carried 50,000 gallons of whisky in cars. In the 1850s many small distilleries closed, left behind by the big boys who were producing whisky in bulk and selling it cheaper. At the same time, after Upper and Lower Canada became one in 1840, the government introduced severe taxes, which also had an adverse effect on the fortunes of the little guys.

Into this changing environment stepped Hiram Walker who crossed the border from the United States into Canada in 1856.

Hiram Walker was born in 1816 and at the age of nine his father died. By the time he was twenty he had left his native town of Douglas in Massachusetts and started working in a grocer's shop in Boston. In 1838 he

moved again, this time westwards to Detroit. This was an exciting time for Detroit City; businesses were springing up and the population of 9,000 was increasing every day, as people came to seek their fortunes.

Hiram quickly capitalized on this growth and by 1846 he was able to start his own grocery and spirits store. But the Temperance Movement was gaining ground and the local government stepped in and banned grocers from selling spirits. Undaunted, Hiram ceased selling liquor and turned his attention to expanding the comestibles

side of his business, marketing his own Walker vinegar. Vinegar was widely used to preserve meat and vegetables and there was a high demand for a good quality unadulterated product, which Hiram was able to provide. He also worked as a grain merchant providing millers in the surrounding area with wheat. His grain sales extended into Canada and he started to explore the business potential of this expanding country.

Labor and grain were readily available and the completion of the Great Western Railway from Niagara Falls to

Right: The entrance to the Hiram Walker Distillery.

Windsor, Ontario in 1854 meant that most of Canada was now linked directly to Portland and New York on the other side of the border. The fact that the Temperance Movement didn't have such a strong hold on daily life must also have been an attraction. So it was that in 1856 Hiram purchased some land in Windsor and by 1858 had set up the Windsor Distillery and Flouring Mill. He started to produce his own whisky and it wasn't long before the fame of Walker's whisky had spread.

In 1859 he moved to Windsor, Ontario, with his family, but either he or his wife and children seemed to have hankered after Detroit, for five years later they all moved back. This meant that Hiram had to travel for six hours each day by ferry and coach from Detroit to Windsor and back again to get to work. No one should ever complain of commuting again after considering this journey.

The distilling and milling business expanded considerably over the next few years and by 1870 Walkerville was born with, among other buildings, maltings, a cooperage, brick and timber yards and a dairy farm, and had extended to include housing for the company's employees. In 1870 a church was built with a school in the crypt. This burgeoning business started to produce its own Club brand whisky in 1884.

Hiram spent much of his time looking at ways of improving the quality of the whisky he produced. He discovered that extremes of temperature during maturation, particularly excessive cold, slowed the process down. He therefore started to introduce heating into the warehouses, so that the spirit could mature at a more consistent temperature throughout the year.

He was also interested in the purity of his whisky and spent much of his time experimenting with filtration

techniques. In 1838 Gooderham & Worts, the first major Canadian distillers, had started using powdered charcoal to filter their whisky. Hiram also built rectifiers with charcoal to filter his new spirit, but his experiments included a wide range of other materials, many of which seem rather bizarre today. "The rectifiers were constructed in the following manner. A few inches above the true bottom of the casks was a perforated bottom. Upon this bottom a woollen blanket or a cleanly-carded cotton was spread, then came a stratum of gravel or pebbles the size of large peas. Upon this was placed six inches of charcoal, then a layer of barley malt, and again charcoal up to a foot and a half from the top; then another woollen blanket, and another layer of gravel and finally more gravel to within eight inches of the top. These rectifiers were placed in series, every one being connected with the next succeeding one by means of a faucet, until the liquid finally reached the common reservoir at the bottom."

However, the two major contributions which Hiram made to Canadian whisky production are the creation of multiple-column distillation and the art of blending. Evidence of his invention of the first is very easy to substantiate, as his multiple-column distillation process is still in use today. The system is made up of three columns; an extraction column, an alcohol column and a recovery column, the principle being that whisky is produced continuously and not in small batches as previously. The second blending is rather more difficult to prove, as by the 1880s other great distillers like Joseph Seagram were marketing their own blends. Whatever, Hiram's experimentation and the blending of his small batch rye whiskies and that produced from his continuous stills meant that the final products were

Above: A portrait of Hiram Walker, the founding father of the Canadian distillery.

lighter and fresher than those normally sold at the time. It is interesting to speculate what the early whiskies were really like. We will probably never know. Indian corn, rye and other cerials have changed genetically and for the most part recipes have been lost.

Hiram Walker died at the age of 83 in 1899. His three sons, Edward, James and Franklin, took on the task of the ever expanding company. In a handsome obituary to Hiram Walker in the *Detroit News* in 1899 the writer commented on the fact that under Hiram's leadership the company had already marked itself out as progressive and innovative in its marketing. "Mr Walker began to advertise in that judicious and permanent fashion characteristic of the British manufacturers of great staples, which does not seek so much as to shock the public for a day or a week, as to increase from year to year a fixed impression regarding the advertised article… Wherever you ask for American whisky today, in Europe, Asia or Africa, you are offered not Yankee spirits, but Walker Club. It is as staple as Cross & Blackwell's pickles. You can drink it in Paris, London, St Petersburg, Berlin, Singapore, Trincamalee, Hong Kong, and in the interior of South Africa. It has even made its way into the United States, and has overcome with many the natural American taste for Bourbon and American Rye."

This popularity with the American public was not to everyone's liking. In the late 1890s, under pressure from local distillers, the United States government tried to curb imports by introducing legislation demanding that all products should show the country of origin. So the Hiram Walker company simply added the word "Canadian" to the whisky label; thus was born "Canadian Club."

Unfortunately for the Americans, this seemed to have the reverse effect to that intended and Canadian Club became ever more popular. The home market didn't like this at all and struck back by marketing their own brands of "Club" whiskies "produced in Canada" or so the labels showed. With over 40 different "Club" whiskies available on the U.S. market, sales of the real Canadian Club started to decline, so the company retaliated with its own very different advertising campaign on billboards. The copy read, "A Swindle! These people sell bogus liquors, George Bowes, Nick Newcomb, 302 East Second Street, Davenport, have been selling a spurious whisky labelled thus Canadian Rye Whisky... after being plainly informed by registered letter that there are no such distillers in Canada, and that the whisky is therefore fraudulent. Notwithstanding this warning Bowes and Newcomb have continued to sell the abominable stuff as genuine Canadian Whisky. We expose their rascality because the bogus whisky is bottled in very close

resemblance to our celebrated 'Canadian Club Whisky... other spurious Canadian whiskies...the other fakes are labelled thus Castel's Toronto Club Whisky...' and finally the 'People of Davenport' were exhorted to seek out only Canadian Club Whisky as manufactured by Hiram Walker & Sons, Lim'd."

By 1910 the position was reversed and Canadian Club was once again Canada's leading whisky export and one of the most popular brands in the United States. The advent of Prohibition in the U.S. and the difficulties this presented to legal distillers across the border led to Hiram's grandsons, Harrington E. Walker and Hiram H. Walker selling the company to a group of businessmen with Harry Hatch at the helm. How this entrepreneur and his successors continued to expand the Hiram Walker empire is another story.

The legacy of its founder Hiram Walker lives on in Walkerville, where whisky is still distilled today – the only distillery founded in the great heyday of Canadian whisky in the 1850s and still producing on the same site. The distilling empire which bears his name is now part of Allied Domecq.

Myths, ghosts and stories of whisky
There are stories surrounding some distilleries and individual single malts, which also add romance and interest to the culture of whisky. Some have already been referred to in the opening chapters of this book.

Given that many distilleries are situated on sites which have very ancient histories, it is not surprising to discover that there are many stories of ghosts and strange meetings. For example, Aberlour is in a valley previously home to a druid community and Glen Moray, Scotland is situated on the old road into Elgin which runs

Above: An illustration of the Podhreen Mare.

straight through the distillery in the lea of Gallow Crook, a site used for executions until the end of the 1600s. At Bowmore distillery on the Isle of Islay they talk of an imaginary walkway from the Giant's Causeway in Northern Ireland to the island. The giant Ennis (Angus) crossed over this route and when he was crossing Loch Indaal, on which the distillery is situated, his dogs were killed by a dragon who had been woken from his slumbers. This is why the sea at Bowmore turns red when the sun is setting.

In the village of Broughshane, County Antrim in Northern Ireland, they tell the story of the Podhreen Mare. In the 1760s this village was well-known as a center of horse racing and one horse's fame spread far and wide. This was the Podhreen Mare, which was owned by a Mr Charles O'Neill. This horse was previously known as The Broughshane Swallow. Her name was changed by an old lady wearing a saffron yellow shawl who placed a string of carved beads around the mare's neck and said that providing the beads stayed there O'Neill and his mare would enjoy good luck. Charles O'Neill was a sporting man and the renown of his horse spread far and wide.

On June 7, 1769, a race was held at Broughshane race course with a record crowd of gambling men from the surrounding towns. Unfortunately, the Podhreen Mare didn't seem to respond when the gun went off and took her time to set a good pace. She soon recovered and overtook the competition to win by a head, but as she crossed the line she stumbled and died. Charles O'Neill also died later that day.

When the Podhreen Mare was taken away her groom was heard to cry "The beads have gone." They were never found and so the old lady's prophecy came true. The Podhreen Mare lives on in a whisky which can be purchased at the Thatch Inn – a special single malt produced for the Inn's owner by the Cooley distillery, Ireland.

At Cardhu distillery in Scotland they tell the story of footsteps, which were heard time and time again in the mashing area some 30 years ago. No one knew who they belonged to, but it seems that the thought of a ghost walking around the distillery was not

uncommon. Later a pair of boots belonging to a distillery worker who had been employed in the mash room and had recently died were discovered. These were burned and from that day the sound of footsteps stopped. Recently another mash room distillery worker appears to have started frequenting Cardhu. He died in 1994 prior to his retirement and obviously didn't want to leave.

In an article for the *Scotch Malt Whisky Society*, Charles MacLean writes of the tale of Bye-way or Biawa Makalanga who appeared in the Glenrothes distillery in 1978. Bye-way had come to Scotland in 1894 from Africa with Major James Grant the owner of the Glen Grant distillery. A great hunter, Grant frequently traveled abroad and brought home many trophies from his journeys. He had discovered the orphaned Bye-way while traveling in the region of Makalanga. As he could find no one to care for him, he brought the young boy home. He went to the local school and worked as Grant's butler until the Major's death in 1931. Bye-way was well provided for in Major Grant's will and he stayed in

Scotland until he died in January 1972 at the age of around 84. He was a well-respected man and it is recorded that "he spoke with a broad Rothes accent, was gentle, kind, and a quiet soul who won the affection of the whole community." Bye-way was laid to rest in Rothes cemetery.

The question had to be why did Bye-way choose to appear at Glenrothes distillery? Why, for instance, hadn't he chosen to visit Glen Grant distillery where he had lived before? Research by Cedric Wilson of University College Dublin, an expert in ley lines and interested in how sometimes spirits can be disturbed, showed that the recent work on Glenrothes distillery had damaged a ley line which ran from Rothes Castle to the cemetery. Ley lines are said to be sources of energy which follow straight lines from one key ancient sacred site to another. Wilson researches ley lines much the same way as dowsers seek water with rods or twigs held above them. By placing the rods that are made of iron above the damaged ley line Wilson was able to correct the fault and the ghost of Bye-way has never again been seen again at Glenrothes.

THE
GLENROTHES
ESTᴰ LIMITED RELEASE 1879
SINGLE SPEYSIDE MALT
Scotch Whisky

The Enjoyment of Whisky

THERE ARE SO MANY WHISKIES FROM AROUND THE WORLD THAT IT IS VERY DIFFICULT TO MAKE A CHOICE. SCOTLAND IS PERCEIVED AS TRADITIONALLY THE HOME OF GOOD WHISKIES, BUT THIS IS ONLY PARTLY TRUE. YES, THERE ARE SOME FANTASTIC SINGLE MALTS DISTILLED IN SCOTLAND AND SOME GOOD BLENDS TO CHOOSE FROM; THERE ARE, HOWEVER, SOME REALLY BEAUTIFUL WHISKIES PRODUCED IN THE UNITED STATES, CANADA AND IRELAND. TO AVOID TASTING A BOURBON, FOR EXAMPLE, IS TO MISS AN IMPORTANT PART OF THE WORLDWIDE WHISKY KALEIDOSCOPE. BY REFERRING TO THE TASTING NOTES IN CHAPTER 3 AND THE DIRECTORY AT THE BACK OF THIS BOOK YOU WILL BE ABLE TO LEARN MORE ABOUT THE WIDE RANGE OF WHISKIES. AN OLD SCOTTISH LAMENT STATES THAT "A WHISKY BOTTLE'S AN AWFUL INCONVENIENT THING; IT'S OWER MUCHLE FOR ANE, AN'NAE ENEUCH FOR TWA!" THIS MEANS THAT A WHISKY BOTTLE IS TOO MUCH FOR ONE TO DRINK, BUT NOT ENOUGH FOR TWO. I WOULD COUNSEL READERS TO TASTE THE WHISKIES DESCRIBED HERE WITH FAR MORE CAUTION.

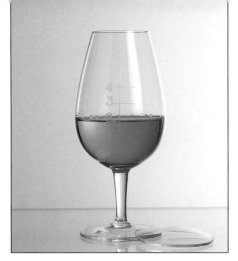

Tasting whisky

T o evaluate a whisky properly you need to employ all the senses, in particular the sense of smell. Professional tasters don't talk about "tastings" they talk about "nosings" and are known as "noses." It is possible to make an informed description of the contents of a glass without even tasting the whisky. Indeed, when selecting single malts and grain whiskies for a blend, a blender will nose them and not taste them at all.

The choice of glass for a whisky nosing is very important. The ideal choice would, of course, be a nosing glass, which has a round bowl and narrows toward the top. This ensures that the aromas are trapped inside the glass. If you don't have a nosing glass, a sherry copita will do very well. If possible, avoid a wide open tumbler because this makes nosing quite difficult.

The first thing to do is to look at the whisky. Hold it to the light to see how the color is reflected in the glass. The depth of color tells a great deal about the whisky. If it is very pale straw in color it has probably been matured in new oak casks and the barley dried without a hint of peat. Another reasonable assumption would be that it is a triple distilled whisky. If the liquid

Top: A nosing glass captures the whisky aroma with its narrowing sides.

Right: George S. Grant of Glenfarclas nosing his company's single malt.

Above and right: The author looking at the color and body of whisky in a nosing glass.

has a warm coppery hue, the whisky could have been matured in old sherry casks and may have been matured for longer. Or a deeper color is often the trademark of a Bourbon, which has been matured in charred barrels. Whisky with deep red flashes of color may well have been stored for a while in old port pipes, which impart the ruby richness of the original spirit to the final maturation.

Swirl the whisky carefully around the glass and see how the spirit clings to the inside. If the whisky drops straight down the sides it is probably young. If it clings to the inside and drips down slowly it is said to have "legs" and has a fuller body. This oiliness, which it has gained from maturation in the wood, means that it takes longer to settle back down. Such oiliness is also the trademark of the peaty Islay malts, which are usually relatively easy to identify by their aroma.

Thus, if you have a pale-blackcurrant-colored single malt whisky, which clings to the sides of the glass when you swirl it around, you could guess it to be a Glenmorangie with final maturation in port pipes without even smelling or tasting it – and what is more you would have a fair chance of being right!

The next step is to nose the whisky. Nosing requires concentration and because your sense of smell is acute you shouldn't nose too many whiskies at a time. The sense of smell is much finer than the sense of taste and by nosing a whisky you can capture a wide spectrum of aromas all of which contribute to the special pleasure of drinking it. When you taste something you discover whether it is sweet or sour, bitter or salty. It is your sense of smell that tells you, for example, that the sweet taste is vanilla.

The aromas you encounter when you nose a whisky will be particularly special to you. We use our sense of smell all the time, indeed we take it for granted, yet a scent can be very evocative. I defy anyone to say that there isn't a perfume that reminds them of their first love or perhaps their home. For me, when I nose a glass of Highland Park single malt the first aroma is heathery and almost immediately come to mind pictures of walking along the shore with my good friends Matthew Gloag and Patrick Gallagher, the heather-covered peat bogs behind and the sound of the sea. During my first visit to the Orkney Isles – the home of Highland Park – the sun shone every day, even though it was February, and this has obviously colored my memories. I wonder what sort of image would be evoked if it had rained all the

Left: Holding the cover on a nosing glass helps you to trap the aroma inside.

Below: There's nothing better than tasting a good whisky and savoring the finish.

time? If you smell Highland Park you will certainly encounter other aromas, which will trigger different images.

The first scents to reach your nose will be the stronger elements such as peat, caramel, maybe lemon or vanilla. Then swirl the glass around; if you like put your hand over the top of the glass to keep the aromas inside, then take your hand away and smell again. (This certainly helps if you haven't been able to find a suitable nosing glass.) This time you will notice other subtler scents such as orange blossom, woods in spring, musky oak or maybe old socks or even cheese.

Adding a little water to your whisky also helps to release the different aromas, although there are some whiskies I believe to be better without water. One of these is the new Auchentoshan Three Wood. The

perfect water would be water from the same source as the whisky you are nosing, but this is not normally practical. Those living in an area of soft water who have their own well can use it straight from the faucet, but for the rest of us still bottled mineral water has to suffice.

It is difficult to describe the smell of a particular whisky since everyone's senses are different. All whisky writers can do is guide you by trying to describe the differences among the whiskies from around the world. For example, in a whisky from the Isle of Islay off the west coast of Scotland you would expect to smell the phenols from the peat over which the water used in the making of the spirits has flowed, and which is used on the fire in the kilns to dry the malted barley.

The next step is to taste the whisky. When tasting a whisky it is as well to know its alcoholic strength. Most whiskies are bottled at either 40 percent or 43 percent by volume. Undiluted cask-strength whiskies, which are bottled at around 60 percent by volume, can be something of a surprise when first tasted; the alcoholic strength can mask the taste and it may be wise to add a little water. Sip the whisky slowly, roll it around your mouth, feel the spirit as it unfolds in your mouth. Some whiskies feel meaty, others thin, others smooth, still others oily in the mouth.

And then feel the glow as the whisky slips down your throat!

Even then the tasting isn't over for much of the pleasure in drinking a single malt is in the finish. As a general rule the more full-bodied the whisky, the longer the finish. The final taste will probably be different than the first flavors you noticed. This explains why you don't spit out whisky when attending a tasting as you would at a wine tasting and also why you can't

taste more than four or five properly at one sitting. At formal tastings guests are encouraged to sip a little water and eat a dry biscuit to keep their palates clean between each whisky. But this doesn't counteract the alcoholic content of whisky, the cumulative effects of which could lead to confused tasting notes at the very least.

Whisky tasting is not an exact science and efforts to categorize whiskies have in my opinion not succeeded. Recently Dr David Wishart of Edinburgh presented a paper attempting to classify single malt whiskies into 10 cluster groups using tasting details from eight books (including my previous publication *The Single Malt Whisky Companion*). All eight authors have queried his results, which are yet to be published. None of us has refuted the validity of his research, which will certainly provide a useful tool in the future.

The Internet is providing some interesting sites for the whisky connoisseur. Many brands such as Laphroaig and The Famous Grouse have their own web sites. In 1998 the Glengoyne distillery launched an Internet-based tasting to celebrate Robbie Burns Night on January 25. I wasn't part of the tasting but representatives from Israel, Iceland and the United States joined a team in Glengoyne with the aim of choosing a special cask for bottling to celebrate the event.

When enjoying whisky with friends it is just as well to have a toast or two up your sleeve. From Ireland, "You must never steal another man's wife, and you must never water another man's whisky!" From the United States, "Here's to beefsteak when you're hungry, whisky when you're dry, all the girls you ever want and heaven when you die."

A glass, a dram or a wee drink?

T radition would have it that whisky is drunk from a small cut-glass tumbler. A cut-glass decanter filled with whisky surrounded by several tumblers can be very beautiful when the refracted light changes the whisky from golden to ruby through amber. There are many prestigious glassmakers throughout the world – Edinburgh Crystal for example has been in production for over 125 years, but its origins can be traced back to the 17th century.

Right: From Edinburgh Crystal traditional images of fine cut glass and whisky while writing in an oak-paneled library.

Below: When a piper has finished playing the bagpipes he is rewarded with a quaich full of whisky, which he is expected to down in one.

Plain glass

Some whisky drinkers prefer to use a plain glass so that they can see the color more clearly, and professional tasters use a nosing glass which has a distinctive shape and is also supplied with a glass cover to allow the aromas of the whisky to be trapped inside.

Quaich

Centuries ago the favorite drinking cup throughout Scotland was the quaich (from the Gaelic *cuach*, shallow cup). Originating in the western Highlands, certain sizes became recognized whisky measures and one of these was generally used when offering the cup of welcome to the visitor and serving the farewell or parting cup. The primitive wood form was superseded by the use

of horn and then silver. Its simple shape with its two handles or ears, colloquially known as lugs, remains unchanged.

Dram

"A wee dram" is widely and cheerfully interpreted, not only in Scotland, to mean a small glass of whisky. In the early eighteenth century a dram was used throughout Scotland as measurement for any type of alcohol and it wasn't until the 1750s that it seems to have become peculiar to whisky. The size of a dram very much depends on where you are and who is treating you. The Scotch Whisky Association determines that "A dram can only apply to a measure of Scotch Whisky, the size of which is determined by the generosity of the pourer."

Dram shops

William Teacher, founder of the great whisky family, started selling whisky from his mother-in-law's grocery shop in 1830. He later opened his own shop in Cheapside Street, Glasgow, selling whisky in bottles. This was followed by several others including one opened on May 6, 1856 by his son William at 450 Argyle Street, Glasgow, and another in 1861 by his son Adam at 136 New City Road, Glasgow. It was around this time that shops starting selling whisky on the premises. These premises were known as "dram shops" and were run on very strict lines and bore little resemblance to today's inns. As described in Geoffrey Cousins' book on the history of William Teacher, *A Family of Spirit*, "A customer laid his money on the counter, a dram of whisky was poured into a thick glass, and the customer, having drained it, went his way. Treating [Trading] was not allowed, and for this reason William and his son on one occasion were congratulated by the licensing magistrates on being temperance reformers!"

Above: Glengoyne the only single malt to be produced without peat.

Right: The Scots would have it that everything is better north of the border with England. One thing is for sure – you get more in a measure of whisky in Scotland.

The English told us we could only serve **THE GLENLIVET** in tiny, **25** milliliter portions. We think you know how we feel about the **ENGLISH.**

One plac

WHISKY IN MUSIC

References to whisky can be found in songs and opera (and opera singers...). Madam Adelina Patti-Nicolini, a singer in London in the 1880s; The *Figaro*, a London newspaper of the time, reported in 1888 that she "... drinks exclusively at her meals whisky and water; all orators and all persons who require to make use of their voice have adopted in this country this drink."

Songs such as *Cigarettes and Whisky and Wild, Wild Women* and *Whisky in the Jar* spring to mind, as well as Don McLean's song, *Bye Bye Miss American Pie*: "So bye, bye, Miss American Pie, Drove my chevy to the levee, But the levee was dry, Them good old boys were drinkin' whisky and rye..."

In *The Compleat Imbiber* by Spike Hughes he talks about the works of Puccini who included whisky in two of his operas, *Madam Butterfly* and *The Girl in the Golden West*. In the latter in the first act visitors to the Polka Bar are offered "Wisky per tutti!" – only the hero asks for it to be served to him with water.

A Scottish or an English measure?

When it comes to asking for a drink of whisky the visitor would be well advised to ask for one in Scotland rather than in England. In Scotland the measure is 35 ml (1¼ oz) which is equivalent to the old Scottish ¼ gill. In England the measure is 25 ml (⅞ oz) which equals the old English measure of ⅙ gill.

Whisky, whisky and soda, whisky with food

How you choose to drink your whisky is a personal matter. On its own is my preferred choice with maybe a little still water. Some add sparkling water, lemonade, ginger ale or green ginger wine. A hot toddy of whisky and boiling water with sugar was a favorite drink in the 18th century. Another was a "het pint," a mixture of whisky and hot ale with sugar and beaten eggs, which was often served at weddings and on New Year's morning.

Perhaps the most traditional use of whisky with food is on St Andrew's night (celebrating the patron saint of Scotland) on November 30, or at a traditional Burns Supper, held on January 25, when it is customary to pour a glass of whisky over the haggis. (A haggis is a large round sausage made with spices, oatmeal and lamb.)

Left: Laphroaig, one of the unique peat-laden malts from the Isle of Islay.

One whisky.

Where to enjoy whisky

he number of bars, restaurants and hotels throughout the world offering a choice of whiskies is growing. I have selected just a few to whet your appetite. The following listings are divided into two sections, the first dealing primarily with venues in Europe, second with those in the United States and other parts of the world.

THE CANNY MAN'S PUB
Morningside, Edinburgh, Scotland
Telephone 011 44 131 447 1484
This inn was first known as The Volunteer's Rest and was started by John Kerr in 1871. Three years later the original premises were demolished and the existing building erected in its place. The Canny Man belongs to J. Watson Kerr who is the grandson of the founder and the inside reflects the history of the pub and also the family's interest in collecting. Every room has its own name and collection of memorabilia. The Canny Man is a special place, where the owner is king and where people who cannot hold their drink are not encouraged to stay. The whisky drinker will be rewarded with a choice 250 single malts to try and the family's own

blended whisky – the only one they sell – The Golden Drop Scotch Whisky.

THE NOBODY INN
Doddiscombsleigh, near Exeter, England
Telephone 011 44 1647 252393,
email Inn.nobody@virgin.net
This little wayside inn is a world away from The Canny Man and the heart of residential Edinburgh, for it is tucked away on the edge of the Dartmoor National Park. But drinking whisky is taken extremely seriously here too. Nick Borst-Smith, the owner, has a wide

selection of single malts and blends behind the bar, he is also an award-winning wine merchant, selling fine wines as well as whiskies from most of the Scotch whisky distilleries at special ages and strengths. A wide range of local cheeses is also for sale in this quiet village.

THE ATHENAEUM HOTEL
Piccadilly, London, England
Telephone 011 44 181 499 3464
email info@athenaeumhotel.com
This hotel, in the heart of London's West End, has a very special Malt Whisky Bar with over 70 different malts.

Right: It would take a very long time to taste all the whiskies behind the bar at the Canny Man in Edinburgh.

Cafe d'es Casal Solleric
Borne, Palma de Mallorca, Spain

This bar is built inside the old palace Solleric on the main street of Palma. The beautiful building also houses a museum and a bookstore. A close inspection of the bar on a recent visit identified 10 single malts, among them Knockando, Cardhu and Glenmorangie; 20 blends including Cutty Sark Emerald, Ballantine's Gold Seal and White Horse; five American, two Canadian and two Irish whiskies.

Above: The Passport bar in the Athenaeum Hotel, a haven for whisky drinkers in London.

Left: Wine buff and whisky connoisseur Nick Borst-Smith in front of part of his wide range of fine whiskies at the Nobody Inn (below).

Hotel Mona Lisa
Borgo Pinti 27, Florence, Italy
Telephone 011 39 55 247 9755

This hotel's bar is an old confessional which is perhaps a particularly good place to drink whisky! The choices range from single malts from Scotland, bourbons from the U.S. and whiskies from Ireland. The Glen Grant was one of the single malts behind the bar.

WALDHAUS AM SEE HOTEL
Waldhaus am See, 7500 St Moritz,
Switzerland
Telephone 011 41 81 833 6666
http://www.waldhaus-am-see.ch
Claudio Bernasconi-Mettier runs the
largest whisky bar, the "Devils Place" in
Switzerland, stocking over 1,300
different whiskies. He also keeps an
extensive wine cellar. The hotel
publishes a magazine called *The Post*,
which keeps the guests in touch with
the hotel's program of activities.

FEATHERS
962 Kingston Road,
Toronto, Canada, M4W 1S7
Telephone 416 694 0443
More than 20 single malts and a range
of different single malts at cask strength.

C'EST WHAT?
67 Front Street East
Toronto, Ontario M5E 1B5
Telephone 416 867 9499
email info@cestwhat.com
Downtown restaurant and whisky bar

has a changing selection and regular
tastings. Focus on micro-distilleries and
unusual offerings.

WHISKY CAFE
5800 St Laurent Blvd
Montréal, Quebec H2T 1T3
Telephone 514 278 2646
email info@whiskycafe.ca

THE PURPLE ONION CLUB
15 Water Street
Vancouver, BC V6A 1A1

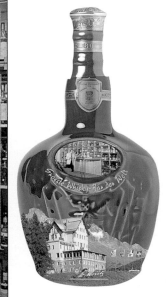

Far top left: Waldhaus am See Hotel, St Moritz, Switzerland.

Far bottom left: Signatory whiskies are appreciated by connoisseurs the world over.

Center: Sea, sun and whisky await the visitor to the beautiful island of Mallorca.

Above: Claudio Bernasconi-Mettier with some of the 1,300 different whiskies he stocks at the Waldhaus am See Hotel.

Left: Sample a whisky at the confessional bar at the Hotel Mona Lisa.

Telephone 604 602 9442
http://www.purpleonion.com
Live jazz club with large selection of scotches.

THE UNITED STATES

Among the hotels and bars are the Tavern on the Green, the Post House and Keen's Chop House, all in New York City. There are also cigar bars that offer customers a selection of single malts. These include Beekman Bar and Books (four locations), and Club Macanudo in New York, Three of Clubs and Bar Marmont in Los Angeles, Berlin Bar in Miami Beach, Occidental Grill in San Francisco, and Fumatore Cigar Bar & Club, Chicago.

For more information, check out *Whisky Magazine* (http://www.whisky-world.com), which regularly features a selection of whisky bars from around the world.

TAVERN ON THE GREEN
Central Park at West 67th Street

New York, NY 10023
Telephone 212 873 3200
http://www.tavernonthegreen.com

POST HOUSE
28 East 63rd Street
New York, NY 10021
Telephone 212 935 2888

BEEKMAN BAR AND BOOKS
889 First Avenue
New York, NY
Telephone 212 980 9314

Whisky clubs and societies

T here are a number of clubs and societies throughout the world, offering a special service to whisky lovers. The following are a selection of recommended establisments, but the list is by no means definitive.

LA MAISON DU WHISKY
20 rue d'Anjou, 75008 Paris, France
Telephone 011 33 14265 0316
In 1996 La Maison du Whisky launched Le Club Maison du Whisky. The club now has over 500 members who receive a copy of the quarterly newsletter *Le Still* and can attend monthly whisky tastings held at various venues.

THE SCOTCH MALT WHISKY SOCIETY
The Vaults, 87 Giles Street, Leith, Edinburgh, EH6 0JS, Scotland
Telephone 011 44 131 554 3451
This society was founded in 1983 and offers its members a choice of malts taken straight from the cask. These are stronger than standard bottlings and because each cask is different, the range of malts is considerable. Its members receive a quarterly newsletter and list of bottlings; single malts are defined by region and a number only. Some of the descriptions are quite diverting in themselves: "Cask No. 11·9 ... before you add water has a citrus, polished wood nose but with quite a prickle. Water brings

out peach skins which then turns to peach stones." Or "Cask 41·13 ... Buttercups and Café Noir biscuits (the ones with coffee-flavored icing sugar); sharp and sweet; a transient whiff of sulphur and smouldering ashes."

Members can also visit the Society at its prestigious base in Leith, the old port of Edinburgh, where they can use the lounge bar, tasting room and other facilities. The Society also offers tastings throughout the United Kingdom. There are overseas branches of the Society that operate independently, but can offer members Scotch Malt Whisky Society bottlings.

AN QUAICH – THE SCOTCH MALT WHISKY SOCIETY OF CANADA
198 Promenade des Bois
Russell, Ontario
Canada K4R 1C4
Fax 613 445 2628
http://www.interlog.com/~contech
Founded in Ottawa, Ontario in 1983. There are now 22 chapters in Ontario with approximately 1,000 members and associate members throughout Canada. It offers its members tastings, the opportunity to buy unique single malts and an annual tour of Scotland.

THE INTERNATIONAL ORDER OF COMPANIONS OF THE QUAICH
Ed Patrick, 206-219 Dundonald Street, Toronto, Ontario, M4Y 1K3

Telephone 416 964 8180
email quaich@interlog.com
The order was founded by Ed Patrick, a well-known writer and journalist in Canada. There are branches throughout Canada from the Society's home base in Toronto, from Montreal to Vancouver. Membership is around $50 and Companions meet up to 12 times a year for tastings and other events and can purchase aged single malts at cost.

SINGLE MALT WHISKY SOCIETY
9838 West Sample Road
Coral Springs, Florida 33065
Telephone 1 954 752 7990

SOCIEDAD BRASILIA DU WHISKY,
Av Rui Barbosa 830, Ap 102, Rio de Janeiro, Brazil
Telephone 011 55 21 551 2297
Founded in 1988 by friends interested in Scotch whisky, the society has grown and has branch offices in other Brazilian Cities. Tastings and monthly meetings are held and members keep in touch through the Society's newsletter.

Above: The headquarters of the Scotch Malt Whisky Society in Edinburgh.

Right: Fine bottles of whisky adorn a well-stocked bar at the William Grant & Sons' distributors offices.

Single malts, cask-strength malts or blends?

Single malts

At present some 80 single malts are bottled by the distillers themselves and many of these can be found in retail outlets around the world. Bottles bear the name of the distillery, the age of the youngest whisky included in the bottle and the designated whisky area – Highland, Islay, Speyside. Single malts are normally bottled at 40 percent for the European market and 43 percent for overseas markets. In the United States whiskies are usually bottled at 43 percent.

From time to time a distillery launches a special bottling, often to commemorate an event, such as Highland Park's 200th anniversary in 1998.

So many different single malts are available because, not only do individual distilleries bottle their own malts at several ages, but from time to time specialist bottlers will bottle a malt at a different age, and also offer customers single cask or cask-strength bottlings. So you may find, say, 15 different malts from any one distillery.

Vatted malts

A vatted malt is produced by marrying various malt whiskies of different ages from several distilleries. Vatted malts often reflect the distilleries from a

Right: Highland Park Distillery gates.

Far right: Whether it's a bottle of Imperial single malt or blended Chivas Regal whisky – the choice is yours.

particular region, such as Pride of the Lowlands from Gordon & MacPhail, and are labeled "Pure Malt" or "Scotch Malt Whisky." Some very special vatted malts are available such as Chivas Century which is made up of 100 single malts.

Cask-strength whiskies are sold at 68·5 percent or about 120° proof. United Distillers, part of the Diageo group, offers a Rare Malts Selection from some of its finest distilleries, among them Caol Ila, Teaninch and Dailuaine. Cask-strength whiskies are stronger than a normal bottling and a little will go a long way. They are also available from specialty retailers and whisky clubs, more of which later.

Single-cask malts are also sold at cask strength and are bottled from just one cask from an individual distillery. Single-casks malts vary considerably, depending on whether the cask has been used before or whether it is a "first-fill" cask. A single-cask malt will probably not taste or smell entirely like the usual bottling, there will be many similar elements but there will be differences. Tasting a single-cask malt can be a voyage of discovery for the whisky connoisseur. As with cask-strength whiskies these single-cask malts are obtainable from the distillery as well as specialist bottlers and whisky clubs.

Blended whiskies

These offer the perfect introduction to drinking whisky and in some countries are the only whiskies produced locally. Some blends, such as Teacher's, contain a higher percentage of malts than others. Deluxe blends also include a high proportion of malt whiskies and often show an age on the label, which reflects the age of the youngest whisky in the blend. Deluxe blends include Johnnie Walker Black Label 12 years, J. & B. Reserve 15 years, and The Famous Grouse Gold Reserve 12 years.

"Hey, look everybody, I found where George keeps the Chivas."

Where to buy whiskies

Europe

In the U.K. there has been a tradition for hundreds of years of selling fine wines and whiskies by the bottle or in casks and many of the specialty retailers in business now were founded many years ago. The Nobody Inn, mentioned on page 170, has a mail order catalog worth requesting if you are looking for something different. Two such retailers, Gordon & MacPhail (George House, Boroughbriggs Road, Elgin, Scotland, Telephone 011 44 1343 545111) and Berry, Bros & Rudd (3 St James's Street, London SW1A 1E, England, Telephone 011 44 171 396 9600) are described in more detail in Chapter 4 and both offer a very good selection of whiskies to try.

CADENHEADS
172 Canongate, Royal Mile, Edinburgh, EH8 8DF, Scotland
Telephone 011 44 131 556 5864
William Cadenhead Limited was founded in 1842 by Mr George Duncan, a vintner and distillery agent in Aberdeen. In 1858 his brother-in-law William Cadenhead joined the business and, on the death of George, he took over the company and changed the name to his own. William was popular in the local community not least because he was a great poet. He was succeeded in 1904 by his nephew, Robert Duthie, who developed the company's whisky portfolio.

MILROYS OF SOHO LTD
3 Greek Street, London W1V 6NX, England
Telephone 011 44 171 437 9311
Perhaps the most famous High Street retailer in London, Milroys of Soho Ltd has an extensive selection of whiskies from all major distilleries in Scotland, Ireland, and around the world, with many special bottlings. I am extremely grateful to them for lending us so many bottles for the photography in this book.

Top left: A quick call to Signatory will help you find the perfect gift for a whisky connoissseur.

Above: Berry, Bros & Rudd.

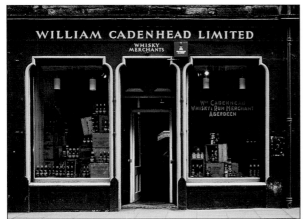

Left and below: William Cadenhead's retail outlet in Edinburgh, close to the Castle and Holyrood Palace.

Robert Duthie was killed in 1931 by a tram on his way to discuss the company's financial problems. A bachelor, Duthie left the business to his two sisters who, knowing nothing about the business, asked employee Ann Oliver to take over. She wasn't a particularly good manager and was asked to retire so that the trustees could sell the business. The warehouses were full of spirits of every variety but there were no stock records. Christie's, the auctioneers, managed the sale in October 1972 and the value of the stock was so high that the amount raised exceeded the company's liabilities. The goodwill and premises were eventually purchased by J. & A. Mitchell & Co. Ltd who own the Springbank Distillery.

Today the company operates from 9 Bolgam Street, Campbeltown, Argyll, Scotland, and has a retail outlet in Edinburgh. Cadenheads offers a wide range of single malts, many at ages and strengths not normally available. For example the Authentic Collection includes Coleburn 1978 from a distillery which closed in 1985, and Glen Mhor 1976 which closed in 1983. The Chairman's Stock includes 26 year old Benrinnes and a 27 year old from the Inverleven stills at Dumbarton distillery. Their cask-strength collection includes Bourbon from Kentucky as well as Lammerlaw from New Zealand and single grain whiskies.

Whisky connoisseurs can purchase single casks of malt whisky from the Springbank distillery and can choose whether their whisky is matured in refill or fresh Bourbon, whisky, sherry, port or rum butts, hogsheads or barrels. In July 1997, the owners J. & A. Mitchell produced the first run of a new single malt, Hazelburn, named for one of the old Campbeltown distilleries. This triple distilled, Lowland style single malt is also available in a variety of casks.

La Maison du Whisky

20 rue d'Anjou, 75008 Paris, France
Telephone 011 33 1 4265 0316

La Maison du Whisky was started in 1956 by George Benitah at the age of 27. He was an importer of blended Scotch, Vat 69 and The Antiquary. He took the unusual step in 1961 of opening a retail whisky shop in Paris – unusual because whisky at the time was not the popular drink it is today. Sales in the early 1960s were around 1.5 million bottles; today they reach nearer to 150 million bottles. Benitah started learning about single malts and by the end of the 1960s was offering several leading brands such as The Glenlivet, Bowmore and Highland Park.

In 1994 George was joined by his son Thierry who continues to run the firm. It now markets more than 450 different brands from around the world including bourbon, rye and Tennessee whiskies from the United States as well as Japanese and Irish, and a wide selection of Scotch single malts. Some are specially bottled for La Maison du Whisky and others are supplied by the Scottish specialty retailers highlighted in this book. The company also operates a wholesale and distribution business offering malt whiskies to specialty shops throughout France.

Loch Fyne Whiskies

Inverary, Argyll, PA32 8UD, Scotland
Telephone 011 44 1499 302219

This company was started in 1992 by a fish farmer, Richard Joynson, and Lyndsay Shearer. It stocks a wide range of whiskies and whisky paraphernalia –

quaichs, glasses, decanters and books. Loch Fyne Whiskies can also supply a varied selection of whiskies by mail order.

John Milroy Independent Whisky Purveyor

Top Suite, 3 Greek Street, London W1V 5LA, England
Telephone 011 44 171 287 4925

Many people associate the name Milroy with whisky. John has been associated with whisky retailing for many years and his brother Wallace is a well-known whisky expert and the author of *The Malt Whisky Almanac,* already in its seventh edition. John offers a special range of single malts as the John Milroy Selection and he and his brother are launching a range of older whiskies under the Milroy Brothers Selection label. Both of these are offered at what the brothers describe as "Golden Strength" 50 percent.

Signatory Vintage Scotch Whisky

7 & 8 Elizafield, Bonnington Industrial Estate, Newhaven Road, Edinburgh EH6 5PY, Scotland
Telephone 011 44 131 555 4988

This family-owned business was started in 1988. It bottles its own range of carefully chosen cask-strength whiskies as well as special whiskies at 43 percent in 70cl bottles and miniatures. Although

This page: Specialist whisky retailers can find bottles from distilleries which are merely sleeping or are now closed.

Opposite page: Whiskies from around the world in New York City.

the bottling is semi-automated, it is very much a hands-on operation, with hand labeling and packaging of products.

Among others, I have tried a 1965 from Littlemill distillery, 49·1 percent, which was fresh, lightly smoky on the nose and honeyed with spice and malt on the tongue. The 1968 from Bruichladdich 52·9 percent on Islay (sadly closed at present) proved a light peaty malt on the nose, slightly sweet on the tongue and has a long warm, slightly smoky finish.

Caledonian Connection

Inglostadt, Germany
Telephone 011 49 84 16 90 55

Whiskey & Co

Munich, Germany
Telephone 011 49 892 161700

The Whisky House

Affligen, Belgium
Telephone 011 32 62 582 1188

Juul's Vinhandel

Vaernedarnsvej 15, 1819 Frederiksberg, Denmark
Telephone 011 45 33 31 13 29

This large wholesaler and retailer on the outskirts of Copenhagen stocks some 350 different whiskies.

WHISKYSLIJTERIJ DE KONIG
Hinthamereinde 41, 5211 PM's
Hertogenbosch, The Netherlands
Telephone 011 31 73 614 3547
This retail store has around 900 whiskies.

CANADA

CHATEAU LOUIS LIQUOR STORE
11727 Kingsway NW
Edmonton, Alberta, T5G 3A
Telephone 780 452 2337
Don Koziak stocks as much as he can
get. Currently 110 single malts and a
wide range of bourbons and other
American, Canadian and Scotch
whiskies.

WILLOW PARK WINES AND SPIRITS
10801 Bonaventure Drive SE
Calgary, Alberta, T2J 6Z8
Telephone 403 396 1640
A wide range of whiskies, including
many fine single malts.

USA

In the United States many liquor stores
sell a wide range of whiskies. This list is
compiled from information from friends
in the trade and I am also indebted to
Malt Advocate for some of the names.

Arizona:

SPORTSMAN'S FINE WINE & SPIRITS
Phoenix
Telephone 602 955 7730

California:

BELTRAMO'S WINE & SPIRITS
Menlo Park
Telephone 650 325 2806

CHALET GOURMET
West Hollywood
Telephone 800 307 3332

D&M WINES & LIQUORS

San Francisco
Telephone 415 346 1325

FIRESIDE CELLARS
Santa Monica
Telephone 310 393 2888

GREEN JUG FINE WINE & SPIRITS
Woodland Hills
Telephone 818 887 9463

HI-TIME WINE CELLARS
Costa Mesa
Telephone 1 800 331 3005

JACKSON'S WINE & SPIRITS
Lafayette
Telephone 510 284 4100

Colorado:

LIQUOR MART
Boulder
Telephone 1 800 597 4440

Florida:

SUNNY ISLES LIQUORS
Sunny Isles
Telephone 305 932 5782

Illinois:

BINNY'S BEVERAGES
Naperville
Telephone 630 717 0100

SAMS WINE'S & SPIRITS
Chicago
Telephone 1 800 777 9137

Indiana:

JOHN'S SPIRITS
Indianapolis
Telephone 317 637 5759

Kentucky:

CORK 'N' BOTTLE
Covington
Telephone 606 261 8333

LIQUOR OUTLET
Louisville
Telephone 502 491 0753

Texas:

POGO'S WINE & SPIRIT
Dallas
Telephone 214 350 8989

SIGEL'S LIQUORS
Dallas
Telephone 214 350 1271

SPEC'S LIQUOR WAREHOUSE
Houston
Telephone 1 800 526 8787

Washington DC:

CENTRAL LIQUORS
Telephone 202 737 2800

Specialist retailers

PARK AVENUE LIQUORS
292 Madison Avenue
New York City, NY
Telephone 212 685 2442
Park Avenue's customers are not just from Manhattan, many of them order their whiskies from around the world because there are over 380 single malts from Scotland and 55 bourbons as well as many blends and Irish whiskies. All are chosen by Herb Lapchin, their

whisky specialist who researches rare whiskies and special bottlings.

WINE AND LIQUOR DEPOT
16938 Saticoy Street
Van Nuys CA 91406
Telephone 818 996 316
email winedepot@wine-and-liquor-depot.com

Buying whisky as an investment
If you buy whisky, buy it because you enjoy drinking it and do not see it as an

Above: Rare whiskies with their original labels command high prices.

Above right: Grants' whisky for sale.

Left: The duty free shop at London Heathrow

Below left: Duty free outlets often have special whiskies on offer.

investment for the future. Purchasers of a cask of whisky should also bear in mind that when the whisky is bottled it will become eligible for excise duty (tax) at the current rates, not the rate of duty applicable when the cask was purchased.

Investment in whisky is currently the subject of some debate. Companies outside the Scotch whisky industry are suggesting that buying whisky is a lucrative investment. It may seem an attractive proposition, but investors should be warned that some of the companies offering casks of whisky, Champagne, cognac and port for sale are doing so at inflated prices and their activities are currently being investigated by the authorities. The Scotch Whisky Association has published a leaflet *Personal Investment in Scotch Whisky in Cask*, which warns investors that "the industry does not work in a way which is conducive to investment. It is unregulated and there is no whisky exchange on which to trade."

However, if you do wish to buy a cask you should talk to any of the specialty retailers identified above, for they know the market and are able to obtain casks from selected distilleries. Broaching your own cask in 2010 could offer a good excuse for a party. I look forward to receiving lots of invitations!

It is comparatively easy to find special bottlings and limited edition packaging for a malt whisky collection, though of course you must not drink the whisky and should keep the packaging as clean as possible. Collecting miniatures is fascinating because many malts are bottled as souvenirs and a number of different bottlings many be produced for each malt.

On January 25, 1999 a bottle of 1869 Old Tobermory was found in the garden of a bar on the Island of Mull, Scotland by its owner Robert MacLeod. Is this the oldest bottle of whisky in the world? Whatever Robert says he doesn't have any plans to sell the bottle. If you are lucky enough to have a very old whisky bottle in your possession or would like to purchase one, Christie's the auctioneers hold regular whisky sales at their Bath Street showrooms in Glasgow, Scotland. Contact Martin Green at 011 44 141 332 8134 for details.

When collecting whiskies, do not emulate the burglar who stole from a liquor store in Edmonton, Alberta, early in January 1999. When the owner, Don Koziak, noticed his store had been broken into, he thought it was just an ordinary heist, but further research revealed that only one bottle had been stolen. This was a 44 year old single malt whisky from the Bowmore Distillery on Islay. One of a limited edition of 306 bottles from one cask, the bottle has a serial number, which is like having its own fingerprint, so should be pretty difficult to sell. The robber sent a note demanding $4,000 Canadian for the release of the bottle. Mr Koziak then received a telephone call telling him that the Bowmore had been stolen to order and was being offered as a lot in a local club auction. The caller suggested that if Mr Koziak would like to make his own bid he could secure it for about $3,500 Canadian!

Buying whisky from duty-free shops

Duty on spirits continues to be a contentious issue. Once the liquor has been distilled and turned into a spirit the local customs and excise people step in and the whisky has to be carefully controlled through a spirit safe so that the appropriate amount of duty or tax can be levied when it is bottled. The vexed question of duty has long influenced the growth and decline of the whisky industry worldwide.

Most whisky companies produce special blends or malts, at strengths or ages not normally bottled, for the duty-free market. Every year a fair is held in the second half of October in Cannes, France, where whisky distillers and other producers of spirits, beers, perfumes and manufacturers of goods destined for duty-free outlets present their offerings for the international traveler.

Some special bottlings are marked "Exclusive to Duty Free." A triple pack "Whiskies of the World" from Bacardi, for example, includes Aberlour 100 single malt from their Speyside distillery in Scotland at 100° proof (57·1 percent by volume). Another special three-pack comes from Laphroaig, the Islay distillery, which offers its single malt whisky as a standard 10 year old, Laphroaig straight from the cask and Laphroaig 15 year old.

The blended whiskies in the duty free stores at London's Heathrow and Spain's Barcelona airports recently offered some interesting choices. For example, everyone knows of Johnnie Walker Red or Black, but Blue or Gold labels? Or how about selecting from Chivas Regal, Chivas Royal Salute 21 year old, Chivas Royal 18 year old or even Chivas The Century of Malts, a blend of 100 single malts? If you prefer Cutty Sark you could choose from the standard blend or Cutty Sark Imperial Kingdom or Cutty Sark Emerald 12 year old. Then if your taste is for an Irish whiskey you would have a choice of Jameson Standard, Jameson 1780 12 year, or even Jameson Gold.

Distillery Destinations

A unique introduction to Scotland's Whiskies

Visiting whisky distilleries

 Many of the single malt whisky distilleries in Scotland welcome visitors. A selection is listed below with opening times where available. Distilleries in other countries also welcome visitors – details of some in North America and Japan are also included. It is always advisable to telephone before you go because not all distilleries are open all year round and visitor facilities are periodically closed for refurbishment. Some distilleries charge an entrance fee, which is often refundable against a purchase in the distillery shop.

A number of specialty travel companies have been set up to help visitors to Scotland to select and plan their trips to distilleries.

DISTILLERY DESTINATIONS LTD
304 Albert Drive,
Glasgow G41 5RS, Scotland
Telephone 011 44 141 429 0762
Distillery Destinations organizes specialist tours for connoisseurs, amateurs and those who would just like to know more about whisky. Tours are tailored to individual requirements and include visits to distilleries that are not normally open to the public.

THE SCOTCH WHISKY ASSOCIATION
14 Cork Street
London W1X 1PF
Telephone 011 44 171 629 4384
email london.office@swa.org.uk
Publishes free annual directory and map of Scottish distilleries that offer tours.

Distilleries and whisky visitor centers normally open to the public

Please telephone the distillery beforehand to check that it is open.

CANADA

CANADIAN MIST
Collingwood, Ontario
Telephone 705 445 4690

GLENORA DISTILLERY
Inverness
Nova Scotia
Telephone 902 258 2662

IRELAND

LOCKE'S DISTILLERY MUSEUM
Kilbeggan, County Westmeath
Telephone 011 353 506 32134

Open April–October, 9:00 am–6:00 pm daily and November–March, 10:00 am–4:00 pm daily. Groups please book in advance.

IRISH WHISKEY CORNER
The Old Jameson Distillery, Bow Street, Smithfield, Dublin
Telephone 011 353 725566
Tours Monday through Friday 3:30 pm, group bookings at other times.

Far left: Visitors are welcome at Jack Daniel's in the USA.

Center: The Jameson Heritage Center, Midleton, County Cork.

Above: Glendronach Distillery, near Huntly, Scotland.

THE JAMESON HERITAGE CENTRE
Midleton Distillery, County Cork
Open throughout the summer every
day 10:00 am–4:00 pm.
Telephone 011 353 216 31821
http://www.jameson.ie

JAPAN

NIKKA SENDAI MIYAGIKYO DISTILLERY
Nikka I-Banchi, Sendai-shi
Telephone 011 81 22 395 2111
Open all year round.

NIKKA YOICHI
**Hokkaido Distillery, Kurokawa-cho 7,
Yoichi-gun**
Telephone 011 81 135 23 3131
Open all year round.

SUNTORY MUSEUM OF WHISKY
HIGHLIGHTS
**Hakushu Distillery and Hakushu
Higashi Distillery, 2913-1 Toribara,
Hakushu-cho, Kitakoma-gun,
Yamanashi 408-0316**
Telephone 011 81 551 35 2211
Open 10:00 am–3:00 pm. Please book.

SUNTORY YAMAZAKI DISTILLERY
**5-2-1 Yamazaki, Shimamoto-cho,
Mishima-gun, Osaka 618-0001**
Telephone 011 81 75 962 1423
Open 10:00 am–3:00 pm. Please book.

UNITED KINGDOM

Northern Ireland

BUSHMILLS
Bushmills, County Antrim
Telephone 011 44 1265 731 521
http://www.bushmills.com
Open Monday to Thursday 9:00 am–
12:00 pm, 1:30–4:00 pm and in summer
9:00 am–4:00 pm plus Saturdays
10:00 am–4:00 pm.

Left: Bushmills Distillery in
Ireland.

Below: The Suntory Museum of
Whisky in Yamanashi, Japan

SCOTLAND

Campbeltown

SPRINGBANK DISTILLERY
Campbeltown, Argyll
Telephone 011 44 1586 552085
By appointment only 2:00 pm weekdays
June–September.

Edinburgh

SCOTCH WHISKY HERITAGE CENTRE
354 Castlehill, The Royal Mile,
Edinburgh, EH1 2NE
Telephone 011 44 131 220 0441
Open from September–March every day
from 9:30 am–5:00 pm except Christmas
Day. Extended hours during the summer. A visit here gives a great introduction to the world of Scotch whisky. Information on single malts, blends, regional characteristics, a "barrel ride" through history in eight languages and a shop and a tasting bar with 180 whiskies are all on offer.

Left and below: The history of Ireland's whisky making is waiting to be discovered in Campbeltown.

Highlands

BEN NEVIS DISTILLERY
Fort William, Inverness-shire
Telephone 011 44 1397 702476
Open Monday through Friday,
January–October 9:00 am–5:00 pm.

BLAIR ATHOL DISTILLERY
Pitlochry, Perthshire
Telephone 011 44 1796 472161
Open Easter–September, Monday
through Saturday 9:00 am–5:00 pm
Sunday 12:00–5:00 pm, October–Easter,
Monday through Friday 9:00 am–
5:00 pm, December–February tours
by appointment only.

CLYNELISH DISTILLERY
Brora, Sutherland
Open Monday through Friday,
March–October 9:30 am–4:00 pm,
November–February by appointment
only.

DALMORE DISTILLERY
Alness, Ross-shire
Telephone 011 44 1349 882362
Only by appointment.

DALWHINNIE DISTILLERY
Dalwhinnie, Inverness-shire
Telephone 011 44 1528 522208
Open Easter–October, Monday through
Friday 9:30 am–4:30 pm other times by
appointment.

THE EDRADOUR DISTILLERY
Pitlochry, Perthshire
Telephone 011 44 1796 472095
Open Monday through Saturday,
10:30 am–5:00 pm and Sunday
12:00–5:00 pm. Large groups are
advised to ring for an appointment
because this is Scotland's smallest
distillery.

From top to bottom: Distilleries on the Highland trail include Glengoyne, Dalwhinnie and Glenturret.

GLENGOYNE DISTILLERY
Dumgoyne, Stirlingshire
Telephone 011 44 1360 550254
Open Monday through Saturday 10:00 am–4:00 pm and Sundays 12:00–5:00 pm, April–November.

GLENMORANGIE DISTILLERY
Tain, Ross-shire
Telephone 011 44 1862 892477
http://www.glenmorangie.com
Open April–October, Monday through Friday 10:00 am–4:00 pm, tours at 10:20 am and 2:30 pm. November–March, Monday through Friday 2:00–6:00 pm tours at 2:30 pm. Please call in advance.

GLEN ORD DISTILLERY
Muir of Ord, Ross-shire
Telephone 011 44 1463 870421
Open Monday through Friday 9:30 am–4:30 pm all year and in July and August, Saturday 9:30 am–4:15 pm, Sunday 12:00–5:00 pm. Please call call for bookings.

GLENTURRET DISTILLERY
The Hosh, Crieff, Perthshire
Telephone 011 44 1764 656565
Open Monday through Saturday 9:30 am–6:00 pm and Sundays 12:00–6:00 pm, and January–February Monday through Friday 11:30 am– 2:30 pm.

OBAN DISTILLERY
Stafford Street, Oban, Argyll
Telephone 011 44 1631 572004
Open all year round Monday through Friday 9:30 am–5:00 pm and Saturdays from Easter–October. Please telephone in advance.

OLD FETTERCAIRN DISTILLERY
Distillery Road, Laurencekirk, Kincardineshire
Telephone 011 44 1561 340205 in advance.
Open Monday to Saturday 10:00 am–6.30 pm.

ROYAL LOCHNAGAR DISTILLERY
Crathie, Ballater, Aberdeenshire
Telephone 011 44 1339 742273
Open Easter–October, Monday through Saturday 10:00 am–5:00 pm and Sunday 11:00 am–4:00 pm. November–Easter, Monday to Friday 10:00 am–5:00 pm.

TOMATIN DISTILLERY
Tomatin, Inverness-shire
Telephone 011 44 1808 511444
Open Monday through Friday 9:00 am–
4:00 pm February–December and
Saturdays 9:30 am–12:30 pm
May–October. Large groups please
telephone in advance.

Isle of Arran

ISLE OF ARRAN DISTILLERY
Lochranza, Isle of Arran
Telephone 011 44 1770 830264
Open all year round 10:00 am–4:00 pm.

Isle of Islay

ARDBEG DISTILLERY
Port Ellen
Telephone 011 44 1496 302244
http://www.ardbeg.com
Open all year Monday through Friday
10:00 am–4:00 pm June–August, Monday
through Saturday 10:00 am– 4:00 pm.
Regular tours from 10:30 am, last full
tour 3:30 pm. Pre-booking advisable.

BOWMORE DISTILLERY
Bowmore
Telephone 011 44 1496 810441
http://www.morrisonbowmore.co.uk
Open all year Monday through Friday
9:00 am until last tour 3:30 pm and
Saturday 10:00 am–12:00 pm.

BUNNAHABHAIN DISTILLERY
Port Askaig
Telephone 011 44 1496 840646
Open by appointment only.

CAOL ILA DISTILLERY
Port Askaig
Telephone 011 44 1496 840207
Open all year Monday through Friday
by appointment only.

Below: Bowmore's malt whisky matures in warehouses below sea level.

Right and far right: The Isle of Mull is home to Tobermory Distillery and Tobermory and Ledaig single malts.

LAGAVULIN DISTILLERY
Port Ellen
Telephone 011 44 1496 302400
Open all year round but only by
appointment.

LAPHROAIG DISTILLERY
Port Ellen
Telephone 011 44 1496 302418
http://www.Laphroaig.co.uk

Open Monday through Friday 10:00 am–
12:00 pm, 2:15–4:00 pm all year, but July
and August by appointment only.

Isle of Jura

ISLE OF JURA DISTILLERY
Craighouse, Jura
Telephone 011 44 1496 820240
Open by appointment only.

Isle of Mull

TOBERMORY DISTILLERY
Tobermory
Telephone 011 44 1688 302645
Open April–September, Monday
through Friday 10:00 am–4:00 pm.

Isle of Skye

TALISKER DISTILLERY
Carbost
Telephone 011 44 1478 640314
Open April–October, Monday through
Friday 9:00 am–4:30 pm.

Lowlands

GLENKINCHIE DISTILLERY
Pencaitland, East Lothian
Telephone 011 44 1875 342004
Open all year round although it is
advisable to check times.
December–February, Monday through
Friday 9:30 am–4:00 pm. Museum of
Malt Whisky Production.

Above: Cardhu Distillery.

Orkney Isles

HIGHLAND PARK DISTILLERY
Holm Road, Kirwall
Telephone 011 44 1856 878619
http://www.highlandpark.co.uk
Open April–October, Monday through
Friday 10:00 am–5:00 pm in July and
August also Saturday and Sunday
12:00–5:00 pm November, December
and March tours Monday through
Friday 2:00 and 3:30 pm. Closed
December 25 and 26 and all January
and February.

Speyside

ABERFELDY DISTILLERY
Aberfeldy, Perthshire
Telephone 011 44 1887 820330
Open Monday through Friday,
Easter–October, 10:00 am–4:00 pm,
advance booking preferred.

ABERLOUR DISTILLERY
Aberlour, Banffshire
Telephone 011 44 1340 871204
Open Tuesday and Friday,
Easter–October by appointment only.

CARDHU DISTILLERY
Knockando, Banffshire
Telephone 011 44 1340 872555
Open all year Monday through Friday,
9:30 am–4:30 pm and on Saturday in
May–September, 9:30 am–4:30 pm.
December–February by appointment
only.

DALLAS DHU DISTILLERY
Forres, Morayshire
Telephone 011 44 1309 676548
The distillery is closed and is now run
by Historic Scotland as a "living
museum." Open April–September,
9:30 am–6:30 pm Sunday 2:00–6:30 pm,
October–March 9:30 am–4:30 pm and
Sunday 2:00–6:30 pm. Closed Thursday
afternoon and all day Friday.

THE GLENDRONACH DISTILLERY
Forgue, Huntly, Aberdeenshire
Telephone 011 44 1466 730202
Tours at 10:00 am and 2:00 pm.

GLENFARCLAS DISTILLERY
Ballindalloch, Banffshire
Telephone 011 44 1807 500257
http://www.glenfarclas.co.uk

Open Monday through Friday, 9:00 am–
4:30 pm all year round and Saturdays
10:00 am–4:00 pm June–September.

THE GLENFIDDICH DISTILLERY
Dufftown, Keith, Banffshire
Telephone 011 44 1340 820373
http://www.glenfiddich.com
Open all year round weekdays (except
Christmas) 9:30 am–4:30 pm, Easter to
mid-October Saturday 9:30 am–4:30 pm
and Sunday 12:00–4:30 pm.

GLEN GRANT DISTILLERY
Rothes, Morayshire
Telephone 011 44 1542 783318
Open mid-March–end October,
Monday through to Saturday
10:00 am–4:00 pm and Sunday
11:30 am–4:00 pm. Open one hour later
June–end September.

GLEN KEITH DISTILLERY
Station Road, Keith, Banffshire
Telephone 011 44 1542 783042
Open all year by appointment only.

THE GLENLIVET DISTILLERY
Ballindalloch, Banffshire
Telephone 011 44 1542 783220
http://www.theglenlivet.com
Open mid-March–end October
Monday through Saturday 10:00
am–4:00 pm, Sunday 12:30–4:00 pm.
July and August open till 6:00 pm daily.

THE MACALLAN
Craigellachie, Banffshire
Telephone 011 44 1340 871471
http://www.themacallan.co.uk
Visits by appointment only.

STRATHISLA DISTILLERY
Seafield Avenue, Keith, Banffshire
Telephone 011 44 1542 783044
Open mid-May–end October, Monday
through Saturday 9:30 am–4:00 pm and
Sunday 12:30–4:00 pm.

UNITED STATES OF AMERICA

Kentucky

http://www.straightbourbon.com
For information, including directions,
on major Kentucky distilleries.

ANCIENT AGE
1001 Wilkinson Blvd
Leestown, Frankfort
Telephone 502 223 7641
9:00 am–2:00 pm Monday through
Friday except national holidays.

EARLY TIMES
850 Dixie Highway
Louisville
Telephone 502 585 1100
http://www.earlytimes.com
Call for appointment.

FOUR ROSES DISTILLERY
Lawrenceburg
Telephone 502 839 3436
Open 8:00 am–2:00 pm by appointment.

HEAVEN HILL
1 Barton Road, Highway 49, Bardstown
Telephone 502 348 3921
Tours at 10:30 am and 2:30 pm Monday
through Friday except national holidays.

JIM BEAM
Clermont Visitors Center
Telephone 502 543 9877
http://www.jimbeam.com
Open 9:00 am–4:30 pm Monday through
Saturday and 1:00–4:00 pm Sunday.

LABROT & GRAHAM DISTILLERY
Millville, Frankfort
Open 9:00 am–4:00 pm Tuesday

through Saturday; tours 10:00, 11:00
am, 1:00, 2:00 and 3:00 pm.

MAKER'S MARK DISTILLERY
Loretto
Telephone 502 865 2099
http://www.makersmark.com
Tours Monday through Saturday
between 10:30 and 3.30 pm all year,
Sunday tours at 1:30, 2:30 and 3:30 pm.

OSCAR GETZ WHISKY MUSEUM
Telephone 502 348 2999
Open 10:00 am–4:00 pm Tuesday
through Saturday; 1:00–4:00 pm Sunday.

WILD TURKEY DISTILLERY
Lawrenceburg Visitors Center
Telephone 502 839 4544
Open 8:00 am–4:30 pm most days.

Tennessee

JACK DANIEL'S DISTILLERY
Lynchburg
Telephone 615 759 6180
Open daily 8:00 am–4:00 pm, check
website for details.

Left and below: In the States don't forget to call
on two distinguished old gentlemen – Jack Daniel
and Jim Beam.

Directory

M ANY OF THE WHISKIES ALREADY MENTIONED IN THIS BOOK CAN BE FOUND IN BARS, HOTELS, LIQUOR STORES AND OTHER RETAIL OUTLETS IN THE UNITED STATES, CANADA AND EUROPE; THEY MAY NOT BE READILY AVAILABLE IN OTHER COUNTRIES. THERE ARE HUNDREDS OF WHISKIES PRODUCED AROUND THE WORLD BUT SOME CAN ONLY BE FOUND IN THEIR COUNTRY OF ORIGIN. FOR EXAMPLE, IN CHINA AS IN MANY OTHER COUNTRIES, A SCOTTISH COMPANY, IN THIS CASE BURN STEWART, HAS ENTERED INTO A JOINT VENTURE AGREEMENT TO PRODUCE BLENDS OF SCOTCH AND LOCAL DISTILLATIONS. THE PRODUCT CREATED AT THE WULIANGYE DISTILLERY IS SOLD AS AMPRESS WHISKY.

I DON'T BELIEVE YOU WILL BE ABLE TO FIND AMPRESS ANYWHERE OTHER THAN IN CHINA, ALTHOUGH I UNDERSTAND THEY DO BOTTLE IT AS EMPRESS FOR EXPORT.

A selection of the best whiskies from around the world

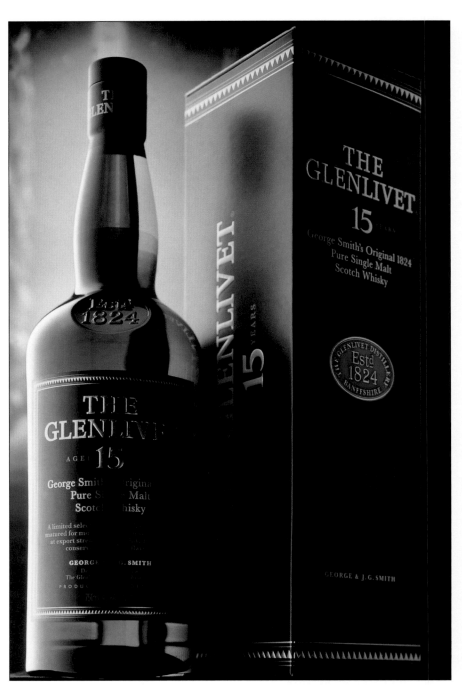

In this directory I've given details of some blended Scotch whiskies, whiskies from other parts of the world and single malts from distilleries in Scotland.

The whiskies chosen are a selection of those produced worldwide and are intended as a representation of the range of production methods and the different styles available to the connoisseur. There will be some notable exceptions and there are two reasons for this. Firstly, tasting notes for certain whiskies are given elsewhere in this book, where they either illustrate a particular region, such as The Glenlivet or Canadian Club, or where they are linked to a family such as William Grant & Sons and The Glenfiddich, and Berry Bros & Rudd and Cutty Sark. A quick look in the index should tell you whether the whisky you are looking for has been featured in the book. Secondly, I've tried to choose whiskies which should be reasonably easy to find.

As with all tasting notes in this book, the comments are the author's own and you may or may not agree with my views.

Left: The Bowmore Distillery.

Blended Scotch Whisky

Ballantine's Finest

If you were to visit the Dumbuck warehouses where whisky is matured for Ballantine's Finest you would be welcomed or should I say warned off by a flock of Chinese white geese known as The Scotch Watch.

Nose: Oak and honey.

Taste: Slightly smoky, well rounded with hints of sweetness and vanilla and a long warming finish.

Bell's

Arthur Bell became a partner in a whisky merchant and blending company in 1851. The trademark for Bell's Extra Special blended whisky was registered in 1895.

Nose: Smooth with a warm nutty aroma.

Taste: Medium bodied with a full flavor with hints of nutmeg, cinnamon and honey.

Black Bottle

Black Bottle was first blended in 1879 in Aberdeen. This is one of the smokiest blended whiskies on the market using nearly all seven of the single malts from the island of Islay.

Nose: Peat and honey.

Taste: This is full bodied slightly smoky yet sweet with a long dry finish.

Dewar's White Label

John Dewar founded his company in Perth in 1846. He was one of the guiding forces in the development of whisky blending and he traveled the world promoting his own brands.

Nose: A hint of smoke and malt.

Taste: Medium bodied with honey, citrus and malt on the tongue and a long dry finish.

The Famous Grouse

Matthew Gloag set up business in Perth in 1800 as a wine merchant. In 1896 his family launched Gloag's Grouse Brand, which was soon known as The Famous Grouse. Today the company belongs to Highland Distillers, but there's still a Matthew Gloag – the sixth in direct succession – associated with this special blend.

Nose: Warm scented.

Taste: Medium bodied with a sweet yet slightly smoky flavor and a long honey finish.

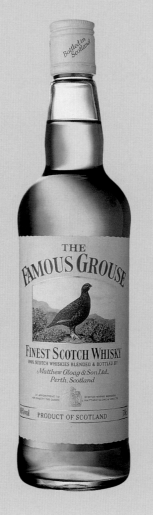

The Famous Grouse Gold Reserve

Many companies have in recent years introduced blends containing specially selected aged whiskies. The Famous Grouse Gold Reserve is aged for 12 years in oak casks before bottling.

Nose: Full bodied with caramel and malt.

Taste: Full bodied with oak and caramel and a warm long finish.

J. & B. Rare

The background to J. & B. Rare is a romantic one. Giacomo Justerini came to London from his home town of Bologna in Italy in pursuit of an Italian opera singer. He set up business as a wine merchant in the 1850s and from there developed his world-renowned blended whisky.

Nose: A light soft aroma with hints of malt.

Taste: This is a smooth whisky with plenty of character and a fresh finish.

Johnnie Walker Red Label

Johnnie Walker started working as a grocer in Kilmarnock in 1820. Today the portfolio of Johnnie Walker blends are the world's biggest-selling brands.

Nose: Fresh with smoke and malt.

Taste: A full-flavored malty blend with honey and vanilla and a hint of smoke and a long warm finish.

Teacher's

William Teacher was a pioneer in the world of whisky and introduced dram shops in Glasgow so that whisky could be made more freely available. The company he founded continued to be innovative and introduced "The Self-Opening Bottle" in 1913, which meant dispensing with the conventional bottle cork and corkscrew.

Nose: Full malty with caramel and oak.

Taste: An exceptional full-bodied blend with plenty of malt, honey and spice on the tongue and a long full finish.

Vat 69

In 1860 the wine and spirit merchants Sandersons of Leith started blending whisky. As already described in this book Vat 69 was chosen from an experiment with numerous blends and launched by William Sanderson in 1882.

Nose: Light malt aroma.

Taste: Medium-bodied with warm oak and spice and a medium malty finish.

White Horse

The original "White Horse" was a coaching inn on the outskirts of Edinburgh. Peter Mackie registered the name for his blended whisky for this famous hostelry in 1861.

Nose: A smoky aroma with malt.

Taste: This is a smooth full-bodied slightly peaty blend with a long clean finish.

Booker's, U.S.

One of the legendary figures of bourbon in more recent years is Booker Noe. He has retired now, but his name lives on in this special distillation from Jim Beam's Boston distillery.

Nose: Full-flavored fruity.

Taste: A warm, nutty bourbon with a full body and a long finish.

Cameron Brig, Scotland

Since 1929 only grain whisky has been distilled at Cameron Brig; before then both grain and malt whiskies were produced. Part of the United Distillers company, Cameron Brig is used in many of their blended brands as well as being bottled as a single grain.

Nose: Intense, slightly sharp.

Taste: Single grain whiskies tend to lack the intensity of flavor of a single malt; this however is quite full of flavor with a smooth finish.

Crested Ten, Ireland

From Jameson and thus now produced at Irish Distillers Midleton distillery in County Cork, Crested Ten is a blended Irish whiskey.

Nose: Smooth malty aroma.

Taste: At first, honey, caramel and malt on the tongue and then a drier finish.

Four Roses, U.S.

A Kentucky Straight Bourbon from a distillery which looks more like a Spanish hacienda with its arched windows and painted façade. This is a whisky available worldwide from Seagram, but not very often in its home town.

Nose: Light malty.

Taste: A light-flavored bourbon with plenty of rye and a dry finish.

The Invergordon, Scotland

Invergordon is another grain distillery producing whisky for blends such as Whyte & Mackay as well as its own single grain whisky. One of the largest grain distilleries in Europe it was built in 1957 in the northeast of Scotland.

Nose: Light delicate.

Taste: Clean and fresh yet sweet with a short, quite intense finish.

Jameson, Ireland

John Jameson founded his distillery in Bow Street, Dublin, in 1780. The whiskies contained in the blend are at least 12 years old, much of which is matured in old sherry casks.

Nose: Light malty with sherried overtones.

Taste: Medium-bodied smooth with caramel, hazelnuts and oak.

Kessler American Blended Whiskey, U.S.

Julius Kessler first distilled his blended whiskey in the late 1800s and launched it under the trademark "Smooth as Silk."

Nose: Honey, rye and cinammon.

Taste: A real mixture of dryness from the rye and honey with a short yet full finish.

Kilbeggan, Ireland

Kilbeggan is Gaelic for "little church." In the 12th century monks in the quiet village of Kilbeggan created a center for religious learning. In 1757 John Locke started distilling whiskey here and built his distillery with stones from an old Cistercian monastery.

Nose: Smooth with malt, honey and spice.

Taste: Medium-bodied with hints of honey and oak and a long finish.

Locke's, Ireland

Another Irish whiskey from the Kilbeggan distillery. Locke's whiskey was exported to the U.K., the United States of America and Australia during the 19th century.

Nose: Fresh, light with hints of oak, vanilla and citrus.

Taste: Medium-bodied with malt and honey and a long oak finish.

Nikka Single Malt, Japan

In 1918 Masataka Taketsuru, the son of a sake brewery owner, came to Glasgow University to learn about whisky. Masataka returned to Japan several years later with his Scottish bride, Jessie Rita. He opened his first distillery in 1934. Sendai distillery, which produces Miyagikyo, was built by his company in 1969.

Nose: Warm sherry.

Taste: Light with sherry, malt and vanilla and a crisp finish.

Noah's Mill, U.S.

The Willett distillery near Loretto, Bardstown has started distilling again where two special whiskies Johnny Drum and Noah's Mill will be produced once more. Up until now they have been produced at nearby Heaven Hill.

Nose: A strong oak aroma.

Taste: This is a big whiskey with a lot of oak and a little sweetness. I am hopeful that the new distillations will recover some of this whiskey's former glory.

Old Grand-Dad, U.S.

Old Grand Dad distillery on the side of the Elkhorn River near Frankfort, Kentucky is no more. The company is now part of Jim Beam brands and they have retained stocks and the recipe for producing Old Grand-Dad.

Nose: A powerful bourbon aroma, especially the older bottlings.

Taste: Plenty of rye which gives it a dry flavor with malt and citrus.

Redbreast Pure Pot Still Whiskey, Ireland

A pot still whiskey from Jameson's, which came to be known as the priest's tipple, for every time you visited your local spiritual counselor Redbreast was on the sideboard.

Nose: Oak and spice.

Taste: Malt and burnt caramel on the tongue then lots of oak and a short sweet yet dry finish.

Seagram's VO, Canada

The Seagram distilleries in Canada produce a wide range of whiskies and this has to be one of the best and perhaps one of the more widely available around the world.

Nose: Deceptively light with malt, caramel and a hint of smoke.

Taste: A full-bodied whisky with lots of flavor and a warm finish.

Suntory Royal, Japan

This is available at both 12 and 15 years and is marketed by the company as one of Japan's finest blended whiskies. With more than 1.6 million barrels maturing in warehouses the blender has a wide range of single malts to choose from.

Nose: Light delicate with hints of citrus.

Taste: Medium-bodied with malt and oak.

Suntory Hibiki, Japan

Hibiki means "harmony" in Japanese and the blender defines this whisky as a harmony of malts many of which have been matured for 20 years.

Nose: Malt and smoke.

Taste: A medium-bodied malt with caramel, vanilla and oak.

Scotch Single Malts

Aberfeldy

Aberfeldy distillery was founded in 1896 by John Dewar & Sons Ltd, just outside of Aberfeldy, Scotland, on the south bank of the River Tay. The label on a bottle of Aberfeldy single malt depicts a red squirrel; there is a colony of these animals nearby. This malt is a beautiful sun-gold color streaked with red.

Age: 15 years 43%.

Nose: Warm; sherry and nutmeg.

Taste: Medium-bodied with a hint of smoke.

Aberlour

The Gaelic translation of Aberlour is "Mouth of the Chattering Burn." The Aberlour distillery is situated at the foot of Ben Rinnes not far from the Linn of Ruthie which tumbles down 30 feet into the Lour Burn. Aberlour is a beautiful amber single malt.

Age: 10 years 40%.

Nose: Heady malt and caramel aroma.

Taste: Medium-bodied with hints of peat and honey.

An Cnoc

Knockdhu distillery was built in 1893 for Haig's, when springs containing pure, clear, crystal water were discovered running down the southern slopes of Knockdhu – also known as the Black Hill. An Cnoc is a very pale gold malt whisky and is bottled by Inver House at 12 years old.

Age: 12 years 40%.

Nose: Soft, very aromatic with a hint of vanilla ice cream and smoke.

Taste: A clean malt with a full range of fruit flavors from dry citrus to warm tropical, with a long, smooth finish. A malt for every occasion.

Ardbeg

As the Island of Islay slips into view from the sea, long low distillery buildings appear on the shore. These are known as the Kildalton distilleries and the farthest to the east is Ardbeg. Distilling at Ardbeg started around 1798, but it was only in 1815 that the MacDougall family began commercial distilling.

Age: 1974 40%.

Nose: A full, peaty aroma, slightly medicinal.

Taste: Smoky rich with an excellent rounded finish. Worth seeking out.

The Balvenie

The Balvenie Distillery occupies a site near the ancient Balvenie Castle and was built alongside Glenfiddich distillery by William Grant in 1892. Both distilleries still belong to the same family firm. The Balvenie single malts vary in color from pale straw through golden honey to deep amber with a hint of copper.

Age: 15 years Single Barrel 50.4%.

Nose: Pungent and dry with a little sweetness.

Taste: 15 years' maturation creates a rich mellow malt with a full caramel aftertaste.

Ben Nevis

Ben Nevis is the only distillery to obtain its water from Britain's highest mountain. It was built in 1825 by one John Macdonald, known as "Long John," whose name is still linked with whisky today. Ben Nevis was purchased by the Nikka Whisky Distilling Company Ltd of Japan in 1989, thus ensuring the future of distilling in Fort William.

Age: 1970, 26 years old.
Cask No. 4533 52.5%.

Nose: Very fragrant with a sweet, full malt aroma.

Taste: A full-bodied malt, very flavorful – sherry, caramel and peat – with a long, sweet finish. An exceptional after-dinner malt.

Blair Athol

Blair Athol distillery was founded in 1798 by John Stewart and Robert Robertson. The label on a bottle of Blair Athol single malt depicts an otter. The distillery's water supply is from the River Allt Dour Burn or The Burn of the Otter. Blair Athol is a warm amber single malt.

Age: 12 years 43%.

Nose: A cold hot toddy – fresh honey and lemon.

Taste: A warm malt with a hint of sweetness and smoke.

Bowmore

Like all Islay distilleries, Bowmore distillery is built close to the seashore. At Bowmore, however, a warehouse is built below sea level and the Atlantic waves break against the thick walls imparting a special flavor to the whisky in the barrels. Bowmore produces a wide range of truly distinctive malts from its own in-house maltings which are dried over peat-fired kilns, and matured in a mix of bourbon and sherry casks. The malts range in color from light gold to amber and bronze, reminiscent of the colors of a Bowmore sunset.

Age: 12 years 43%.

Nose: A light, smoky nose with a stronger hint of the sea.

Taste: The heather of the peat and the tang of the sea combine to give a round, satisfying taste with a long finish.

Bunnahabhain

Distilling has been part of life in Islay for more than 400 years. Bunnahabhain was built in 1883 to satisfy the blenders' demand for fine malt whiskies and in particular those from Islay. Initially, sales were made solely to the wholesale market for blended whisky. In the late 1970s the owners, Highland Distilleries, launched a 12 year old Bunnahabhain, a lightly peated malt with a soft, mellow character and a golden corn color.

Age: 12 years 40%.

Nose: Definite aroma of sea and summer flowers.

Taste: A surprise for an Islay malt with just a hint of peat, light and malty.

A richer stronger finish. A favorite with overseas drinkers as an after-dinner drink.

Caol Ila

One of the finest views on the island of Caol Ila is from the stillhouse looking out across the water to the mountains known as the Paps of Jura as they appear in and out of the mist. This is the largest distillery on the island and the modern buildings seem a little incongruous in the remote Islay countryside.

Age: 20 years Distilled 1975, 61.12% Rare Malts Selection.

Nose: Stronger peatier aroma.

Taste: Mellow, dry, with a peaty, slightly salty taste. A hint of sweetness and a long smooth finish.

Cardhu

John Cumming started farming at Cardow in Upper Knockando in 1813. Like many other farmers Cumming began distilling because the isolated location meant he could do so without drawing the attention of the exciseman. In 1981 the name of Cardow was changed to Cardhu.

Age: 12 years 40%.

Nose: Warm honey and spice – a hint of winter sunshine.

Taste: Fresh on the palate, a hint of honey and nutmeg, with a smooth finish.

Cragganmore

Cragganmore distillery was founded in 1869 by John Smith. An experienced distiller, he managed the Macallan distillery in the 1850s, founded Glenlivet in 1858, then managed Wishaw distillery and finally went back to Speyside in 1865 as lessee of Glenfarclas. Cragganmore is marketed by United Distillers as one of their "Classic Malt" range.

Age: 12 years 40%.

Nose: Dry honey aroma.

Taste: A pleasant medium-bodied malt with a short smoky finish.

The Dalmore

The Dalmore means "the big meadowland" and takes its name from the vast grassland of the Black Isle, which lies opposite the distillery in the Firth of Cromarty. Whisky at Dalmore matures in a mixture of American white oak and Oloroso sherry casks.

Age: 12 years 40%.

Nose: A full fruity aroma with hints of sherry sweetness.

Taste: A good full-bodied malt with overtones of honey and spice with a dry finish.

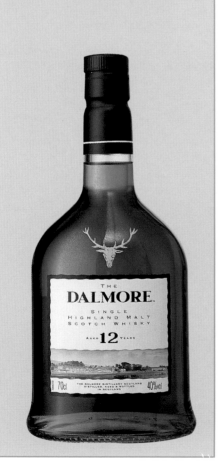

Dalwhinnie

Dalwhinnie single malt is part of United Distillers' "Classic Malt" range. Dalwhinnie distillery began operations as the Strathspey distillery in 1898, and stands at a popular meeting place for drovers from the north and west (Dalwhinnie is Gaelic for "meeting place"). Dalwhinnie distillery is also the site of a meteorological office and the distillery manager is also responsible for taking daily readings.

Age: 15 years 43%.

Nose: Dry, aromatic, summery.

Taste: A beautiful malt with hints of honey and a lush sweet finish.

The Deanston

Deanston distillery is unique, as it is housed inside an historic building, an old cotton mill which was designed by inventor Richard Arkwright. Cotton mills and whisky distilleries have a common requirement – a source of pure water.

Age: 12 years 40%.

Nose: A truly cereal aroma.

Taste: The malt flavor hits the palate first and then citrus and honey notes come into play.

Age: 25 years 40%.

Nose: The longer maturation produces a fuller, sweeter malt with a rich aroma.

Taste: The oak tannins hover around the mouth, while the overall taste is full-bodied and creamy with a smoky finish. A rare and exquisite malt.

Drumguish

The story of Drumguish distillery is also the story of one family and, in particular, one man. The Christie family started to build Drumguish in 1962 close by the original distillery, which closed in 1911. Much of the work was carried out by George Christie himself and the building was completed in 1987. The new distillery produced its first spirit in December 1990.

Age: Unaged 40%.

Nose: A light aroma with hints of honey and fruit.

Taste: Soft on the palate with a little honey and a long smooth finish.

Dufftown

The Dufftown-Glenlivet Distillery Co. was founded in 1896 when the distillery was built inside an old meal mill. The label on a bottle of Dufftown features the kingfisher, a local bird with brilliant plumage that can be seen along the Dullan River which flows past the distillery buildings.

Age: 15 years 43%.

Nose: Warm, fragrant.

Taste: Smooth, slightly sweet with a hint of fruit. A delicious light malt.

The Edradour

Edradour distillery is Scotland's smallest distillery. Edradour, founded in 1825 on land rented from the Duke of Athol, has changed little since then and is a good example of a working Victorian distillery.

Age: 10 years 40%.

Nose: Delicate sweet with a hint of peat.

Taste: Dry slightly sweet with a nutty smooth finish. A malt for any occasion.

The Glendronach

Distilling at The Glendronach was practiced illegally for many years. In 1826, James Allardes and his associates were the second distillers to take out a license to distil whisky legally. All casks at Glendronach are still stamped with the first two letters of Allardes' name – AL.

Age: 12 years 40% Traditional.

Nose: Sweet, smooth aroma.

Taste: A long, sweet taste with smoky overtones and a pleasant finish.

Glen Elgin

Glen Elgin was designed by Charles Doig during the whisky boom of the 1890s. The boom ended when Pattisons of Leith, a firm of whisky-blenders, declared bankruptcy in 1899.

Age: no age 43%.

Nose: Smoky aroma with a hint of honey.

Taste: Medium-bodied malt with a peaty taste, a hint of sweetness and a long finish.

Glen Garioch

Records show that Glen Garioch was founded by Thomas Simpson in 1798. It is reputed, however, that Simpson was producing spirit in 1785, but whether at Glen Garioch or not is unclear.

Age: 15 years 43%.

Nose: Warmer, fruitier aroma with hints of oak.

Taste: A warm glowing whisky with citrus and smoke and a long mellow finish.

Age: 21 years 43%.

Nose: Honey and peat with a slight hint of chocolate.

Taste: Full-bodied, sweeter with a hint of smoke and a warm, mellow finish. A good after-dinner malt.

Glengoyne

A license was issued to Burnfoot distillery in 1833 and leased to George Connell. From 1851 to 67 the distillery belonged to John McLelland and was then taken over by Archibald C. McLellan, who sold the distillery to Lang Brothers in 1876. The distillery was then renamed Glen Guin. The name was changed again in 1905 to Glengoyne.

Age: 10 years 40%.

Nose: A clean, sunny, floral aroma.

Taste: Medium-bodied malt with hints of honey and a slight hint of fruit. A good all-round malt whisky.

Glen Grant

Glen Grant was founded by John and James Grant in 1840. In 1872, Glen Grant was taken over by his son Major James Grant; a colorful figure who had traveled widely. Major Grant ran Glen Grant for nearly 60 years. During that time he created a beautiful garden with a waterfall, ponds, rhododendron banks, and extensive orchards.

Age: unaged 40%.

Nose: Dry, slightly tart.

Taste: A light dry malt with a faint hint of fruit in the finish.

Glen Keith

One of the first new distilleries to open in the twentieth century, Glen Keith was built on the site of a cornmill in 1958. The distillery is an attractive building constructed from local stone, located near the ruins of Milton Castle and a beautiful waterfall, the Linn of Keith.

Age: 1983 43%.

Nose: Warm, scented with hints of oak and peat.

Taste: A delicate malt with fruit and a hint of caramel and a long medium finish.

Glenkinchie

Glenkinchie was founded in 1837 by John and George Rate, who had been operating the distillery under the name Milton from 1825 to 1833. The Museum of Malt Whisky Production is located inside the old maltings facilities and includes a model of a Highland malt whisky distillery. Glenkinchie distillery is located amid beautifully kept grounds and is open all year round to visitors.

Age: 10 years 43%.

Nose: Orange blossom and honey.

Taste: A smooth, light malt with a rounded flavor with a hint of sweetness and smoke and a long finish. A malt for any time of day.

Glenlossie

Glenlossie is situated near Elgin, a town synonymous with whisky, and is adjacent to Mannochmore. The spirit stills have purifiers just between the lyne arms and condensors, which add something different to this light fresh malt with a light lemon-gold color.

Age: 10 years 43%.

Nose: A light, fresh aroma with a delightful hint of honey and spice.

Taste: Smooth with honey, smoke, and a little oak.

Glen Moray

Glen Moray is located in the middle of one of the best farming areas of Scotland. The distillery began as a brewery and was converted in 1897 by the Glen Moray Glenlivet Distillery Co. Ltd. At Glen Moray there is a sense of timelessness and the distillery still looks reminiscent of a Highland farm, constructed with buildings around a courtyard.

Age: Glen Moray 12 years 40%.

Nose: Delicate, hints of summer.

Taste: A medium-bodied malt with a hint of peat and a warm, slightly sweet finish. A good after-dinner malt.

Glen Ord

Ord distillery was founded in 1838 by Robert Johnstone and Donald McLennan in an area renowned for whisky distilling.

Age: 12 years 40%.

Nose: Full-bodied, warm, spicy.

Taste: Flavorful with caramel, nutmeg, and a long, smooth finish. Try Glen Ord in a cocktail.

The Glenrothes

The Glenrothes distillery was built in 1878 by W. Grant & Co. beside the Burn of Rothes, which flows from the Mannoch Hills. The water supply comes from The Lady's Well. Records show that this was where the only daughter of a 14th-century Earl of Rothes was murdered by the "Wolf of Babenoch" while attempting to save her lover's life.

Age: 1982 43%.

Nose: Warm caramel nose.

Taste: Full-bodied with toffee and vanilla and a long flavorful finish.

The Glenturret

Built in 1775, Glenturret is Scotland's oldest Highland malt whisky distillery. Research shows that distilling began in this area in 1717. Glenturret is one of the smallest distilleries in Scotland. It is situated near the Turret Burn, which flows down from Turret Loch, a source of cool, clear water.

Age: 12 years 40%.

Nose: Aromatic, hints of sherry and caramel.

Taste: A full-bodied malt with wonderful warming flavor and a long, satisfying finish.

Inchmurrin

Inchmurrin distillery was founded in 1966 by the Littlemill Distillery Co. Ltd. Two types of single malt were produced by Littlemill – Inchmurrin and Rosdhu.

Age: 10 years 40%.

Nose: Malty, spicy.

Taste: A light-bodied spicy malt with a hint of lemon and a short finish.

Isle of Jura

On the west coast of Scotland, across the Sound of Islay, the mountain peaks of the Paps of Jura are a unique feature. Jura is one of the least populated Scottish islands with only some 200 inhabitants. The Isle of Jura distillery is one of the main employers.

Age: 10 years 40%.

Nose: A golden malt with a peaty aroma.

Taste: A light malt suitable for drinking as an aperitif yet with a full flavor and undertones of honey and smoke.

Knockando

Knockando is Gaelic for "little black hill." The distillery, which was built in 1898, is situated on the banks of the River Spey. In 1905 the distillery was connected to the Great North of Scotland Railway, so that Knockando could be delivered more efficiently throughout Britain.

Age: Distilled 1982
Bottled 1996 43%.

Nose: Fragrant, spicy.

Taste: A syrup-flavored malt with undertones of spice, vanilla and hazelnut.

Lagavulin

Lagavulin distillery is situated on a bay at Port Ellen with the ruins of Dunyveg Castle at its mouth. Lagavulin used small coasters to transport barley, coal, and empty casks from Glasgow, returning with full casks. These coasters were known as pibrochs and were used until the early 1970s when roll-on roll-off ferries were introduced to Islay.

Age: 16 years 43%.

Nose: A very powerful, peaty smell.

Taste: Full-bodied, pungent peat flavor with undertones of sweetness and a long finish. A perfect after-dinner malt.

Longmorn

Longmorn distillery was built in 1894 by Charles Shirres, George Thomson, and John Duff. Power was provided by a large water wheel and the first distillation was produced in December 1894.

Age: 15 years 43%.

Nose: Fragrant, delicate, slightly fruity.

Taste: Full of flavor with hints of fruit, flowers and hazelnuts with a long, sweet finish.

The Macallan

The Macallan distillery was founded in 1824 by Alexander Reid at the site of a ford across the River Spey at Easter Elchies. The Macallan is matured in old oak sherry casks, which impart a special flavor to the malt whisky.

Age: 10 years 40%.

Nose: Light, fragrant sherry.

Taste: Full-bodied sherry with hints of vanilla and fruit, a long smooth well-rounded finish. A malt to savor before or after dinner.

Mannochmore

Mannochmore 12 year old single malt has a drawing of a great spotted woodpecker on the label, an inhabitant of the Millbuies Woods which are next to the distillery.

Age: 12 years 43%.

Nose: Delicate, springlike, with a hint of peat.

Taste: A fine malt with a clean, fresh taste with a lingering, slightly sweet aftertaste.

Mortlach

Mortlach distillery was founded in 1824 by James Findlater. In the early days the distillery was still a farm and waste barley was fed to the farm animals.

Age: 16 years 43%.

Nose: Fruity, warm with a hint of peat.

Taste: Full-bodied with caramel and spice, and a long, sherry and honey finish.

Oban

Oban distillery is one of United Distillers' "Classic Malt" range. Oban was founded in 1794 by the Stevensons, who were local businessmen with interests in quarrying, housebuilding, and shipbuilding. The buildings at Oban have remained virtually unchanged for nearly 100 years and are nestled right up against the cliffs, which rise 400 feet above the distillery.

Age: 14 years 43%.

Nose: Light with a hint of peat.

Taste: Medium-bodied malt with a hint of smoke and a long, rewarding finish.

Old Fettercairn

Although legend tells of an earlier distillery in this area, some miles further up into the Grampian Mountains, no written documentation exists. However, records show that this distillery was built on this site at the foot of the hills in 1824 by Sir Alexander Ramsay.

Age: 10 years 43%.

Nose: Delicate, fresh with a hint of smoke.

Taste: A good introductory malt with a full flavor, undertones of peat, and a dry finish.

Royal Brackla

Royal Brackla single malt whisky is marketed as "The King's Own Whisky," for the distillery was granted the Royal Warrant in 1833 by King William IV. Brackla was founded in 1812 by Captain William Fraser.

Age: Unaged 40%.

Nose: Peat, honey, and spice.

Taste: A medium-bodied malt with a spicy sweetness and a clean, slightly fruity finish.

Royal Lochnagar

In 1848 John Begg wrote to Queen Victoria telling her about his spirit and extended an invitation to visit his distillery. The Queen, Prince Albert, and their family arrived the very next day and thus Royal Lochnagar was born.

Age: 12 years 40%.

Nose: Warm, spicy aroma.

Taste: A whisky to savor, with fruit, malt, and a hint of vanilla and oak. Sweet, long-lasting finish.

Scapa

Scapa is one of Scotland's northernmost distilleries, situated on the banks of the Lingro Burn, and overlooking Scapa Flow on the Island of Orkney.

Age: 12 years 40%.

Nose: The Island of Orkney in a bottle – sea, peat, and heather.

Taste: A mix of salt and citrus with a long-lasting, crisp finish. Try Scapa before dinner for a different cocktail.

The Singleton

The Singleton Distillery is a relative newcomer to the malt whisky industry. Founded in 1974, it was first marketed in the United Kingdom as a single malt whisky in 1978.

Age: 10 years 43%.

Nose: Rich, warming, with sherry notes.

Taste: Full flavor on the tongue with hints of tangerine and honey, deliciously smooth in the mouth and a warm, long finish. Recommended as an after-dinner malt.

Speyburn

Speyburn distillery was founded in 1897 by John Hopkins & Co., and is situated in a picturesque position nestled in the rolling hills of the Spey Valley. Tradition has it that distillation started before the building work had been completed and it was so cold that employees were forced to work in their overcoats.

Age: 10 years 40%.

Nose: A dry, sweet-scented aroma.

Taste: A warm, flavorful malt with hints of honey and a herbal finish. A malt to be savored after dinner.

Strathisla

Strathisla was founded by George Taylor and Alexander Milne in 1786 as the Milltown distillery. At that time the town of Keith was renowned for its linen mills.

Age: 12 years 43%.

Nose: A beautiful aroma full of summer fruit and flowers.

Taste: Light, sweet on the tongue with hints of peat and caramel. Long, smooth, fruity finish.

Tamdhu

In 1863 the Highlands along the Upper Spey became more accessible to tourists with the opening of the Strathspey Railway from Boat of Gaten to Craigellachie. In the early 1890s blended whisky was increasing in popularity and businessmen were encouraged to invest in new distilleries. Tamdhu is the only Speyside distillery to malt all its own barley on site.

Age: Unaged 40%.

Nose: A light, warm aroma with a hint of honey.

Taste: Medium flavor, fresh on the palate with overtones of apple and pear orchards and a long, mellow finish. Suitable for drinking at any time.

Tobermory

Tobermory has one of the most beautiful distillery locations at the southern end of the famous harbor on the Hebridean island of Mull. The only distillery on Mull, it was founded in 1795 by John Sinclair, a local merchant.

Age: Tobermory unaged 40%.

Nose: The island in a bottle – a light, soft, heathery aroma.

Taste: Light, medium-flavored malt with undertones of honey and herbs and a soft, smoky finish.

Tomatin

Tomatin distillery, which stands at 1,028 feet (313 meters) above sea level, was founded in 1897. In 1956 the number of stills was increased from two to four and further stills were steadily added until in 1974 there were a total of 23. It is one of the largest distilleries in Scotland.

Age: 10 years 40%.

Nose: A delicate aroma with hints of honey and smoke.

Taste: Light and smooth with a hint of peat.

Tomintoul

Tomintoul is a modern distillery built in 1964. Tomintoul is the second-highest village in Scotland, at 1,100 feet (335 meters), and had a reputation in the past for illegal distilling.

Age: 10 years 40%.

Nose: Light, sherry.

Taste: Sweet on the tongue with smoky undertones.

The Tormore

Tormore was the first new distillery to be built in the 20th century in Scotland. Designed by Sir Alfred Richardson, it is an architectural gem. The distillery buildings and housing are built around a square with a belfry, which has a chiming clock.

Age: 10 years 40%.

Nose: A dry aroma with a slightly nutty overtone.

Taste: Soft on the tongue, a well-defined medium-flavored malt with a hint of honey.

Acknowledgments

Where do I start? It is very difficult to write a list of acknowledgments when I have received so much suppport from the whisky industry. However, at the risk of offending anyone, here goes. Thanks to Sarah Moody at Berry Bros & Rudd Ltd, James McEwan of Morrison Bowmore Distillers, Lynette Fox and Rick Bubenhofer of the Brown-Forman Corporation, Geraldine O'Shea of Cooley Distillery plc, Charo Rojo at Destilerias y Crianza del Whisky, Mary Darling at Glenkinchie Distillery, Cathy Law at Glenmorangie plc, Philippa Ireland at Glenturret Distillery, Leslie Duroe at Gordon & MacPhail, Malcolm Greenwood at J.&G. Grant, Pat Grant at William Grant & Sons Ltd and their public relations consultant Stephanie Renouf at BMA, Mhairi Graham at Highland Distillers, Jacqui Stacey of Inver House Distillers Ltd, Eily Kilgannon at Irish Distillers Ltd, Neil Clapperton of Cadenheads and J. &A. Mitchell & Co Ltd, Rachael Dutton of Seagram, Andrew Symington at Signatory, Shuna Mitchell at Suntory and Jonathan Driver at United Distillers. And then special thanks go to Iain Russell at Longmorn Distillery for his painstaking research, my whisky colleague Caroline Dewar, the well-known brothers Jack and Wallace Milroy, and my very good friends Bill Bergus of Allied Distillers and Alan Rutherford, all of whom put up with my queries and reviewed some of the copy for me. And, of course, apologies for anyone I have omitted.

Picture Credits

The Publisher would like to thank all the individual distilleries and their owning companies for contributing illustrative material to support their stories in this book. Additional picture credits go to the following:

Whyte & Mackay Group pp 8, 68, 114, 115, 116, 117; Coffey Distillery p 27 (t); Glenrothes Distillery p 27 (b); Laphroaig Distillery pp 28, 43 (t); Highland Park Distillery pp 7, 48; Life File Photographic Agency pp 39, 41, 70, 74, 75, 78, 81 (b), 83; Springbank Distillery p 45 (c); Glenfiddich Distillery p 46 (t); Glenmorangie Distillery p 47 (b); Morrison Bowmore Distillery p 53; Jack Daniel Distillery pp 66, 67, 69; Archie Miles p 86; Sally Green p 191 (t).

Index